CHARLES BROCKDEN BROWN

SERIES PREFACE

Gothic Authors: Critical Revisions is dedicated to publishing innovative introductory guides to writers of the Gothic. The series explores how new critical approaches and perspectives can help us to recontextualize an author's work in a way that is both accessible and informative. The series publishes work that is of interest to students of all levels and teachers of the literary Gothic and cultural history.

SERIES EDITORS

Andrew Smith, University of Glamorgan
Benjamin Fisher, University of Mississippi

EDITORIAL BOARD

Charles Brockden Brown

Jeffrey Andrew Weinstock

UNIVERSITY OF WALES PRESS
CARDIFF
2011

www.uwp.co.uk

British Library CIP Data
A catalogue record for this book is available from the British Library

ISBN   978-0-7083-2420-2 (hardback)
         978-0-7083-2419-6 (paperback)
e-ISBN 978-0-7083-2422-6

Typeset in Wales by Eira Fenn Gaunt, Cardiff
Printed by CPI Antony Rowe, Chippenham, Wiltshire

ACKNOWLEDGEMENTS

A number of people contributed valuable advice, time and assistance toward the completion of this book. I would like to thank Andrew Smith and Benjamin Franklin Fisher IV for inviting me to serve as author for this volume, and the team at the University of Wales Press for overseeing the manuscript's production. Stephen Shapiro, Mark Kamrath and Philip Barnard, from whose work on Brown I have benefited greatly, were each kind enough to answer questions about Brown's potential influence. Janie Hinds, whose work on Brown I have also enjoyed, was kind enough to send a copy of her book when my university library could not obtain one.

Central Michigan University facilitated the completion of this project with a course reduction and my colleagues in the English department, especially Ari Berk and Kris McDermott, have always been supportive.

Most crucially, my wonderful wife Astrid, my son William and my parents Alan and Madeline supported me every step of the way and make everything possible.

CONTENTS

A Polemical Introduction

ဆာလ

This book is a contribution to the University of Wales Press's Gothic Authors: Critical Revisions series, which has among its objectives to offer new perspectives on and to reinvigorate discussion of canonical and neglected Gothic authors. Late eighteenth- to early nineteenth-century American Gothicist Charles Brockden Brown has the odd and seemingly paradoxical distinction of arguably being *both* canonical – an established figure within the American literary tradition – and, simultaneously, neglected. This contradictory duality in large measure has to do with the critics' suspicion that although Brown was first in many things, he was not among the best. As Bernard Rosenthal pointed out in the introduction to his collection of critical essays on Brown in 1981, Brown, like a musician who invented an important new instrument that he himself could not play especially well, has again and again been honoured by critics more for what he initiated than for what he achieved.[1] Widely regarded, according to Paul Lewis, as the 'first serious, complex, and/or interesting American novelist',[2] Brown is repeatedly addressed as a point of origin rather than a destination. Not only is he considered the United States's first professional writer – the first American author who attempted to earn a living through his pen – but, according to Michael Davitt Bell, the 'real history' of 'serious' American literature begins with Brown, the 'American Byron', whose six novels set the stage for the blossoming of American Romanticism later in the century.[3] Brown is thus figured as a sort of Aristotelian 'prime mover' of American fiction, the 'Father of the American Romance'.[4]

First among firsts

But Brown apparently went beyond pioneering the American romance. A brief survey of the critical literature on Brown yields an impressive range of claims made concerning his foundational status. For the purposes of this study focusing on Brown as writer of Gothic tales, it is significant to note that the 'Father of American letters'[5] also set the American Gothic into motion – an achievement trumpeted by the title of H. R. Warfel's seminal 1949 study, *Charles Brockden Brown: Pioneer American Gothicist*. In Leslie Fiedler's estimation, Brown single-handedly solved the key problems of adapting the European conventions of the Gothic to American shores and, through his influence on Poe and Hawthorne, 'determined . . . the future of the Gothic novel in America'.[6] Peter Kafer forcefully reiterates this when, in the introduction to his biography of Brown, *Charles Brockden Brown's Revolution and the Birth of the American Gothic* (2004), he states baldly that with the publication of Brown's first novel *Wieland* in 1798, 'at the age of twenty-seven Charles Brockden Brown invented the American Gothic novel'. Kafer goes on to make the sensational claim that Brown 'was the only man or woman in 1790s America with the requisite Gothic imagination to sense the dark histories already weighing down on the American republic'.[7]

Brown's trailblazing, however, extends in the estimation of the critics far beyond his dark Gothic vision and his adaptation of the European Gothic novel to American shores. For William Hedges, what is notable about Brown is his intuition that 'derivative and discredited fictional forms' including the romance and the melodrama were particularly well suited to conveying 'deep American impulses',[8] while for Charles Carpenter, Brown's magazine the *Literary Magazine and American Register* which he ran from 1803 until 1806 and then again in a different form from 1807 to 1809 establishes his credentials as a pioneer American historian; and further, according to Carpenter, Brown's early nineteenth-century political pamphlets entitle him to a place as one of the early American republic's 'most articulate political theorists'.[9]

Romanticist, Gothicist, sentimentalist, historian, political theorist – Brown was there at the start. Again and again, Brown is heralded as having been first (or at least among the first), if not best. His first novel, *Wieland* (1798), arguably inaugurated the Gothic novel in America and its narrator, Clara Wieland, presents us with the first case of an unreliable narrator in American literature.[10] His second novel, *Ormond* (1799), offers what Kristin Comment characterizes as the 'first extended fictional portrayal . . . [of] "romantic passion" between women'[11] – that is, it was the first American novel to represent what we today call lesbianism – and Bill Christophersen proposes that the work is perhaps the first 'symbolist work' in American fiction.[12] *Arthur Mervyn*, his third novel (or, since it was published in two parts [Part I 1799, Part II 1800] with another novel, *Edgar Huntly* [1799], intervening, possibly his fourth depending upon how one counts) has the distinction of offering according to Hedges the 'first significant representation of the American in his "solitary condition", the hero beset by the contradictions of the new-world culture'.[13] And *Edgar Huntly*, Brown's fourth (or, again, third depending on how one counts) novel must be ranked as a first on several counts: the first American novel to mine the raw material of the American frontier for fictive purposes, in the process making it the first to create a 'specifically American psyche';[14] the first American novel to adapt the European tradition of the picturesque travel narrative;[15] the first important American use of the Gothic device of the double or doppelgänger;[16] and a story that pioneers both the detective story genre[17] and the style of narration now referred to as free indirect discourse (a 'revolutionary' achievement in Hagenbüchle's estimation).[18]

Summarizing this impressive array of achievements, Kafer notes the arguments for Brown's inauguration of the American traditions of the romance, the Gothic, the 'highbrow' novel and the 'Adamic myth',[19] while Verhoeven observes the characterizations of Brown as the first American novelist, the inventor of the American writer, the first professional man of letters in America and the father of American letters.[20] Brown is variously claimed by critics and historians as the starting point for American feminism, American nationalism, the American Gothic and even American realism.[21] This is a significant list of firsts, which would seem in and of itself to warrant affording Brown canonical status – or, at the very least, an American postage stamp with his face on it!

Success or sham?

Yet Charles Brockden Brown, even in America, is far from being a household name today. The best that can be said of Brown's literary status is Verhoeven's cautiously tepid appraisal that 'it would not be a gross exaggeration to say that Brown [has risen] in the ranks from a forgotten author to being one of the more distinguished ancestors of "major" American writers such as Cooper, Poe, Hawthorne, Melville, and James'.[22] And there is even debate concerning the extent to which Brown, first among firsts, actually influenced anyone. On the one hand, in his own time and later in the nineteenth century, it appears he was read and admired by Percy Bysshe Shelley, Mary Shelley (who read Brown's first novel *Wieland* just before starting work on *Frankenstein* in 1816),[23] John Keats, William Hazlitt and Thomas Peacock.[24] In America, according to Donald Ringe, writers as diverse as Poe, Hawthorne, Whittier and Fuller admired his fiction.[25] Poe borrowed from Brown's *Edgar Huntly*,[26] as did James Fenimore Cooper,[27] and Hawthorne included Brown in his 'Hall of Fantasy' sketch in his 1846 *Mosses from an Old Manse* – the only American author to be included in Hawthorne's pantheon of literary giants![28] Indeed, according to Fiedler, Brown essentially 'invented' Poe.[29] But on the other hand, Fiedler notes that Brown's first four novels, despite their unprecedented 'vigor', 'didn't sell'.[30] And then there is Hedges's assertion that Brown 'had hardly any major influence on subsequent American fiction'.[31] Paradoxically, Brown seems to have influenced everyone and no one, to be simultaneously crucial and dispensable – to be the most important American author no one has ever heard of.

In an interesting way, debates over Brown's position in the literary canon sound remarkably like the debates over the nature of his character Arthur Mervyn from his novel of the same name. Emory Elliott observes that critics have been divided on the question of the character of *Arthur Mervyn*'s titular protagonist to such an extent that, at times, they almost seem to be reading different books. 'Some view him', writes Elliott, 'as the prototype of the successful American Adam – a young innocent who receives a just reward for a life of virtue – while others see him as a scoundrel, an opportunist, a "double-tongued deceiver".'[32] Reading critical appraisals of Brown, similar questions arise: is he the father of American literature, an American Adam dedicated to inventing a new literature and instrumental in directing the subsequent course of American letters? Or is he a sham, a failed author with no lofty ambitions who didn't really influence anyone? From this perspective, to offer a 'polemical introduction' to Charles Brockden Brown here is apparently redundant – the argument has been going on for a long time. Any introduction to Brown is seemingly of necessity polemical.

And this debate about Brown's achievement brings one inevitably back to the issue of *quality*. Brown may have been first in many things, but at the end of the day is his fiction any good? Another way to put the same question: Brown and his novels may be historically significant for their innovations, but do the works possess any intrinsic literary merit? Here as before, much of the time the critics seem frankly uncertain just what to do with Brown and how to answer these questions. Rosenthal is again instructive with his summation of the critical literature when he notes that 'Brown's detractors [see] chaos of narration, an inability to delineate characters, and a body of fiction that depend[s] too heavily on improbable events. His admirers [tend] to grant these objections but [feel] that they [are] secondary considerations in responding to Brown's merits'.[33] So on the one hand there is Fiedler who paints Brown as a writer 'careless to the point of shamelessness'.[34] On the other, there is Norman Grabo whose entire book on Brown, *The Coincidental Art of Charles Brockden Brown* (1981), is devoted to disputing the claim of Brown's carelessness and proposes instead that his narratives are 'intentionally flawed' and his reliance upon coincidence is purposeful.[35] On the one hand, there is Nina Baym who in her 'minority reading' of *Wieland* interprets it as a flawed work and, more generally, counters claims of Brown's artistic merit by suggesting that there is 'no real evidence that his novelistic aims were very high'.[36] On the other, there is Christopher Looby who proposes that *Wieland*, flawed or not, is 'possibly the most profound reflection on the aporias of time, history, language, and knowledge that can be found in the literature of the early national period'.[37]

Although Brown's defenders have mounted an impressive campaign in recent years not so much to rehabilitate as – more accurately I think – simply to establish his reputation, it is still the case that no critical consensus has emerged on what to do with Brown and how to interpret his works. Does Brown's work constitute a conservative defence of tradition or a liberal celebration of modernity?[38] Should Brown's novels be considered poorly plotted, digressive explorations of ideas or rather, as Cathy Davidson suggests, historically anachronistic masterpieces of postmodern metafiction?[39] As David Larsson notes, echoing Emory Elliott in reference to Brown's *Arthur Mervyn*, critics addressing the same text almost seem to be reading different works.[40] Is Arthur Mervyn a naïve innocent with a zeal for good works or a subtle scheming huckster? Is *Wieland* a conservative defence of Federalist policies as Jane Tompkins asserts in *Sensational Designs* (1985), or is it a more subversive undermining of those policies?[41] Or is it the case that Brown's texts, rather than taking any side at all, instead 'allegorize the very disruption, trauma, and ambivalence' of post-Revolutionary political and social shifts?[42]

With Fiedler, I think we are forced to conclude that Brown remains in his own unique and provoking way 'a living writer, because of the polemical tone which a discussion of his work necessarily assumes'.[43] As soon as one begins to speak about Charles Brockden Brown, one is inevitably enmeshed in these debates about quality, significance and influence. The sense that one is participating in an ongoing and still developing conversation, indeed, is part of the fun of reading, discussing and teaching Brown; and it is in this spirit of intellectual contestation that this book, this inevitably 'polemical introduction' to American Gothic author Charles Brockden Brown, will be organized around four central theses. The first is that Brown needs to be recognized as the initiator of, or innovator within, several American subgenres of the Gothic including what will be referred to as the Frontier Gothic, the Urban Gothic, the Psychological Gothic and what has come to be known as the Female Gothic. My second thesis is that Brown represents a crucial transitional figure or 'hinge' between eighteenth-century Enlightenment rationality and nineteenth-century Romanticism who develops a powerful model of what Edgar

Allan Poe subsequently dubs human 'perverseness' almost forty years before Poe. The third argument is that Brown needs to be recognized as a progressive political voice who not only articulated in his *Alcuin* (1798) one of the United States's earliest women's rights platforms, but also spoke out against the slave trade and anti-Semitism – and that his progressive views are clearly evident in his fiction; and finally, that Brown is worth reading in his own right for the narrative force of his stories, their intellectual merit and the insight they provide into the sociopolitical milieu of the early American republic. In my view, Brown was not only first, but also both good and influential.

Before diving into these considerations of his fiction, however, some background to Brown's life and the historical context in which he lived and wrote is both appropriate and necessary. As is the case with any author, Brown's fiction – the forms his works take, the themes he utilizes, the language he employs – was shaped both by his personal experiences and his general milieu. And in Brown's case, given the sensational and even gruesome events he depicts in his Gothic fictions, the links between content and context are interesting indeed.

Brown's biography

Taken together, what the writings of Charles Brockden Brown provide for us is a snapshot of a man growing up and attempting to earn a living by his pen in the midst of one of the most – if not the most – tumultuous periods in American history. Brown was born into a Quaker family in Philadelphia on 17 January 1771. Although the American Revolution was still five years away, Philadelphia – the political and intellectual centre of the thirteen original American colonies (and subsequently the first capital of the newly formed country) – was already a hotbed of political agitation and a place that would become increasingly uncomfortable for pacifist Quakers. Indeed, in what Peter Kafer figures in his biography of Brown as a foundational moment for Brown's development – almost as a sort of Freudian primal scene later to echo through his fiction – Brown's father Elijah who, like other colonists, opposed the Stamp Act of 1765 and supported the goals of the Revolution, but as a result of his Quaker religious principles refused to bear arms or to take a patriotic oath of allegiance, was arrested in September 1777 and disappeared for eight months while he was held with other individuals "'dangerous" to the Revolutionary cause' in Virginia.[44]

Unlike his three older brothers who moved into commercial careers as soon as possible, Brown was enrolled in the autumn of 1781 (more or less coincident with the de facto conclusion of the American Revolution) in the Friends' Latin School which he attended until 1786 and at which, in addition to the Bible, he studied Latin, Greek, mathematics, English literature and geography. Under the tutelage of schoolmaster Robert Proud, a Tory sympathizer who later produced a two-volume history of Pennsylvania, the pro-Revolution Brown was initiated into the Quaker tradition of intellectual exchange and dialogue.[45] Critics have noted the influence of Proud's *The History of Pennsylvania* (1797) on *Wieland* and the Quaker model of intellectual investigation on all his writing.[46]

Brown's family seemingly intended him to pursue a career as a lawyer and at the age of sixteen he entered the Philadelphia law office of a non-Quaker, Alexander Wilcocks, in 1787 – the same year the Federal Convention met in Philadelphia to draft the American Constitution. At about this time, Brown also founded the Belles Lettres Club, a group whose goals were 'literary improvement' and 'to enlarge the circle of . . . faculties, of which the human mind is capable'.[47] Including both Quakers and non-Quakers, this group, which sometimes met at the home of Benjamin Franklin and was possibly modelled after Franklin's own Junto, regularly debated issues such as 'the morality of suicide, the imperfections of government, the limits of liberty and the possible rationalizations for lying' – all issues that would surface to varying extents in Brown's later fiction.[48] This group later appears to have morphed in the early 1790s into another intellectual society with which Brown was associated – the Society for the Attainment of Useful Knowledge.

The Belles Lettres Club and his law apprenticeship arguably offered Brown two models of intellectual inquiry that were at variance with each other: the first was open-ended and unstructured, while the second was precedent-bound and rigid. It is clear both from Brown's life and fiction (as many have noted, his novels are built around the asking of questions) which approach he preferred.[49] Reflecting on his time in Wilcocks's law office, Brown wrote in a letter to a friend: '[I] was perpetually encumbered with the rubbish of the law and waded with laborious steps through its endless tautologies, its impertinent circularities, its lying assertions and hateful artifices'.[50] Even while working under Wilcocks, Brown was already pursuing literary interests, noting in his journals ideas for epic poems taking as their foci the discovery of America and the conquests of Mexico and Peru and composing imitations of the Book of Psalms, the Book of Job and a cycle of poems published in 1760 referred to as the Ossian poems.[51] Brown's first literary works, a series of sketches called 'The Rhapsodist' modelled on the works of Rousseau and exploring the temperament of the 'visionary writer', were published on the eve of the French Revolution in 1789 when he was eighteen. He gave up his formal study of the law several years later and in his novel *Ormond* caustically characterizes the law as a 'tissue made up of the shreds and remnants of barbarous antiquity, polluted with the rust of ages, and patched by the stupidity of modern workmen, into new deformity'.[52] Nevertheless, as Laura Korobkin has shown in relation to *Wieland*, Brown's novelistic work is informed throughout by a thorough knowledge of legal affairs. *Wieland*, in Korobkin's assessment, is a novel structured as a trial and 'obsessed with law'.[53]

After leaving Wilcocks's office, Brown took a job in Philadelphia as 'master' at the Quaker Friends' Grammar School and went through a period of intellectual exploration in which he wrote copiously but published little. Pivotal to his future development during this period were the associations he made and the friendships he formed with other intellectuals, most importantly Elihu Hubbard Smith (1771–98), a Yale-educated physician whom Brown first met in Philadelphia in 1790. Smith was an abolitionist and deist committed to progressive ideals, as well as a man of letters who composed opera libretti, authored a biography of the Connecticut Wits and edited an anthology of American poetry.[54] It was Smith who encouraged Brown's literary ambitions, and when Smith established a medical practice in New York City in 1791 Brown visited him frequently before moving in with him in New York in 1797; alas, Smith was to die the very next year from yellow fever.

The friendship with Smith inevitably involved Brown in the Friendly Club, a New York City social group that, like Brown's Belles

Lettres Club and Society for the Attainment of Useful Knowledge, gathered weekly to discuss books, politics, poetry, philosophy and religion. According to Kafer, the group was marked by 'undoctrinaire federalism' and a commitment to free thought.[55] Barnard and Shapiro observe that the group, which included both men and women, was 'invested in progressive intellectual exchange and enlightened models for same-sex and other-sex companionship' and they propose that Brown's association with this group was central to his intellectual development.[56] As part of this group, Brown was first exposed to or had his knowledge deepened of radical democratic writers of the period – especially William Godwin and Mary Wollstonecraft (to be discussed below) – as well as of scientists, philosophers and political thinkers of the day. During 1796 and 1797, Brown shared a number of his own works in progress with this group, including *Alcuin* (1798), his dialogue on women's rights. In April 1799, when the Friendly Club founded a periodical titled *Monthly Magazine and American Review*, the aim of which was to 'extract the quintessence of European wisdom; to review and estimate the labours of all writers, domestic and foreign',[57] Brown became the magazine's editor and a frequent contributor of essays, criticism and fiction.

Starting around 1798 – seemingly touched off by the death of Elihu Smith from yellow fever and Brown's own narrow escape – and lasting into 1801, Brown entered a frantic writing and publication period that is unlikely ever to be matched. Robert A. Ferguson estimates that Brown was at work on all four of what are considered his major novels between September (when Smith died) and November 1798.[58] *Wieland, Ormond, Arthur Mervyn* and *Edgar Huntly* were all written during an eighteen-month period, as were his unfinished works, *Memoirs of Carwin the Biloquist* and *Memoirs of Stephen Calvert*.

Following the publication of the second part of *Arthur Mervyn*, Brown – perhaps exhausted from his unprecedented explosion of writing, perhaps in response to petitions from his family – abruptly returned to Philadelphia, stopped working on the *Monthly Magazine* and proclaimed his intention to give up writing novels altogether. He even went so far as to regret his previous efforts publicly, writing in 1803 in his *Literary Magazine and American Register*: 'I should enjoy a larger share of my own respect at the present moment if nothing had ever flowed from my pen, the production of which could be traced to me'.[59] Nevertheless, he published two more novels in 1801 – *Clara Howard* and *Jane Talbot*, sentimental novels that differ markedly in form and tone from his previous more clearly Gothic novels – and he continued to remain a fixture in the literary world, publishing political pamphlets, including ones arguing for acquisition of the Louisiana Territory and against the Embargo Act of 1807; editing and contributing to two more magazines, *The Literary Magazine and American Register* (1803–6) and *The American Register and General Repository of History, Politics, and Science* (1807–9); authoring a series of historical fictions between 1803 and 1807; and translating and annotating a geographical study of the United States by the French author the Comte de Volney.

After his return to Philadelphia in 1800, Brown also went to work with his brothers in the family business – a mercantile import-export business – and married Presbyterian Elizabeth Linn in 1804 (for which he was formally disowned by the Philadelphia Quaker Meeting House),[60] with whom he had four children. This period of Brown's life has often been interpreted as marking a shift in his philosophical orientation from Enlightenment-influenced religious questioner and political progressive to a more conservative orthodox Christian. Whereas the young Brown had been an avowed Godwinite with pro-Jeffersonian Republican leanings, during the final decade of his life, after Jefferson was elected president, Brown authored a series of pamphlets critical of his administration and vowed that his 1803 publishing venture, *The Literary Magazine and American Register*, would embrace the cause of religion. Brown contracted tuberculosis in 1809 and died in February 1810 at the age of thirty-nine. Less than five years after his death, his friend William Dunlap published the first biography of Brown in 1815.

Brown's historical, intellectual and literary context

As the brief biographical sketch of Brown above suggests, Brown's life and his art, his personal experience and his output of fiction, were intimately interconnected. The characteristic interrogative structure of his works (his characters often run through rapid-fire lists of questions, considering all manner of possibilities before deciding on a course of action) can reasonably be interpreted as reflecting both Quaker religious practice and his legal training; the absent fathers in his work can be traced back to the disappearance of his own for eight months when he was not quite six; many of the themes explored in his fiction, from sexual discrimination to the limitations of Lockean sensationalist psychology,[61] clearly show the influence of Elihu Smith, the Friendly Club and Brown's own reading; and, perhaps most notably, his representations in both *Ormond* and *Arthur Mervyn* of the yellow fever epidemic that decimated Philadelphia in 1793 obviously reflect his own experiences of living through yellow fever epidemics in both Philadelphia and New York throughout the 1790s. As these examples suggest, however, the personal experiences that shaped Brown and his fiction need to be situated within the broader framework of Revolutionary and post-Revolutionary America – a period that Linda Kerber asserts was one of the most intellectually traumatic in American history.[62] As Douglas Anderson proposes, what often seems most personal and inward in Brown's work must instead be seen as reflecting pervasive cultural tensions and anxieties.[63] The fact of the matter is that Brown lived during a period of immense uncertainty and volatile change. In the 1790s, when Brown did the bulk of his writing, the United States was a gigantic experiment and, as Jane Tompkins observes, it was not clear at any given moment that it would still exist at all the next year or the following.[64] Brown's fictions clearly reflect the upheavals of his era as he insistently meditates on both the promise and perils of new systems of governance and thought, as well as on the external forces that constrain and dictate the course of human events.

There is, of course, no way that I can hope to offer a complete portrait of pre-Revolutionary, Revolutionary and immediately post-Revolutionary America in a few pages. Instead, I will focus on a handful of interconnected issues that in significant ways can be seen as both framing Brown's novels and to varying extents being consciously thematized within them. My purpose here is to introduce historical context that in substantive ways informs Brown's fictions and that therefore assists one in making sense of them. I will begin by discussing the political upheavals and radical ideas that were transforming Brown's world and fostering internal American schisms and conspiracy paranoia. I will then discuss the yellow fever epidemics of the 1790s that serve as the immediate context for Brown's second and third novels, *Ormond* and *Arthur Mervyn*, before examining the literary models available to and appropriated by Brown in the production of his fictions.

Political revolutions and radical ideas

Brown was born into a world being reshaped by revolutionary change. During his childhood, the North American colonies transformed from British and European possessions into an independent nation, and Kafer notes that the experience of Revolution in the Philadelphia of Brown's childhood was 'physical, brutal, and morally disorienting'.[65] France, too, underwent a period of revolutionary change starting in 1789. Americans initially greeted the news of the French Revolution joyously as a kindred manifestation of the force of democracy; sympathy with France, however, was reversed in 1793–4 as news of the atrocities of the Reign of Terror reached American shores, only then to revive temporarily in 1795–6 as a result of British naval depredations. More ominously, black insurrection in the West Indies between 1791 and 1803 claimed the lives of over 46,000 whites.[66] The most serious revolt took place in the French colony of Saint-Domingue and led to the formation of Haiti in 1804. As Goudie observes, the violence and rebellion in the West Indies precipitated a flood of West Indian Creole émigrés escaping the carnage into the United States (Philadelphia was a major destination for such refugees) and caused many citizens to become anxious about possible slave revolts in the United States.[67]

The 1780s and 1790s also witnessed the importation and circulation of radical sociopolitical theories, most importantly those of British radical democrats William Godwin and Mary Wollstonecraft and the 'Woldwinites' who orbited around them, including Thomas Paine, Thomas Holcroft, Robert Gage and Helen Maria Williams.[68] As summarized by Barnard and Shapiro, the Woldwinites rejected hierarchically arranged social orders and artificial constraints on human behaviour and proposed that human social advancement and harmony were to be achieved through the application of reason.[69] In Godwin's *An Enquiry Concerning Political Justice* (1793) and his famous 'novel of ideas', *Things as They Are or the Adventures of Caleb Williams* (1794), Godwin articulates his anti-statism and distrust of coercive institutions of all stripes, including organized religion and state as well as church-authorized and -sanctioned rituals such as marriage. In Wollstonecraft's *A Vindication of the Rights of Woman* (1792), the pioneering feminist asserted that women are not naturally inferior to men, but rather are only made to appear so as a result of educational inequalities. Despite commonly held assumptions, Wollstonecraft's treatise was in fact generally favourably received and frequently discussed on both sides of the Atlantic.[70]

These political revolutions and revolutionary ideas impacted directly on Brown in a variety of ways. As a resident of Philadelphia, Brown witnessed at first hand the immigration deluge of the 1790s from France and the French West Indies, as well as from Scotland, England and Ireland.[71] As a citizen of the newly formed United States, he was unavoidably thrust into the middle of post-Revolutionary political debates divided along Federalist and Republican lines and guided by ideological assumptions about human nature (more on this below). And as a young intellectual participating in various reading groups and first publishing in, and then also running his own magazine publications that reviewed and debated philosophical ideas, Brown was clearly exposed to and influenced by these radical doctrines. Indeed, in 1795 Brown referred to Godwin's *Enquiry* as his 'Oracle',[72] and Brown's 1798 dialogue on women's rights, *Alcuin*, is thoroughly Woldwinite in its repudiation of arguments for the natural inferiority of women and its radical critique of marriage and related laws disenfranchising women (to be discussed in more detail in chapter 4). Although Brown's novels have variously been read as supporting and critiquing Woldwinite philosophy, the influence of Brown's exposure to these ideas on his intellectual maturation is undeniable.

Revolutions abroad and the importation of radical doctrines, combined with internal debates over slavery and Indian policy and dramatic shifts in financial policy and industrial production, produced a United States fraught with political tension and extreme factionalism in the 1790s.[73] Vigorous political debates pivoted around issues of how much power the federal government should have, whether the United States should ally itself with Great Britain or France, and – in keeping with the Woldwinite meditations – whether human beings in general possessed the capacity for self-governance. As Clemit explains, the Republicans, led by Thomas Jefferson and James Madison, held an essentially Godwinian optimistic belief in man's innate integrity and envisioned an agrarian nation based on this principle with minimal federal oversight or interference in private affairs. Federalists, represented by George Washington, John Adams and Alexander Hamilton in contrast adopted a more pessimistic attitude toward human nature and argued for the necessity of external controls to maintain law and order and to regulate the economy.[74] This ideological debate over the power that the government should have, which indeed shaped the American Constitution and has resonated ever since, was sharpened in the 1790s by a series of events linking the domestic and international spheres that further factionalized the United States almost to the point of civil war. To a certain extent this schism divided along political lines of supporting either England or France.

In 1794, the United States signed the Jay Treaty with Great Britain, which defused growing political tensions, resolved many issues left over from the American Revolutionary War and opened up a ten-year period of peaceful mercantile trade between the two nations. Because France had declared war on Great Britain in 1793, from the British perspective it was important to form an alliance with the United States if for no other reason than to prevent France from doing so. The Jay Treaty averted possible war between America and Great Britain, but became a central issue in domestic politics and was roundly condemned by Thomas Jefferson and James Madison who sided ideologically with the ideals of the French Revolution and feared the treaty would strengthen the Federalist grip on power.

Political events in the international sphere really heated up beginning in 1798 with what was known as the XYZ Affair, which was followed closely by the domestic imposition of the Alien and Sedition Acts and the Virginia and Kentucky Resolutions. In 1798, to a certain extent in response to the Jay Treaty signalling the Anglo-American alliance, the French government attempted to extort funds from the United States government. France's representatives, publicly referred to as X, Y and Z (hence the title, the XYZ Affair) made it clear that unless certain 'loans' were made available to France, United States shipping would be interrupted and the nation isolated. The United States refused to capitulate to France's demands, and when news of the affair broke a wave of anti-French sentiment swept across the United States, damaging the public image of the pro-French Jeffersonian Republicans and helping to ensure the election of Federalist John Adams as president in 1796.

In the wake of the XYZ Affair and the election of Adams, the Federalist-controlled Congress passed four bills in 1798 collectively known as the Alien and Sedition Acts. Proponents of these acts claimed that they were necessary measures designed to prevent alien citizens of enemy powers from weakening the United States government. Opponents attacked them as unconstitutional infringements of individual liberty and states' rights. The Naturalization Act of 1798 extended the duration of residency requirement to apply for citizenship to fourteen years; the Alien Friends Act authorized the president to deport any resident alien determined to be dangerous; the Alien Enemies Act authorized the President to deport resident aliens if their home countries were at war with the United States; and the Sedition Act made it a crime to publish writing deemed false, scandalous or malicious in relation to the government or its officials. Jefferson, Madison and the Republicans, who rightly perceived these pieces of legislation as constraints on free speech muzzling expressions of dissent, countered the Alien and Sedition Acts with the Virginia and Kentucky Resolutions calling upon the states to declare the federal legislation null and void.

Not surprisingly during this feverish period of political jockeying, conspiracy theories in the 1790s were rife and both Federalists and Republicans accused their opponents of subterfuge and devious dealing. As Levine explains,

> federalists made nervous by the French Revolution and its aftermath insisted that the riotous enthusiasm greeting Genêt's audacious visit, the insurrectionary spirit of the Whiskey Rebellion, and the increasingly virulent opposition of the Jeffersonian Republicans were all secretly kindled and enflamed by Jacobin subversives. In contrast, Jeffersonian Republicans proclaimed that Federalist policies of economic centralization reflected the corruption of an oligarchical ministry deviously plotting to subvert the freedoms achieved by the American Revolution.[75]

Perhaps the most visible manifestation of conspiratorial rhetoric was the Illuminati panic of 1798–9, an event that clearly informs Brown's *Ormond* and his *Memoirs of Carwin the Biloquist* which both feature individuals who are members of Illuminati-like secret societies.

As Christophersen explains, the Order of the Illuminati, a fraternal society promoting rationalist ideals, was founded to combat the stifling power of the Bavarian Jesuits in 1776 by Adam Weishaupt, a law professor at the University of Ingolstadt.[76] Two European books written independently of each other, Abbé de Barruel's *Memoirs Illustrating the History of Jacobinism* (1797–8) and John Robison's *Proofs of a Conspiracy against All the Religions and Governments of Europe, carried on in the Secret Meetings of the Free Masons, Illuminati, and Reading Societies* (1797), purported to trace all the revolutionary upheavals of the current age to the clandestine machinations of this secret society 'dedicated to the general destruction of government and religion, and that now operated through its covert agents in all the nations of Europe and in the United States'.[77] American Congregationalist minister Jedidiah Morse used the theme of alien infiltration in May 1898 to decry the effects of Enlightenment rationalism. According to Morse, French agents, controlled by the Bavarian Illuminati, had infiltrated America with the ultimate aim of undermining American civic and political institutions: 'Hostile to true liberty and religion, the conspirators were ready to launch an all-out assault on the institutions the founding fathers had so painstakingly established'.[78] As Bradshaw notes, these warnings about French subterfuge only further agitated a public already disgusted by the excesses of the French Revolution, enraged by political events including the XYZ affair and violence in the West Indies, and unsettled by internal dissent manifested through the Whiskey Rebellion.[79]

By mid-1798, as historian Richard Buel observes, 'Illuminati became a household word in America'[80] and in Brown's home city of Philadelphia, a major destination in the 1790s for political refugees of all stripes, 'the end result of the repeated declarations of French, Illuminati, Federalist-aristocratic, and even Irish conspiracy was a near panic situation'.[81] Summarizing the tensions of post-Revolutionary America that swirled around Brown, Frank Shuffelton writes that in the dozen years before Brown's novels appeared, Americans had put down two rebellions, seen Europe thrown into self-devouring revolutionary turmoil, and become more fully aware of their relative powerlessness on the international scene. Anxieties heightened and given shape by the traditional fear of conspiracy that lay at the center of Whig ideology, they felt themselves beset from both within and abroad and were ready to find hidden connections among the host of threatening circumstances.[82]

Yellow fever

During his lifetime – and especially during his explosion of creative energies in the late 1790s and early 1800s – Brown was unavoidably at the centre of this swirling maelstrom of sociopolitical events and philosophical ideas. Revolutions were taking place overseas and re-bellions at home. Émigrés were flooding Philadelphia, as were new and radical doctrines. The American government was divided, as were the American people, and conspiracy theories were widespread and frightening; as we shall see, these themes repeatedly play out in Brown's fiction. Christophersen contends that Brown's fiction is 'remarkable, even unique for its time, in its reflection of the nation's identity'.[83] Brown's life, however, was also influenced by a separate set of circumstances that made especially clear the limitations of human autonomy and must have called into question faith in divine providence: that was disease, and most importantly yellow fever.

Both Brown's second and third novels, *Ormond* and *Arthur Mervyn*, have at their centres Gothic pictures of a Philadelphia decimated by yellow fever, and while in both these novels the spread of plague symbolizes moral degradation and social crisis, Brown also draws from accounts of and his own experience with actual pestilence. As will be discussed in greater detail in chapter 2, during the summers of the 1790s yellow fever epidemics occurred annually in large Ameri-can cities, especially those along the Eastern seaboard. In 1793, the period dramatized in *Ormond* and *Arthur Mervyn*, the disease claimed over 2,500 lives in a roughly six-week period between late August and September, and more than 5,000 died overall – almost one tenth of Philadelphia's total population.[84] Brown himself contracted yellow fever in 1798 and the disease killed his close friend Elihu Smith. Indeed, his manic period of feverish writing began not long after the death of Smith and his own recovery.

Literary influences

One last piece of the puzzle that needs to be supplied here is some information about the literary models available to Brown in the late eighteenth century. Brown, as a young intellectual with a sound classical education and a pronounced interest in literature, read deeply and widely. He had learned Greek and Latin in school and was clearly fluent enough in both French and German to undertake translations. Philadelphia's status as a major seaport ensured a steady stream of books and his participation in various intellectual societies, as well as his authorship of book reviews and his editing of magazines, kept Brown abreast of new literary and intellectual sensations, shifts in the literary landscape and responses to those shifts.

Brown had a variety of literary models available to him during his lifetime and these helped to frame his own innovations. While traces are apparent in his work of many different literary forms reflecting his wide-ranging intellectual tastes and investigations, Brown argu-ably draws upon, blends and innovates most substantially upon three popular eighteenth-century categories of literature: sentimental romances, Gothic romances, and what were known as 'novels of purpose'. As Russel B. Nye explains in his 'Historical Introduction' to the Bicentennial Edition of Brown's *Ormond* (1982), the most popular variety of fiction available to Brown as a model was the sentimental romance associated with British authors such as Samuel Richardson, Henry Fielding and Laurence Sterne. In novels along the lines of Richardson's *Pamela, or Virtue Rewarded* (1740), virtue is pitted against vice as innocence is attacked in scenes staged to evoke emotional responses from readers of 'fine sensibility'.[85] Nye com-ments that Richardson's influence on virtually every American nov-elist before 1820 can be taken for granted[86] and Lulu Rumsey Wiley, in her book-length study of influences on Brown, observes that the epistolary form used by Brown in four of his novels 'unquestionably follows the precedent of Richardson, Fielding, and Sterne'.[87] The influence of the sentimental novel is readily apparent throughout Brown's body of work but most of all in *Ormond*, in which his female characters all seem derived from this tradition, and in his two final epistolary works, *Jane Talbot* (1801) and *Clara Howard* (1801).

The second major literary form clearly influencing Brown and from which he undoubtedly drew inspiration was the literary craze of the 1790s, the Gothic novel, as epitomized by Ann Radcliffe and Matthew 'Monk' Lewis. Popular magazines in the 1790s, according to Nye, 'overflowed with stories crammed with haunted castles, secret passages, ghosts, damp tombs, mysterious chests, [and] unearthly shrieks',[88] which Brown, who particularly esteemed Radcliffe, adapted into his tales of murder, insanity, confinement, sleepwalking, pestilence, attempted rape and other lurid subject matter. Connected to Brown's appropriation and manipulation of Gothic themes and tropes is also the influx of sensationalist German romances which began to filter across the Atlantic in the 1790s. Like their British Gothic counterparts, these tales of murder, torture and rape were often criticized for their perceived immorality even as they were widely distributed and eagerly consumed. Warfel has noted Brown's familiarity with this form and the possible influence of German 'terror novels' including Friedrich von Schiller's *The Ghost-Seer* (1789) and Cajetan Tschink's *The Victim of Magical Delusion* (1795) on his fiction, especially *Wieland*.[89]

Less lurid and more intellectually engaging were writings by the Enlightenment-influenced French *philosophes* and British 'novelists of purpose'.[90] Brown at various times in his journals and letters mentions French authors Montesquieu, Helvétius, d'Holbach, Diderot, d'Alembert, Fénelon, La Bruyère, Voltaire and La Rochefoucauld,[91] and it is clear that he was heavily influenced by Rousseau. Brown's very early 'Henrietta Letters', a sort of epistolary romance, appear to be modelled after Rousseau's epistolary *Julie, ou la nouvelle Héloïse* (1761), by far the most popular novel of the eighteenth century;[92] and his 1789 'Rhapsodist' sketches seem to be a take on Rousseau's unfinished *Reveries of a Solitary Walker* (1782).[93] According to Kafer, Brown's earliest fictions were attempts to model himself after Richardson and Rousseau.[94] Later, Brown appears to have swapped the French *philosophes* for the British novels of purpose. Popular during the 1790s and after, these were productions by socially conscious writers in England who believed that the novel could be used as a medium through which to debate contemporary issues and as an instrument of social protest and change.[95] Foremost among the novels of purpose was William Godwin's *Caleb Williams.*

As Nye notes, by the end of 1797 – before Brown got underway on the novels for which he is remembered (when in fact he is remembered at all) – he had tried his hand at the epistolary form, the dialogue, the third-person point of view and the 'involved narrator'. He had appropriated from the Gothic novel, the sentimental novel and the novel of purpose, and had 'exchanged Rousseau for Godwin'.[96] The novels he subsequently produced were conscious attempts to combine elements from these various traditions into something new, something intrinsically American – an 'American novel, built around native scenery, native incidents, blended into the form and style of his European models'.[97] As I shall discuss in the next chapter, Brown's awareness of pioneering a new literary form in a new country seeking to define itself is both a conscious and unconscious theme throughout his work, but is made most explicit in his 'To the Public' note at the start of *Edgar Huntly* where he proposes that the American Indian and American wilderness will substitute in his novel for 'Gothic castles and chimeras'.[98]

This author's note to *Edgar Huntly* foregrounds one other literary model available to Brown that clearly finds its way into his writing: the Native American captivity narrative. Extending back to Mary Rowlandson's thrilling 1682 publication of *The Sovereignty and Goodness of God: Being a Narrative of the Captivity and Restoration of Mrs Mary Rowlandson*, captivity narratives were accounts of persons of European or, on rare occasions, African descent held captive for a period of time by indigenous North American tribes. While more or less 'factual', such accounts also generally reflected the prevailing ideological beliefs of the author and the author's culture, thus furthering the political designs of the author's culture by reinforcing convenient stereotypes concerning Native Americans. Because the accounts were considered factual, they also avoided the eighteenth-century stigma associated with imaginative fiction. Captivity narratives thus constituted thrilling reading that one could consume without guilt. As we shall see, embedded within *Edgar Huntly* is precisely such an account.

The polemics

As noted above, this polemical introduction to Charles Brockden Brown is organized around four central arguments: first, that Brown needs to be recognized as the initiator of or innovator within the Gothic traditions that I will refer to as the Frontier Gothic, the Urban Gothic, the Psychological Gothic and the Female Gothic; second, that Brown represents a crucial transitional figure or 'hinge' between eighteenth-century Enlightenment rationality and nineteenth-century Romanticism; third, that Brown needs to be recognized as a surprisingly progressive political voice who used his fiction to address issues of women's rights, slavery and anti-Semitism; and fourth, that in addition to his historical significance as first among firsts, Brown is worth reading in his own right because his fictions, while indisputably flawed, are nevertheless fascinating.

The first of these arguments, that Brown must be recognized not just as an essential American Gothic author but as an innovator within four specific subgenres of the Gothic – the Frontier, the Urban, the Psychological and the Female – organizes the structure of this book as chapters 1 to 4 will be dedicated respectively to Brown's contributions to each of these forms. Chapter 1 on the Frontier Gothic begins with the observation that Brown is the first American novelist to dramatize frontier violence between settlers and Native Americans, 'Gothicizing' the American landscape through depictions of tortuous pathways through dense wilderness, craggy eminences and dark caverns and caves. This chapter will then explore Brown's characterization of the frontier in *Edgar Huntly*, his 'Somnambulism. A Fragment', and to a lesser extent his novel *Wieland* as a perilous 'liminal zone' between reason and madness, life and death. Brown's depictions of the landscape and of native inhabitants will be addressed and his influence on subsequent Romantic depictions of the landscape – among them Hawthorne's *The Scarlet Letter* (1850) and 'Young Goodman Brown' (1835), Melville's *Pierre: or the Ambiguities* (1852), Cooper's Indians, Irving's 'The Legend of Sleepy Hollow' (1820), the blasted landscapes of Poe, Bierce, Richard Henry Dana Sr and others – will be argued.

Chapter 2 on the Urban Gothic will shift focus from forest to city and from *Edgar Huntly* and *Wieland* to Brown's novels *Ormond* and

Arthur Mervyn, both of which treat to varying extents the disastrous yellow fever epidemic of 1793 in Philadelphia. In these two works, Brown – prior to Dickens, George Lippard, Poe and subsequent Gothic authors who situate mysterious goings-on in the city – depicts the city itself as a Gothicized site of secrets, vice and peril, and thus pioneers the Urban Gothic form. Brown's eerie renderings of the city will be discussed and their influence on subsequent romancers, including Lippard and Poe, will be asserted.

In chapter 3, the emphasis will shift from Gothicized exterior landscapes to the haunted interior of the human mind and to the strange forces that impel human behaviour. Readers of Edgar Allan Poe's fiction, especially his 'The Black Cat' (1843) and 'The Imp of the Perverse' (1845), will be familiar with Poe's uncanny representations of individuals compelled to perform actions – sometimes self-destructive ones – purely because they know they should not. Students of American literature and the Gothic, however, may be surprised to learn that this idea of the mind divided against itself (as well as many other typically Poe-esque themes such as doppelgängers, premature burial, detectives, psychological obsession and so on) can be found in the work of Brown some forty years before Poe got to them. This chapter on the Psychological Gothic will focus on Brown's development of a model of human cognition that, both pre-Poe and pre-Freud, emphasizes the power of the human unconscious. Emphasized here with special attention to *Wieland* and *Edgar Huntly* will be Brown's use of what have become stock Gothic features such as doubles and twins, sleepwalking, prophetic dreams and locked doors, chests and cabinets. This chapter will also explore Brown's critique of Enlightenment rationality by examining the ways his protagonists are strangers to themselves and make faulty decisions as a result of incomplete knowledge, inaccurate interpretations of sensory data and irrational impulses. The argument will be presented here that Brown clearly serves as a hinge between the legacy of Enlightenment rationality and the full-blown Romanticism of Poe, Melville and Hawthorne.

While chapters 1 to 3 with their respective emphases on the Frontier Gothic, the Urban Gothic and the Psychological Gothic will focus on Brown's best-known works (*Wieland, Ormond, Arthur Mervyn* and *Edgar Huntly*), chapter 4 will examine Brown's representations of women with particular attention to some of his lesser-known works, including his dialogue *Alcuin*, and some discussion of one of his epistolary novels, *Clara Howard*. This chapter will start by offering an overview of his radical ideas concerning female independence and the restrictions marriage places on it in his Wollstonecraft-influenced feminist dialogue, *Alcuin* – one of the earliest expressions of such viewpoints in American history. The chapter will then go on to explore his representations of women in his fiction, emphasizing the ways in which, in keeping with the arguments expressed in *Alcuin*, his female characters are disempowered and rendered helpless by restrictions on their education and dependence upon men. This chapter will assert that Brown can be considered as a participant in the Gothic subgenre that has come to be known as the Female Gothic – the category that utilizes Gothic themes in order to address specifically female concerns.

Rounding out this study of Charles Brockden Brown, his works, his characteristic themes and his innovations will be some consideration in the conclusion of his appeal, achievement and continued relevancy. Brown, I will argue, deserves to be read today for multiple reasons – not only was he first in many things, which makes him historically significant, but his articulation of what we have come, post-Freud, to consider the 'uncanny' is arguably as prescient, evocative and effective as anything in the canon of American literature. At his best moments, Brown is as good at getting under our skin as any of our more famous Gothic authors. He is worth reading today not only because he was there first, but because his moments of brilliance are brilliant indeed.

A note on the text

Quotations from Brown's four Gothic novels in this study all are taken from the scrupulously prepared Hackett Publishing Company editions edited by Philip Barnard and Stephen Shapiro. The Hackett editions have the benefit of being readily available in relatively inexpensive paperback editions. I have however compared all quotations from the Hackett editions with how they appear in the authoritative

Kent State University Press Bicentennial Editions of Brown's works, and note any variants in the endnotes.

Although I offer some discussion of *Alcuin* and *Clara Howard* in chapter 4, for the purposes of this 'introduction' to Brown and his contributions to the Gothic genre I have made the decision to focus my attention primarily on Brown's works that are commercially available (his four Gothic novels and his short story 'Somnambulism').

1

Charles Brockden Brown and the Frontier Gothic

ജഇ

Into the woods

Since this chapter is about getting lost in the American woods, it seems appropriate that I take a somewhat circuitous path to get to Charles Brockden Brown, and begin by briefly discussing three contemporary films that share the conceit of the haunted American wilderness: Tim Burton's *Sleepy Hollow* (1999), Daniel Myrick and Eduardo Sánchez's *The Blair Witch Project* (also 1999) and M. Night Shyamalan's *The Village* (2004). Burton's *Sleepy Hollow* purports to be a film adaptation of early American author Washington Irving's classic, 'The Legend of Sleepy Hollow', first published in 1820 as part of Irving's *The Sketch-Book of Geoffrey Crayon, Gent*. In Irving's much-beloved comic tale, gawky and generally unlikeable itinerant teacher Ichabod Crane is either manipulated by the fetching Katrina van Tassel and victimized by the rough and ready Brom Bones or he is spirited away by the iconic headless horseman of Sleepy Hollow, the ghost of a German Hessian who allegedly lost his head to a cannonball during the Revolutionary War. Tim Burton's reimagining of this tale transforms Irving's misfit pedagogue into a bumbling yet somehow still savvy detective (played by Johnny Depp) sent from New York City to investigate murder in Sleepy Hollow, and ultimately affirms what Irving's tale leaves ambiguous: the Gothic intervention of malevolent preternatural forces. In Burton's hands, Irving's classic

comic tale transforms into a supernatural thriller in which the decapi-
tated rider emerges from the Western woods to wreak havoc on the
town.

The supernatural ambiguity that Burton drains away from the
New York woods in *Sleepy Hollow* is intriguingly relocated to the
Maryland forests in the smash hit released the same year, *The Blair
Witch Project*. In this low-budget release famous for its wobbly cam-
corder aesthetic and infamous for not showing the viewer anything
especially gory or frightening, three college students making a docu-
mentary about the Blair Witch, a mythic figure said to haunt the
forest in the foothills of the Appalachian Mountains, find themselves
increasingly lost until they move off the map entirely and disappear,
leaving only their film as testimony to their terrifying ordeal. At the
end of the film, like Ichabod Crane in Irving's original, they may
or may not have encountered the ghostly presence haunting the
woods and their current whereabouts are unknown.

As in *Sleepy Hollow* and *The Blair Witch Project*, the forest in M. Night
Shyamalan's *The Village* is also a haunted place, home to horrible
creatures referred to simply as 'Those We Do Not Speak Of'. Circum-
scribing the late eighteenth-century or early nineteenth-century
American village of Covington, the forest defines the limits of the
civilized world. According to the elders of the town, it is taboo to
enter the woods because this would encroach upon the creatures'
territory and violate the fragile truce that exists between the villagers
and the forest dwellers; the edge of the forest thus is presented as a
volatile contact zone, a guarded place where offerings are left to
propitiate the monsters. The trick to *The Village*, unlike *Blair Witch*,
is not that Those We Do Not Speak Of are never shown, but rather
that they are in fact not real. In Shyamalan's cynical post-September
11th envisioning of American society, the elders of Covington have
populated the woods – the outside – with monsters that function
as a cohesive force of social control.

The Village has not one trick but two. The other trick of *The Village*
is that the viewer discovers that the film is not in fact set 200 years
in the past as it first appears; rather, the film is set in the present. The
elders of Covington are modern, everyday people traumatized by
various acts of violence who have removed themselves from the
world altogether and created an insular society on a sort of desert

island in the middle of a nature reserve. For our purposes here, this temporal dislocation, this overlapping of past and present, eloquently condenses the central premise of this chapter that has already been gestured to by the introduction of *Sleepy Hollow* and *The Blair Witch Project*: that at the heart of the haunted psychic space of American identity remains the immemorial forest – the Western Woods that stretch all the way back to the first contact between Old World and New and are, to borrow from poet Robert Frost's famous formulation, inevitably dark and deep, if not always so lovely.

Indeed, all three of these modern films function as sorts of uncanny time machines that interrupt linear temporality as they foreground the Gothicized space of the American frontier. The Western Woods in *Sleepy Hollow* are a place populated by witches where the dead rest uneasily. Although Burton's adaptation is remarkably *un*faithful to Irving's original, it forcefully retains Irving's emphasis on the forest as a space of bewitchment in which we, like the inhabitants of Sleepy Hollow, New York, 'inhale the witching influence of the air, and begin to grow imaginative, to dream dreams, and see apparitions'.[1] With *Blair Witch*, we are not so much transported into the past as the past is dragged into the present. We are in Sleepy Hollow all over again, bewitched, bothered and bewildered by an undifferentiated smooth space in which linear time simply seems to have ceased, displaced by an unsettling temporality of repetition. And *The Village* turns out to be an exercise in double vision, an overlapping of eighteenth-century New York State and twenty-first-century Pennsylvania in which only the woods stay clearly in focus.

What these three modern films emphasize is the persistent power of what David Mogen, Scott P. Sanders and Joanne B. Karpinski refer to as the 'Frontier Gothic' in the introduction to their edited collection of the same name. From their perspective, the 'most fundamental conflict shaping American experience' is 'the battle between civilization and nature, between the mental landscape of European consciousness and the physical and psychical landscape of the New World'.[2] This confrontation between human aspirations and the Gothicized American landscape in their assessment is one that stretches from the present day all the way back to the earliest forays of European immigrants into North America. At the heart of American literature from its very beginnings are figurations of wilderness and the frontier as spaces of danger, savagery and violence. Indeed, the frontier is arguably the original American Gothic symbol, one evoking 'supernatural terror',[3] and *Sleepy Hollow, The Blair Witch Project* and *The Village* all support Mogen, Sanders and Karpinski's contention that frontier settings 'continue to be adapted to current literary needs, as self-consciously constructed symbolic environments, as threatened territories surviving from older frontiers, as new environments pioneered by science and technology'.[4]

This is important to us here because Charles Brockden Brown, as we shall see, played a foundational role in establishing the haunted American wilderness as an archetype of American Gothic literature. Before we ourselves shift back in time to consider Brown's innovations, however, it is necessary to foreground one crucial transformation that occurs in the contemporary American Frontier Gothic, as exemplified by Burton, Myrick and Sánchez, and Shyamalan. These three films are all to varying degrees about the haunted American wilderness, but what they displace and obscure is the connection between this motif and America's indigenous populations. The never-represented ghost that haunts the margins of these three movies, that is always just beyond the framing vision of the camera, is that of the Native American. As Mogen, Sanders and Karpinski observe – and as we shall see with Brown – in early American representations of the Gothicized wilderness, the encounter with indigenous persons, with the cultural and racial other, is central. The Indian, indeed, is represented in many early American narratives as a type of supernatural agent, as a figurative or literal demonic entity obstructing and actively threatening immigrant agendas in the New World. This vexed and complex interaction with the racial other, however, dissipates in the modern American Frontier Gothic. In Washington Irving's original 'The Legend of Sleepy Hollow', one hypothesis for the bewitching atmosphere of the Sleepy Hollow region is that an 'old Indian chief, the prophet or wizard of his tribe, held his pow-wows there before the country was discovered by Master Hendrick Hudson'.[5] In Burton's updating, the forest is devoid of Native Americans, the Indian wizard having transformed into a white female witch – which also interestingly is the case in *Blair Witch*. And, most fascinating of all, Shyamalan in *The Village* turns Indians literally into 'Those We Do Not Speak Of', monsters clothed in feather and bone that roam the forests but that are not human. In what seems a metatextual gesture almost too suggestive to be accidental, the film foregrounds Indians – and, by extension, racial difference – as precisely the topic that it will not address explicitly and yet that is everywhere present in this allegory of modern paranoia and racial profiling.

The point here is that ideas of the wilderness and the frontier are defining and intrinsically Gothic elements of both American literature and American identity. The forest is a place of monsters, witches and ghosts. And the frontier, the liminal space between wilderness and civilization, is the uncanny contact point at which self confronts other (as we shall see, both the external other and the other within), civilization shades into nature and linear time is interrupted. Among those responsible for naturalizing these historical associations is Charles Brockden Brown, credited as being the first American author to recognize the potency of the wilderness for the self-conscious construction of an intrinsically American Gothic fiction. For the purposes of this polemical introduction to Brown, my argument is that Brown essentially invents the American Frontier Gothic.

Turning now to Brown, I will first comment on the availability of the figuration of the Gothicized American wilderness to Brown as a trope to be appropriated and developed in his fiction. From there I will consider the ways in which Brown expands his Frontier Gothic with reference to his frequently anthologized short story, 'Somnabulism', his first novel, *Wieland*, and his final novel, *Edgar Huntly*. Along the way, I will give some consideration to Brown's appropriations in his fiction both from the European Gothic novel associated with Ann Radcliffe and Matthew Lewis and from the Native American captivity narrative. I will then conclude the chapter with some consideration of the ways in which later authors – notably Cooper, Poe and Hawthorne – themselves range freely across Brown's haunted American landscapes.

Wilderness views

Brown, well read as he was, would have been bombarded with images of the American wilderness and the frontier as dangerous spaces.

Even a cursory analysis of colonial American literature makes immediately obvious the iconic status of the American frontier as an uncanny contact zone fraught with anxiety. In the writings of the earliest American colonizers, including John Smith, John Winthrop and William Bradford, the struggle for survival is a contest with nature and with the 'savage and brutish men',[6] the Indians, who inhabit the forest. Cotton Mather famously figures the American wilderness as the 'devil's territories' in *The Wonders of the Invisible World*,[7] reinforcing the correlation repeatedly made between Native Americans and the devil in Native American captivity narratives such as Mary Rowlandson's popular *A Narrative of the Captivity and Restoration of Mrs Mary Rowlandson* published eleven years before. As Rowlandson details in her account, the frontier outpost of Lancaster, Massachusetts, thirty miles west of Boston, was attacked in February 1676 by merciless heathen 'hell-hounds' as part of what became known as 'King Philip's War' and Rowlandson, who was captured during the attack, spent the next ten weeks sharing her captors' hardships as they moved from place to place and struggled to stay alive during the frigid New England winter.[8] Her account of her experience became one of the most popular prose works of the seventeenth century, both in the American colonies and in England.

Of particular interest to Brown would also have been J. Hector St John de Crèvecoeur's *Letters from an American Farmer*, a series of essays about America based on Crèvecoeur's personal experiences but told from the point of view of a provincial farmer who calls himself simply James. The work was an immediate success when it first appeared in 1782 and presents a very positive appraisal of the newly formed American republic. Of note to us here, however, as we prepare to consider Brown's development of the Frontier Gothic – and especially his *Edgar Huntly* – is Crèvecoeur's representation of the frontier and of frontier settlers. Crèvecoeur's Jeffersonian ideal is the gentleman farmer. The 'great woods',[9] however, in which men exist beyond the reach of law and government, are a place where men 'appear to be no better than carnivorous animals of a superior rank, living on the flesh of wild animals'.[10] By virtue of living in or near the woods, 'their actions are regulated by the wildness of the neighborhood' and children born there 'grow up a mongrel breed, half civilized, half savage'.[11] Removed from the constraints of civilized society, these necessary precursors to civilized society exist 'often in a perfect state of war'.[12] As is the case in Brown's *Edgar Huntly*, the American wilderness in *Letters from an American Farmer* is a lawless place that renders human beings 'ferocious, gloomy, and unsociable'[13] and transforms them into animals. Brown's cynical revision of Crève-coeur, however, will be to suggest that the animal is lurking there all along, even in the midst of civilized society. The gentleman farmer is only ever one small step away from transforming into the lawless savage.

In considering the power that the frontier and the wilderness would have exercised over Brown's imagination, it is also important to consider just what Brown's experience of the world would have been in the decades leading up to the turn of the eighteenth century. Brown, we need to bear in mind, lived in a world in many ways substantially different from the one we inhabit today. Although Philadelphia was rapidly expanding in the late eighteenth and early nineteenth centuries, roads outside the old town centre (roughly between Front Street and Seventh Street running from east to west and Arch Street to Pine Street from north to south) quickly degener-ated into unlit dirt paths. Walking north or west, one could very speedily leave behind urban life and enter unsettled wilderness areas – including picturesque areas celebrated in the writings of authors indebted to Brown, notably Edgar Allan Poe (especially 'Morning on the Wissahiccon' [1844]) and George Lippard.

Brown, in short, lived in a world still surrounded by actual wilder-ness – forested areas still containing dangerous predatory wildlife – and I suspect it is difficult for the contemporary imagination to grasp just how dark it must have been at night in the woods in a world without electric lights, automobile headlamps, flashlights, or any means of illumination aside from candles, oil lamps, lanterns and torches. It was a world in which most people seldom or never ventured more than a few miles from home due to terrible or non-existent roads. And it was a bigger world – the roughly 100-mile trip from Philadelphia to New York which now can be accomplished by car or train in a couple of hours would have taken two days by horse and carriage with overnight accommodation scarce and far between. Without mobile phones and GPS navigation systems available, getting lost or injured – particularly away from more travelled paths – were legitimate concerns.

When one considers the literary precedents available to Brown characterizing the wilderness as dangerous, savage, wild and the 'devil's territories', as well as the much more immediate reality of the wilderness during his lifetime, that Brown should foreground the forest as part of his American Gothic is indeed far from surprising. Brown clearly was not the first to Gothicize the forest, to represent it as a realm of lawlessness and animalistic savagery; this image of the woods was already firmly in place, available for his literary colonization. Brown's achievement was to become the first American author consciously to appropriate the woods and their attendant anxieties for his Gothic romances.

Rude, sterile and lonely: 'Somnabulism. A fragment'

Now let us travel with Brown well past the boundaries of Philadelphia northward to the 'desolate tract' dubbed 'Norwood' by Brown in his 'Somnabulism. A fragment' – a region he depicts as 'rude, sterile, and lonely, bestrewn with rocks, and embarrassed with bushes'.[14] Although 'Somnabulism' was not published until May 1805 in Brown's *The Literary Magazine and American Register*, many scholars believe this most anthologized of Brown's writings to have been written between 1797 and 1799 during the period that Brown was at work on his first novel, *Sky-Walk; or, The Man Unknown to Himself*, the 'lost precursor' to *Edgar Huntly*.[15] It certainly seems to be the case, as we shall see, that Brown incorporated much of this story of nocturnal somnambulistic perambulation (sleepwalking) through a Gothicized wilderness setting directly into *Edgar Huntly*, supporting Barnard and Shapiro's suggestion that the story was a 'draft "fragment"' in the planning of either *Sky-Walk* or *Edgar Huntly*.[16]

'Somnabulism' is a first-person account told by a young male narrator named Althorpe. His household has been entertaining two guests, the lovely Constantia Davis – with whom the narrator is smitten – and her father, both of whom are abruptly summoned away by a letter detailing 'concerns of great importance' (p. 246) that must be attended to immediately. As the two prepare to set out on a twenty-mile night-time journey across wood and field, young Althorpe – who is concerned that if he lets Constantia out of his sight, he will lose his chance at love – begins to conjure up all manner of nocturnal dangers that could greet them along their way and first entreats his guests to wait until morning and then, when they resist this suggestion, to allow him to accompany them. 'My imagination was vivid', he tells the reader, 'my passions, when I allowed them sway, were incontroullable. My conduct, as my feelings, was character-ized by precipitation and headlong energy' (p. 248).

The narrator, alas, is doubly rebuffed. Constantia and her father will neither wait until morning nor permit him to accompany them. They depart and Althorpe, after spending a 'drooping and melancholy evening' (p. 250) in which he envisions every possible obstacle to their progress in his mind's eye, ultimately falls into a 'profound slumber' in which he dreams that he is summoned to defend Constantia from an 'assassin' whom he kills with a pistol shot (p. 251). The next day brings uncanny confirmation of the prophetic nature of Althorpe's dream. Constantia Davis, he learns, was shot on the road during the night and, we are subsequently informed at the end of the story, she died the next morning after lingering for a time in 'dreadful agonies' at the home of a physician named Inglefield (p. 258).

Prefaced as Brown's story is with an 'extract' attributed to the *Vienna Gazette* detailing an account of a young man who allegedly shot the object of his affection while sleepwalking, the obvious 'up-shot' of 'Somnabulism' is that Althorpe is himself the assassin who followed the Davises and shot Constantia in his sleep. As I shall return to in chapter 3, his dream of being summoned to protect Constantia and then shooting her assassin is not then an example of supernatural (if somewhat confused) prophecy, but rather of unconscious 'in-controullable' passions being allowed sway over conscious restraint and reflection. Althorpe, in this drama of the mind divided and turned against itself, is thus simultaneously protector and assassin, the spurned lover whose affection turns to animosity.

For the purposes of this chapter, however, what I wish to emphasize here is not the conflict between the conscious and unconscious mind, but rather the physical landscape on which this contest plays out. What Brown invents in 'Somnabulism' – and then develops much more fully in *Edgar Huntly* – is the theatre of the Gothicized American frontier wilderness, a liminal crepuscular realm that, to borrow from Dennis Berthold, exploits the American landscape for fictive purposes.[17]

The story is an early example of Brown essentially treating geography as a sort of character 'to create both an impetus and an arena for the working out of gothic terror'.[18] The Davises must navigate twenty miles of alien landscape in darkness, hedged in by 'neighboring precipices, and a thick umbrage of oaks' (p. 257). Norwood (the North Woods) is a particularly 'lonely region' (p. 258), sparsely populated and characterized by a 'profound stillness' (p. 257). Travellers must take care to manoeuvre around bridges and sloughs and exercise particular care to avoid an ancient and enormous oak that grows in the middle of the road (p. 250).

While there are apparently no actual Indians haunting the woods in 'Somnabulism', what arguably substitutes for them – like the headless horseman, Blair Witch, or Those We Do Not Speak Of – is a quasi-mythical creature named Nick Handyside who reportedly bedevils travellers for sport. Nick, who loves to scare strangers in the woods, is both physically and mentally 'other'. He is an 'idiot' who 'merited the name of monster, if a projecting breast, a mis-shapen head, features horrid and distorted, and a voice that resembled nothing that was ever before heard, could entitle him to that appellation' (p. 255). 'The propensities of this being', consider Constantia and her father in a line of thought later picked up by Irving's Ichabod Crane, 'might contribute to realize, on an American road, many of those imaginary tokens and perils which abound in the wildest romance' and, their meditation continues, 'no theatre was better adapted than Norwood to such an exhibition' (p. 256). The American woods, in short, are bedevilled by both perils and monsters, and Nick's cries, 'as ferocious as those which are to be heard in Siamese or Abyssinian forests' (p. 256), awaken and transform the landscape from passive obstacle into active threat – a hazard realized when the Davises' coach, pulled uncontrollably by frightened horses, crashes into the same oak about which they were warned and is 'dashed into a thousand pieces' (p. 257).

'Somnabulism. A fragment' is a story about the mind divided and human beings who are strangers to themselves, compelled as we are by unconscious impulses. But what structures the possibility and participates in the development of this story is Brown's creation of a haunted and menacing American landscape. Both figuratively and literally, 'Somnabulism' is a story about being surrounded by darkness and, in this gloom, the land itself manifests what George Toles refers to as a 'capacity for aggression'.[19] Norwood, 'rude, sterile, and lonely', becomes the 'theatre' for the development of the American Gothic and, replacing European castles and abbeys, the sublime geography of precipices and ancient oaks becomes the site of hazard and haunting. The American Frontier Gothic begins in 'Somnambulism' with a midnight murder in the middle of the woods – an event that will be reprised by Brown in *Edgar Huntly*.

Out of Eden and into the wilderness: Wieland

The Gothic potential of the American landscape represented in 'Somnambulism' is developed by Brown most fully in *Edgar Huntly*, a narrative that imports from 'Somnambulism' the device of sleep-walking, transforms Norwood into Norwalk (signalling the increased emphasis on movement), changes oak to elm, and recasts Nick Handy-side in the form of Native Americans. However, before ending up with Edgar, our next stop on this circuitous tour of Brown's Frontier Gothic is to spend a little time with Clara Wieland and Brown's first published novel, *Wieland; or, The Transformation. An American Tale* – 'the founding text of American Gothic' according to Kafer.[20] While I will deal with the psychological aspects of *Wieland* more fully in chapter 3, what I wish to observe here is the role that the American landscape plays in developing Brown's Gothic themes and the impli-cations of this Gothicization of physical geography for those who wish to read *Wieland* as an allegory of the post-Revolutionary American condition.

Wieland, arguably Brown's most famous novel, is the account of a man who hears voices commanding him to murder his family. Like 'Somnambulism', *Wieland* consciously raises questions about the bifurcated nature of the mind and the human ability to interpret sensory data accurately and arrive at sound conclusions. Also as in 'Somnambulism', the landscape itself plays an important role in structuring the action and allowing the horrific events to play out. Indeed, what stands out early on in *Wieland* is the isolated situation of Mettingen, the Wieland family estate purchased by Wieland Sr along the banks of Pennsylvania's Schuylkill River. Although only a few miles from Philadelphia, Mettingen seems a world apart – an impression especially developed through the description of the temple built by Wieland Sr,

> on the top of a rock whose sides were steep, rugged, and encumbered with dwarf cedars and stony asperities . . . The eastern verge of this precipice was sixty feet above the river which flowed at its foot. The view before it consisted of a transparent current, fluctuating and rippling in a rocky channel, and bounded by a rising scene of cornfields and orchards.[21]

The temple is isolated and difficult to reach and it is upon this 'rocky mass' (p. 16) – Brown's dark parody of the Puritan conception of a religious city on a hill – that Wieland Sr meets his doom through what the narrative suggests is spontaneous human combustion.

Despite the tragic circumstances resulting in the death of her father and in turn leading to the death of her mother, Clara Wieland at the start of her tale portrays Mettingen as a placid island of artistic and intellectual contemplation in which she, her brother and his family dwell harmoniously. Her father's property having been divided equally between herself and her brother, Clara lives alone in a 'neat dwelling, situated on the bank of the river, three quarters of a mile' (p. 21) from her brother's dwelling – and apparently at least that far from anyone else's as well. Joined by their friend Henry Pleyel, Mettingen existed for them, Clara explains, as the site of 'six years of uninterrupted happiness' during which the violence of the French and Indian War was so distant as to 'enhance [their] enjoyment by affording objects of comparison' (p. 26). Mettingen in short is initially presented as a sort of idyllic garden of paradise, ripe for the serpent to come calling.

Like the Norwood forest in 'Somnambulism', Mettingen is a haunted liminal space positioned on the border between the real and the fantastic and defined by its isolation and strangeness. The foundational trauma of the story is the midnight spontaneous combustion of a religious zealot initially called to the New World to enter the forest and convert the natives. The blazing light that illuminates the lonely temple during his immolation only serves to magnify the darkness – both literally and, as we shall see in chapter 3, metaphorically – that follows it 'in a tenfold degree' (p. 17).

At several different points in *Wieland* following this mysterious beginning, the isolation of Mettingen – and particularly of Clara's dwelling on her own there (Clemit remarks that Clara's isolated situation is strongly reminiscent of the Radcliffean Gothic plot)[22] – as well as the darkness and hazards of the landscape are emphasized. The first time that Clara hears voices in her bedroom, she is forced to jump out of bed and run the better part of a mile to her brother's house in the dark where she faints on the doorstep (p. 51). Following this event, Clara explains that '[t]hat solitude, formerly so dear to me, could no longer be endured' (p. 53). Several weeks after this event, Clara has another uncanny experience that, as one might expect, takes place in the woods. Seeking out a place even more secluded than her little house, Clara visits a little summerhouse or gazebo in an isolated spot by the river:

> The river bank is, at this part of it, and for some considerable space upward, so rugged and steep as not to be easily descended . . . From a crevice of the rock, to which this edifice was attached, there burst forth a stream of the purest water, which, leaping from ledge to ledge, for the space of sixty feet, produced the freshness in the air, and a murmur, the most delicious and soothing imaginable. These, added to the odours of the cedars which embowered it, and of the honey-suckle which clustered among the lattices, rendered this my favorite retreat in summer. (p. 54)

The scene is sylvan and Clara is soon lulled to sleep, but the seclusion of her retreat elicits unsettling dreams in which the landscape both figuratively and literally becomes threatening. Clara recalls:

> I at length imagined myself walking, in the evening twilight, to my brother's habitation. A pit, methought, had been dug in the path I had taken, of which I was not aware. As I carelessly pursued my walk, I thought I saw my brother, standing at some distance before me, beckoning and calling me to make haste. He stood on the opposite edge of the gulph. I mended my pace, and one step more would have plunged me into this abyss, had not some one from behind caught suddenly my arm, and exclaimed, in a voice of eagerness and terror, 'Hold! hold!' (pp. 54–5)

Clara awakens from her dream to find herself 'surrounded by the deepest darkness' (p. 55). The mysterious voice from her closet speaks to her again, explaining that its purpose had been to murder her but it has repented. Clara is then left in a precarious position:

> I could not take a step without hazard of falling to the bottom of the precipice. The path, leading to the summit, was short, but rugged and intricate. Even star-light was excluded by the umbrage, and not the faintest gleam was afforded to guide my steps. (p. 55)

She is left in 'unintermitted darkness' (p. 55) until Pleyel shows up to rescue her.

Critics have rightly focused on the psychoanalytic implications of Clara's dream in which her brother summons her toward her destruction. Shirley Samuels, for example, has interpreted the dream as suggestive of incestuous desire;[23] Leslie Fiedler, somewhat more circumspectly, has considered it in light of the 'destructive aspects of the brother-sister relationship'.[24] What also should be emphasized here, though, is the role the landscape plays in structuring Clara's experience. Just as the path up to the temple at Mettingen is 'steep, rugged, and encumbered with dwarf cedars and stony asperities', the path down to the summerhouse is steep, rugged and 'embowered' with cedars. Both are isolated locations at which the line between fantasy and reality crumbles. In the temple, the 'inner light' that guides Wieland Sr externalizes itself as spontaneous combustion, while in the summerhouse, the figurative 'gulph' of Clara's dream is paralleled by the literal chasm of her location. And in both locations, profound darkness – again, both literal and figurative – ultimately prevails.

Indeed, as *Wieland* progresses, the darkness enveloping Mettingen only becomes more and more impenetrable and Clara more and more isolated. She becomes increasingly aware of her vulnerable position in her little house with only her servant Judith: 'Whether midnight was approaching, or had passed, I knew not. I was, as then, alone and defenseless' (p. 70). Her lover Pleyel overhears a conversation in the dark and becomes convinced of Clara's perfidity: 'My sight was of no use to me. Beneath so thick an umbrage, the darkness was intense' (p. 107). Following the murders and Wieland's arrest, Clara returns to her 'vacant and forlorn' (p. 146) cottage illuminated solely by a 'kind of twilight ... sufficient for the purposes of vision; but, at the same time, involving all minuter objects in obscurity' (p. 147). Here Carwin emerges from the darkness to plead his case before Wieland himself appears with the intention of completing his bloody work by murdering Clara. Then, following Wieland's suicide and echoing the spontaneous combustion that begins the narrative, Clara's house bursts into flames, again briefly illuminating the darkness. This pattern has led Christophersen to remark that one of the organizing motifs of the novel is a 'flickering light followed by darkness' and to conclude that 'darkness pervades *Wieland*'.[25]

Hinds, noting the 'non-causality' in *Wieland* – the story's random occurrences and digressions – argues that the narrative 'sublimates' the 'local frontier to a discursive wilderness',[26] and her assertion that 'Clara's narrative exists not on Huntly's literal frontier but on the frontier of discourse' is provocative.[27] Nevertheless, I think one can make the case (as Hinds in fact does, though she plays it down in comparison with *Edgar Huntly*) that landscape in *Wieland* remains 'alien' and 'uncontrollable',[28] and I agree with Lisa West Norwood that the narrative in *Wieland* 'revolves around the capacity of the landscape to generate and retain meaning'.[29] Mettingen is Brown's Norwood/Norwalk combined and condensed. Although the farm presumably possesses some tillable ground, Brown's representation of it emphasizes cliffs and chasms, woods, rivers and, above all, darkness. The twenty miles the Davises must traverse in the dark to the ferry in 'Somnambulism' are reduced to the three quarters of a mile Clara must run in the night to her brother's house for help, but the journey seems just as long and frightening and the 'umbrage' every bit as deep. Mettingen ultimately is just as remote and isolated as are the Davises while travelling across Norwood or Edgar while sleepwalking through Norwalk.

Of particular note in *Wieland* are the ease and speed with which an apparent Eden – a 'rationalist's paradise' in Jane Tompkins's estimation[30] – transforms in Brown's 'American Tale' into the site of a holocaust.[31] Tompkins thus reads the novel as an allegory of American colonial history in which the situation of the Wieland family serves as a microcosm for the post-Revolutionary nation at large. Vickers, glossing Tompkins, explains that

> the novel can be read allegorically if we view the plight of the young Wielands as analogous to the plight of the fledgling nation. Thus, the

setting of the deceptively idyllic Wieland home on the banks of the Schuylkill provides a microcosmic parallel for the deceptively idealistic temper of the new republic. The horrific events in the novel are the effects of the self-imposed isolation of the Wielands and the Pleyels.[32]

Tompkins reads the novel as expressing Brown's horror at the 'consequences of independence',[33] his rejection of Jeffersonian Republicanism and his 'plea for the restoration of civic authority in a post-Revolutionary age'.[34] Vickers qualifies this assertion by asserting that *Wieland* offers a more ambivalent critique of both Republicanism and Federalism.[35]

What is interesting about these allegorical interpretations is the extent to which they – and others like them – necessarily overlay a figurative interpretation upon the literal geography in *Wieland*. Tompkins thus discusses *Wieland* in spatial terms: she notes, for example, that 'because the social spaces in *Wieland* are empty, the space of authority is vacant'.[36] This observation then leads her to assert – using language from the novel itself – that 'the absence of "grounds" on which to build either belief or disbelief is the problem that confronts the central characters in this novel'.[37] In terms echoing those of Tompkins, Hagenbüchle (himself borrowing from Ridgely) asserts that the world of *Wieland* is a world of 'terrible emptiness'[38] and goes on to discuss the undermining in the novel of the 'ground' of epistemological certainty and human trust.[39] Making the clearest link between physical geography and allegorical interpretation, Christophersen writes that *Wieland* 'poses a contrary, highly skeptical vision of God and the American experience – one that stresses the abyss on whose verge the nation's temple has been erected'.[40] All of these interpretations depend for their force on Brown's characterization of isolating geographical spaces that turn threatening. Put differently, the bedrock of these interpretations is the landscape. Cathy Davidson, in her seminal study of American literature, *Revolution and the Word: The Rise of the Novel in America*, contends that Brown in *Wieland* 'raises perturbing questions about how much the Gothic might be rooted in the very essentials of American democracy'.[41] What also seems to be the case, though, is that Brown raises perturbing questions about the extent to which the American identity is rooted in a Gothicized American *landscape* and the effect that this

Gothicization of American identity may have on possibilities for harmonious existence. In relation to this, Dennis Berthold asserts in a comment specifically tied to *Edgar Huntly* but that, I would argue, can be extended to Brown's writing in general, that

> savagery – or gothic terror – is not something one can easily avoid in the American landscape. It inheres in the scene as much as in the psyche, and each complements the other to suggest the mixed nature of the American experience. In America, gothic terror is somehow 'natural'.[42]

American possibilities, Brown seems to suggest, are both constructed and constrained by the physical geography of the land itself. The American experience, as a result of American geography, is an essentially Gothic one.

Edgar's musket: planting the seeds of violence

In a strange and striking moment in Brown's fourth novel, *Edgar Huntly*, the eponymous protagonist, having escaped from a cave, eaten a panther and killed four Indian assailants, finishes off a fifth and then 'prompted by some freak of fancy', he explains, 'I struck his musquet in the ground, and left it standing upright in the middle of the road'.[43] According to Harriet Hustis, Huntly's gesture of planting the musket

> symbolically establishes a psychological and textual crossroads where masculinity, narrativity, and American national identity violently and memorably intersect. In effect, the Indian's musquet serves as a signpost, a silent but evocative marker of the repressions and epistemological elisions upon which American literary identity is premised in this novel.[44]

In Hustis's interpretation of *Edgar Huntly*, Edgar's 'hysterical discourse' essentially rationalizes white genocidal intentions towards what Brown depicts as savage and depraved Indians.[45] As I will discuss below, Brown's attitude toward Native Americans, especially as represented in *Edgar Huntly*, has been a contentious issue. Before turning to that topic, however, I would like to approach the musket in the road from a somewhat different direction and consider it as a condensed symbolization of Brown's Frontier Gothic.

The gun in the road is arguably the novel's pivot point, the axis around which the narrative rotates. Indeed, it would be hard in all of American literature to find a more evocative symbol of the taming of the wildness through violence. Edgar has conquered the cave, the panther and the Indian, and through his act of planting the musket he essentially now claims this territory as his own. Wrenched away from the Indian who possessed it, the gun (itself a product of white culture somehow appropriated by the Indian) acts as a type of signpost saying 'Edgar was here'. It marks his having crossed over into the wilderness, been baptized in blood and violence, and returned. Edgar does not plant a flag in the ground, claiming 'virgin territory'. Nor does he plant a cross over the body of his fallen foe, reclaiming the territory for God; rather, he plants a gun – perhaps even one fashioned from the very trees torn up to lay down the road – near the corpse of his unburied opponent, suggesting that what grows from this soil is violence. Edgar, blind as he is to what motivates him throughout the tale, doesn't know what compels him to leave the gun standing as he does, essentially announcing his prowess and 'giving the middle finger' to the world. It is merely a 'freak of fancy' to him – like everything that moves him, an unconscious impulse the meaning of which escapes him. This overdetermined symbol of masculine violence, however, seems to loom large over the entire novel – a work that is considered the first to exploit the dangers of the American frontier for fictive purposes.[46] The long path of the American Frontier Gothic stretches back in time to a gun planted in the middle of a road alongside a dead Indian.

According to Kafer, Brown invented the American Gothic with *Wieland*, and with *Edgar Huntly* he 'set out determinedly to write a Gothic novel, American style'.[47] In most cases, ascertaining an author's intentions is a hazardous endeavour; Brown, however, is very clear in the brief note that precedes the text of *Edgar Huntly*. He tells the reader in 'To the Public' that American literature can and must differ from European models and that it is the purpose of his work to 'exhibit a series of adventures, growing out of the condition of our country' (p. 3). His work will engage the reader 'by means hitherto unemployed by preceding authors' and will eschew the 'puerile superstition and exploded manners; Gothic castles and chimeras' of European models. In place of these established conventions, he will substitute devices he feels are more appropriate to the American condition: 'incidents of Indian hostility, and the perils of the western wilderness' (pp. 3–4). For ghosts he will give us Indians, and in place of haunted castles he will substitute haunted forests. True to his word, both of these topics become crucial components of Brown's invention of the American Frontier Gothic.

As I have already gestured toward above (and as is the case with just about every aspect of Brown's writing), there is a well-established debate in the critical literature on Brown concerning just how to interpret his representations of Indians. Critics sympathetic to Brown bend over backwards to exonerate Brown and his protagonist in *Edgar Huntly* from the charge of virulent racism. So Christophersen explains in a roundabout way that Brown, together with some of his contemporaries, was concerned that the integrity of the newly formed country was being eroded by slavery and Native American policy.[48] Sydney Krause argues that *Edgar Huntly*'s oblique references to Native American exploitation and displacement 'awake[n] a compassionate attitude toward the Indians themselves'.[49] And in language clearly indicative of the period of its production, Mabel Morris contends that '*Edgar Huntly* indicates that the writer's attitude was one of sympathy toward the red man'.[50] On the other end of the spectrum, Myra Jehlen asserts that '*Edgar Huntly*'s gothic conventions come alive in an implacable hatred of Indians that the author shares with his characters'.[51] Hustis agrees, arguing that Edgar's murderous rampage 'participates in an early American textual hegemony that repeatedly sanctions and paradoxically rationalizes colonial violence against the "savagery" and "depravity" of the Native Americans'.[52]

A more nuanced position is adopted by those critics who observe that, while Native Americans are presented as savage and animalistic in *Edgar Huntly*, white society – and especially Edgar – are presented as being as bad if not worse. This is the conclusion of Robert Newman, for example, who contends that 'the underlying irony of the novel is the revelation of the savage potential of the white man'.[53] Edgar, once he wakes up in the cave, essentially 'goes Native' to the point of parody. He kills a panther in the dark with a 'tom-hawk', he out-savages the Indians by murdering them in their sleep, and later while being pursued by Sarsefield and a band of white men, he is not surprisingly mistaken by them for an Indian, is fired upon and returns fire, narrowly missing killing his mentor and substitute father, Sarsefield. So, while Indians in the novel are presented as barbaric savages, the text's apparent racism is undercut by the revelation that 'savagery becomes a human characteristic, unrestricted by race'.[54]

It seems clear to me that, while Brown's Indians may indeed gesture toward a tragic history of betrayal, exploitation and genocidal intent on the part of white society and, in keeping with Newman's argument above, barbarism starts at home, Brown's Indians are not finally people but merely plot devices – nightmarish natural forces that are part of Brown's Gothicization of the American landscape. Brown's Indians, like panthers, caves and cliffs, reflect and accentuate the peril of the wilderness. As Grabo observes, Brown's 'brawny and terrific'[55] Indians, denied the power of speech, are not human: 'Those Indians have not come from any Cooper novel but from some nightmare without words. Their lack of speech is their real savageness, and it is this lack that makes them so terrible and so easily destroyed'.[56] Christophersen extends this by proposing that 'it is not the Indian as social victim that appeals to Brown's imagination, but the Indian as projection of natural evil and the id; his red men are therefore treated essentially as animals, living extensions of the threat of the wilderness'.[57] It is no accident, then, that Edgar first encounters Indians like bears asleep in a cave. They are yet another natural obstacle to be overcome on his path back to civilization.

The difficulty of Edgar's quest to return home is that he, like the missing film-makers in *The Blair Witch Project*, has essentially wandered off the map. *Edgar Huntly*, it should be pointed out, is a novel defined by wandering – both, as critics have remarked, in its digressive structure and more literally through Edgar's constant movement. What Edgar primarily does is walk. He walks when he is awake and he walks in his sleep. He walks during the day and he walks at night. He walks until he collapses, then he gets up and walks some more. He walks through underground caves, hikes up mountainsides and then, for a change of pace, floats down a river. He is defined by his passage through space (and, one might add, like some perverse Johnny Appleseed, he leaves dead Indians and plants muskets in his wake). The centrality of movement to the narrative is even signalled by Brown in his transformation of 'Nor*wood*' in 'Somnambulism' into 'Nor*walk*' in *Edgar Huntly*. Edgar is constantly on the move throughout the entire text. The problem for Edgar, though, is that, like attempting to run in a nightmare, all his movement does not really get him anywhere; this is because all his attempts to organize the landscape and his progress through it, to survey and describe – and indeed to stick guns in the road like pins in a map to mark his progress – are frustrated by the dream logic that governs Norwalk. Norwalk is ostensibly part of Pennsylvania, but the Norwalk through which Edgar ventures appears on no map. As Hinds observes, Edgar's confrontation is with a 'large and boundless space',[58] space that, as Downes characterizes it, is 'mazy and impassable'.[59]

Edgar takes pains in Chapter IX to paint a picture of Norwalk as inhospitable and confusing; and either Edgar or the space itself turns out to be inconsistent. He initially describes it as 'a space, somewhat circular, about six miles in diameter, and exhibiting a perpetual and intricate variety of craggy eminences and deep dells' (p. 67). It is a discontinuous, irregular space in which valleys do not connect or connect mysteriously through secret, underground passages:

> The hollows are single, and walled around by cliffs, ever varying in shape and height, and have seldom any perceptible communication with each other. These hollows are of all dimensions, from the narrowness and depth of a well, to the amplitude of one hundred yards. Winter's snow is frequently found in these cavities at midsummer. The streams that burst forth from every crevice are thrown, by the irregularities of the surface, into numberless cascades, often disappear in mists or in chasms, and emerge from subterranean channels, and, finally, either subside into lakes, or quietly meander through the lower and more level grounds. (p. 67)

This unwelcoming location is a space governed by geological, rather than human, time:

> Wherever nature left a flat it is made rugged and scarcely passable by enormous and fallen trunks, accumulated by the storms of ages, and

forming, by their slow decay, a moss-covered soil, the haunt of rabbits and lizards. These spots are obscured by the melancholy umbrage of pines, whose eternal murmurs are in unison with vacancy and solitude, with the reverberations of the torrents and the whistling of the blasts. (p. 67)

And, above all, Norwalk is a labyrinthine, frustrating space that, as described by Edgar, almost consciously thwarts human intentions:

A sort of continued vale, winding and abrupt, leads into the midst of this region and through it. This vale serves the purpose of a road. It is a tedious maze and perpetual declivity, and requires, from the passenger, a cautious and sure foot. Openings and ascents occasionally present themselves on each side, which seem to promise you access to the interior region, but always terminate, sooner or later, in insuperable difficulties, at the verge of a precipice or the bottom of a steep. (p. 67)

As detailed by Edgar, Norwalk is finally a place of mystery and concealment – a site of hidden hollows, numberless waterfalls and underground passages. It is a space outside time, of midsummer snow and 'slow decay' where 'eternal murmurs' whisper across the detritus of 'storms of ages'. And it is a devious space that tempts one with the 'promise' of knowledge, only to frustrate one's designs with paths that ultimately lead nowhere.

Of course, Edgar does manage to access the hidden heart of Norwalk – by accident, as one would expect, rather than conscious design – and what he discovers is what Ichabod Crane will later find in Sleepy Hollow, what Poe's Arthur Gordon Pym will find on the island of Tsalal and the lost *Blair Witch Project* students still later will find in the Maryland woods: an utterly foreign space, sublime, nightmarish and inhuman. Having emerged from the pitch blackness of the underground cave into which he has tracked Clithero and advanced into the interior of Norwalk, Edgar, in another extended meditation on the landscape, attempts to paint a picture of an unexpected topography that is essentially something from a dream. He begins by struggling to give some sense of the landscape's organization:

> I now turned my attention to the interior space. If you imagine a cylindrical mass, with a cavity dug in the centre, whose edge conforms to the exterior edge; and, if you place in this cavity another cylinder, higher than that which surrounds it, but so small as to leave between its sides and those of the cavity, an hollow space, you will gain as distinct an image of this hill as words can convey. The summit of the inner rock was rugged and covered with trees of unequal growth. (p. 71)

As best one can tell, the interior of Norwalk seems to be organized like Chinese boxes or Russian nesting dolls with a mountain within a mountain, and this counter-intuitive space is disarmingly surreal. Edgar continues:

> As I had traversed the outer, I now explored the inner, edge of this hill ... I could scarcely venture to look beneath. The height was dizzy, and the walls, which approached each other at top, receded at the bottom, so as to form the resemblance of an immense hall, lighted from a rift, which some convulsion of nature had made in the roof. Where I stood there ascended a perpetual mist, occasioned by a torrent that dashed along the rugged pavement below. (p. 71)

Edgar is peering down into yet another chasm shrouded in mist through which a river runs, and what he discovers is nature's hidden sanctuary, a natural hall dramatically lit by sunlight streaming down through a rift.

Since this is not a Poe narrative, however, Edgar does not experience the perverse inclination to throw himself into the chasm (although he does encounter an apparently near-sighted panther that does); rather, as a young man of more sensibility than sense, he is moved to reflect on the 'desolate and solitary grandeur in the scene' (p. 71):

> A sort of sanctity and awe environed it, owing to the consciousness of absolute and utter loneliness. It was probable that human feet had never before gained this recess, that human eyes had never been fixed upon these gushing waters. The aboriginal inhabitants had no motives to lead them into caves like this, and ponder on the verge of such a precipice. Their successors were still less likely to have wandered

hither. Since the birth of this continent, I was probably the first who
had deviated thus remotely from the customary paths of men. (p. 71)

That Edgar is wrong in his assumptions is a given; immediately after
speculating on the uniqueness of his situation, Edgar is stunned to
see Clithero in the distance, 'seated where it seemed impossible for
human efforts to have placed him' (p. 72). But rather than detracting
from the surreal hauntedness of this irrational topography, the unexpected presence of Edgar's doppelgänger here only serves to accentuate its uncanniness. Where else would one expect to meet one's
double than among the 'phantastic shapes and endless irregularities'
(p. 71) of this Gothicized landscape?

Also of note in relation to this discussion of the fantastic topography of Brown's American wilderness is the strange fact that, as
the narrative progresses, Norwalk actually seems to expand. Initially
presented as 'about six miles in diameter' in Chapter IX, by Chapter
XVII Edgar is telling us that 'Norwalk is the termination of a sterile
and narrow tract, which begins in the Indian country. It forms a
sort of rugged and rocky vein, and continues upwards of fifty miles'
(p. 115). In the space of eight chapters, Norwalk has expanded over
seven times. This is because the heart of Norwalk into which Edgar
chases Clithero is the epicentre of the Gothic earthquake that shakes
Edgar Huntly and its strangeness radiates outward, eventually engulf-
ing the narrative as a whole; and the ripples are still being felt today.

Brown, note the critics, invented the American Frontier Gothic
with *Edgar Huntly*. The wilderness, according to Paul Downes, 'represents one element in Brown's Americanization of the gothic form'.[60]
Myra Jehlen concurs, observing that the western frontier enters
American fiction in *Edgar Huntly*, and adding – perhaps with Edgar
planting the musket in the road in mind – that in her estimation
the novel is 'the first to envision a specifically American psyche and
also more or less the last to represent taking possession of the continent not as a destined fulfillment but as conquest'.[61] Newman
contends that Brown uses the 'indigenous terrors' of the American
wilderness 'to create a distinctly American Gothic' and notes that,
'by writing in support of the settlement built against the wilderness,
he inverts the radical social order of the European Gothic romance,
which stresses the decay of the aristocracy'.[62] And Seelye observes

that Brown's dark vision of the frontier setting established the 'tone' for much future American fiction.[63]

What these appraisals do not get at, though, is the essential strangeness of Brown's Gothicized American landscape. When one ventures into the American woods, one is leaving behind not only civilization, but logic, reason and conscious deliberation. The two critics who make this connection most explicitly are Elizabeth Jane Wall Hinds and George Toles. Hinds notes the ways in which landscape functions in *Edgar Huntly* essentially as a character in its own right. She observes the ways in which Edgar is 'overcome by his confrontation with frontier spaces' and is 'led passively among uncontrolled forces, as though the landscape itself were in control of the action'.[64] Later, she remarks on the way in which the landscape seems to become 'actively aggressive',[65] and it is this animation of the topography that constructs for the reader Brown's unsettling Gothic atmosphere:

> the terror in Brown's novels lies in the active role these locations play in the undoing of Brown's narrators. These spaces do not exist to be conquered by penetration. Rather, landscape in Brown's work remains at all times alien, and finally, uncontrollable.[66]

In essence, the landscape becomes unstable and irrational – dreamlike – in *Edgar Huntly*, and Edgar's attempt to get back to civilization is the attempt to wake up from a nightmare.

For Toles as well, the 'special quality of terror' generated by Brown's works is a product of his environments that are 'unknowable and wholly beyond control'.[67] Landscapes in Brown's fiction, according to Toles, resist being tamed and mastered. The wilderness harbours mysteries and secrets that it refuses to divulge: 'it must be emphasized that in Brown's fiction the landscape acquires its energy and what one might almost call its will in the process of becoming mysterious – in creating a distance or gap between itself and the mind that wishes to penetrate it'.[68] This irrationality of the landscape, its seemingly wilful resistance to being known and conquered, makes it both frustrating and dangerous. As Seelye notes, 'at the farthest point, Huntly's wilderness quest carries him into the heart of American darkness. The world of nature is both a lunatic asylum and a sanctuary for murderous beasts and men'.[69] In Brown's American Frontier

Gothic, the wilderness does not simply reflect the savage heart of man; it arguably produces it.

The expansive wilderness

I began this chapter by noting the significance of the American wilderness in three contemporary American films: *Sleepy Hollow*, *The Blair Witch Project* and *The Village*. My argument here has been that the path through the woods in these films and others like them goes back and back through time to the Davises' nocturnal journey into the threatening forest in Brown's 'Somnabulism', to the bizarre and possibly supernatural events that occur on the isolated Pennsylvania farm called Mettingen in *Wieland*, and most of all to Edgar Huntly's wanderings through the panther- and Indian-infested forest in *Edgar Huntly*. The trip from Brown's Norwood/Norwalk to Irving's Sleepy Hollow, New York is relatively short and direct. In place of Nick Handyside and Indians, Irving – and much later Tim Burton – substitutes a German Hessian, but the woods remain the theatre for irrational nocturnal predations. What the Maryland woods in *Blair Witch* share most immediately with Brown's Norwalk is the irrationality of the forest. As I have written elsewhere, the three students in the film get progressively more lost – lost in space, lost in time and ultimately lost altogether – as they wander through the undifferentiated smooth space of the forest.[70] Most provocatively, echoing Brown, *The Village* channels not only a sense of the hauntedness of the American forest but also an emphasis on the savagery that underlies the facade of civility. The village of Covington, like Mettingen, is an island surrounded by wilderness, but the attempt to keep the badness of the world at bay only reveals that it has been lurking there all along.

One could of course add any number of other stops on the road of the Frontier Gothic that stretches from Edgar's Pennsylvania gun-planting to the contemporary Pennsylvania community of Covington. The path wanders through Poe's 'Tale of the Ragged Mountains' and Hawthorne's 'Young Goodman Brown' and then westward through James Fenimore Cooper's Leatherstocking tales. The academic collection of essays *Frontier Gothic: Terror and Wonder at the Frontier in*

American Literature considers not just the usual list of canonical American romancers, but extends consideration of Frontier Gothic themes to Mary Wilkins Freeman, Charlotte Perkins Gilman, Edward Abbey, William Gibson, Gerald Vizenor, Leslie Silko and Rudolfo Anaya as well. Ambrose Bierce is notably missing from this list but could certainly be added, as could Jack London, and one could also add any number of authors of Westerns such as Zane Grey and Louis L'Amour. The American woods are emphasized as the source of supernatural activity in cult television favourite *Twin Peaks*, and the isolated cabin assailed by quasi- or avowedly supernatural forces hiding in the woods is a mainstay of the horror genre (think of *Friday the 13th* or *The Evil Dead*).

The point here is that it was Brown who first realized the potential of the American wilderness for constructing an intrinsically American Gothic romance. In so doing, Brown, as Seelye observes, established 'the peripheries of what would become a distinctly American fiction'.[71] In 'commit[ting] himself to exploring a new vein in American literature',[72] Brown through his Gothicization of the American landscape tapped into a potent source of both anxiety and promise that has continued to resonate ever since.[73] Indeed, as the editors of the *Frontier Gothic* collection assert, the Gothicized encounter with the frontier wilderness may be the most fundamental conflict shaping the American experience.[74] Brown was the first to realize this for literary purposes.

2

Charles Brockden Brown and the Urban Gothic

Ωଔ

At the beginning of the last chapter on the Frontier Gothic, I attended briefly to three contemporary American films, *Sleepy Hollow*, *The Blair Witch Project* and *The Village*, each of which illustrates the archetypal significance of the haunted American wilderness to the constitution of American identity. I then traced this theme back to its literary origination in Charles Brockden Brown's 'Somnambulism', *Wieland* and most of all *Edgar Huntly*. My argument in that chapter – in keeping with the assertions of Downes, Hamelman, Newman, Seelye and other contemporary critics, as well as those of Brown himself in his 'To the Public' at the start of *Edgar Huntly* – was that in these works, Brown reconfigures the European Gothic associated with authors such as Radcliffe, Lewis and Schiller better to reflect the American experience. Instead of haunted castles and invidious aristocrats, he gives us haunted forests and dangerous Indians and, in the process, he founds the American literary tradition of the Frontier Gothic.[1]

In this chapter, the action moves from country to town, from the howling heart of the American wilderness to the dark mysteries of the inscrutable city, and I would like to begin here with a similar approach to that employed in the last chapter – that is, by briefly considering the well-established tradition of what will be referred to as the Urban Gothic before following the winding path through the urban jungle back in time to its beginnings with Brown in the city of Philadelphia at the turn of the eighteenth century. My over-arching argument here will be similar to that presented in chapter 1: that Brown needs to be recognized as the American originator of an important subcategory of the Gothic. In his *Ormond* and *Arthur Mervyn*, Brown – preceding Bram Stoker, Charles Dickens, George Lippard, Edgar Allan Poe and others generally associated with de-veloping that branch of the Gothic that Gothicizes the city experience – pioneered the Urban Gothic. In these works, Brown in fact presents the city as a type of wilderness, one that is as disorienting and danger-ous as being lost in the woods.

Eight million stories

Part of the significance of this discussion about Brown and the ori-gination of the category of the Urban Gothic is the fact that the idea is so commonplace to us today that we may not give it a second thought. While there are any number of novels to which one could turn in order to explore representations of the city as a space of danger, mystery and vice, in the twenty-first century we are perhaps most familiar with this idea through the medium of cinema. Two cinematic genres in particular – film noir and science fiction – have naturalized the idea of the city as a space of crime and peril to such an extent that this perception arguably informs our thinking about urban existence in general. I will begin by briefly addressing film noir with some attention to the paradigmatic classic *The Naked City* (1948) and then shift into a more contemporary mode by considering the city in the updated film noir *Blade Runner* (1982) and the comic book noir adaptation *Batman* (1989).

Film noir refers primarily to 'gritty' Hollywood crime dramas produced in the 1940s and 1950s, including *The Maltese Falcon* (1941), *Double Indemnity* (1944) and *The Big Sleep* (1946). Generally making use of a black-and-white visual style and plots often derived from 'hard-boiled' crime stories of the 1930s produced by authors such as Dashiell Hammett, Raymond Chandler and James M. Cain, the genre is conventionally associated with urban settings and stock char-acter types including the cynical private eye and the femme fatale. Hallmarks of the genre include a plot structure employing multiple flashbacks, voiceover narration and a fatalistic mood developed in part through the dramatic and extensive use of shadow. Actors and actresses famed for performances in classic film noir dramas include Humphrey Bogart (*The Maltese Falcon, The Big Sleep*), Robert Mitchum (*Out of the Past* [1947]), Jane Stanwyck (*Double Indemnity*), Rita Hayworth (*Gilda* [1946]) and Lana Turner (*The Postman Always Rings Twice* [1946]).

In place of big-name leading actors and actresses, *The Naked City*, which chronicles the police investigation of the murder of a young female model and was shot on location in New York City, arguably casts the city itself in the leading role. The film, which won an Academy Award for cinematography, begins with a wide shot of New York as the voice of producer Mark Hellinger frames the story. The viewer is then introduced to various denizens of the night going about their business – night workers on the graveyard shift, a radio DJ wondering if anyone is listening, a woman washing floors in an office building – before the camera moves in through the window of an apartment building where a murder is taking place and the voiceover explains that this too is part of the city.

The rest of the film follows the investigation of this murder as world-weary Irish Detective Lt Dan Muldoon (Barry Fitzgerald) and novice Detective James Halloran (Don Taylor) uncover the questionable lifestyle led by the victim, model Jean Dexter. Their search leads them through confidence man Frank Niles (Howard Duff) to ex-wrestler Willie Garzah (Ted de Corsia), who is chased through lower Manhattan onto the Williamsburg Bridge that connects the island with Brooklyn. As Garzah climbs one of the towers, a shoot-out occurs and he is shot and falls to his death. This sordid tale of crime and murder ends with another panoramic shot of New York and Hellinger's famous voiceover pronouncement that 'there are eight million stories in the naked city; this has been one of them'.

I have chosen to offer this brief overview of *The Naked City* here because it provides a clear representation of the idea of the Urban Gothic to be developed in the rest of this chapter. The city in this film – in keeping with representations in film noir more generally – is presented both as a space of concealment and as a kind of labyrinth. At the start, the voyeuristic camera moves silently in through the window of an urban apartment dweller, revealing a murder in progress of which the neighbours are unaware. The implication of this murder and the closing assertion that it is just one of the 'eight million stories of the naked city' is that the thin walls and closed doors of city apartments and townhouses conceal all manner of criminal activity and that attractive exterior facades can conceal the blackest of hearts.

Equally significant in *The Naked City* is the spectacular presentation of the city itself through sweeping documentary-style shots, including long shots from the Williamsburg Bridge, overhead aerial shots and scenes emphasizing the population density of lower Manhattan. The effect of this presentation of New York is to create the impression of the city as an immense and confusing space, and of urban existence as chaotic. The city itself, beyond being a setting for the action, becomes a sort of character that structures the plot and facilitates the action. Taking a direct cue from Brown's *Arthur Mervyn*, as I shall discuss below, *The Naked City* Gothicizes the urban experience by presenting the city as a labyrinthine space that both fosters and conceals vice and plays on the anxiety that, surrounded by strangers, everyone's motives are suspect.

In many respects Ridley Scott's 1982 science-fiction epic, *Blade Runner*, is simply an updated version of 1940s film noir in which hard-boiled detective Rick Deckard, played by Harrison Ford, attempts to navigate the dystopian Los Angeles of 2019. In classic film noir like *The Naked City*, the detective deals with 'confidence men', criminals who mislead and play upon the naïvety of others. The suggestion in these films is that these heartless villains are inhuman. *Blade Runner* literalizes this metaphor by having the detective seek to root out 'replicants' – androids attempting to pass for humans. Fittingly, the primary way to distinguish a replicant from a human is through a test measuring empathic responses: replicants, like confidence men, lack empathy. The difficulty of Deckard's task, of course, is that the population density and the configuration of the city itself make hiding and blending in easy.

In its presentation of the city as well as the confidence man, *Blade Runner* updates and offers a science-fiction twist on classic film noir. *The Naked City* suggests that urban experience is chaotic and the city is a labyrinth concealing vice. *Blade Runner* takes this idea and extends it to the point where the city is virtually incoherent. It sprawls in all directions, including up, and the language of the streets, 'City

Speak', is a mishmash of languages and dialects. Further, the city in *Blade Runner* is a thoroughly Gothic space. It is perpetually dark and rainy and parts of it are deserted and filthy. Appropriately, the final confrontation between Deckard and replicant Roy (Rutger Hauer) occurs in the rain atop a high-rise building – *Blade Runner's* substitute for the typical Gothic cathedral.

I would like to stress the cinematic ubiquity of the Urban Gothic here with one more example: director Tim Burton's 1989 version of *Batman*. Burton's adaptation of the DC Comics superhero, Batman, remains true to a defining aspect of the long-running comic book series – the representation of the city as a place of crime and corruption. As anyone with even passing familiarity with Batman in any form is probably aware, the Batman narratives take place in Gotham City, a decaying urban jungle (and New York City analogue) ruled by criminals and inhabited by citizens who live in perpetual fear. Superhero narratives in general, it should be noted, almost always foreground the urban experience: Superman moves from Smallville to Gotham City's rose-tinted mirror reflection, Metropolis; eschewing generic fantasy cities, the creators of Spiderman place him in New York City, which is also where the Fantastic Four reside; both Anthony Stark (Iron Man) and Steve Rogers (Captain America) are native New Yorkers, and so on. *Batman*, however – both the original comic book series and the recent cinematic adaptations – offers by far the bleakest rendering of the urban experience as it transforms the hard-boiled detective of true crime stories and film noir into a morally ambiguous and revenge-driven hero.

Burton's *Batman* maps the conventions of the classic Gothic novel onto contemporary experience in a straightforward way. As the hero seeks to combat the villain and liberate the lovely damsel in distress, the action moves by way of two castles (Batman's home, Wayne Manor, and an art museum) from the depths of a dungeon (a chemical plant) literally to the spirals of a Gothic cathedral. For our purposes here, what I wish to emphasize about Burton's version of *Batman* is the expressionistic correlation between immorality and urban decay. For the conventional exotic Italian setting of the Gothic novel, Burton substitutes Gotham City; and, borrowing from film noir, the ominous cityscape of Gotham with its decaying buildings, nightmarish industrial parks and filthy, rain-drenched streets, is clearly the 'objective correlative', the physical manifestation, of moral turpitude. As is the case with *Blade Runner*, it seems to be perpetual night in Burton's *Batman* as Michael Keaton's unsmiling caped crusader stalks the streets of a city every bit as diseased as Brown's Philadelphia in *Ormond* and *Arthur Mervyn*.

Origins of the Urban Gothic

The point of this brief discussion of cinema and the city (a discussion which could be expanded greatly to include other film noir films of the 1940s and 1950s and updated film noir variants like *Dark City* [1998] that fuse film noir sensibilities with fantasy and science fiction) is that the idea of the Urban Gothic, of narratives that highlight the anxieties associated with the urban experience and portray cities as dangerous places of mystery and vice, is a commonplace one to us today. This is because it has been repeated and developed so extensively, first in literature and then also in film, since its origins in the nineteenth century – although precisely where and when the Urban Gothic subgenre originated has been a subject of debate, and here is where Brown comes back into the picture.

In his very interesting study of the development of the literary Gothic genre and its negotiation of history and place, *A Geography of Victorian Gothic Fiction: Mapping History's Nightmares* (1999), Robert Mighall gives consideration to the nineteenth-century development of Gothic tales of the city – of the terrors that derive 'from situations peculiar to, and firmly located within, the urban experience'.[2] His analysis begins with G. W. M. Reynolds's *The Mysteries of London*, published in parts between 1844 and 1848, which in Mighall's estimation Gothicizes the labyrinthine city through its emphasis on peculiarly modern anxieties in relation to the 'growth of an information culture, and its correlative production of secrets'.[3] Mighall then backtracks to reference works by Fielding, De Quincey and Hugo (in passing) that predate Reynolds in representing London as a labyrinthine 'figure of tangled impenetrability',[4] before giving extended consideration to the imbrication of urban experience and criminality as represented in the works of Charles Dickens – notably in *Oliver Twist* (1837–9) and *Bleak House* (1854) – which emphasize the city as a site of mystery and danger and thereby relocate the Gothic's fictional horrors into a new urban space. 'With the Urban Gothic', writes Mighall, 'the aristocracy deserts the "House" of Gothic fiction, and its new inhabitants, the outcasts of London, inherit its "heirlooms" as they inherit the (cursed) focus of Gothic representation.'[5] Central to this new Urban Gothic is an attention to filth and stench as low-life characters stalk the back alleys and little-frequented corridors of the mazelike city.[6] Equally significant is 'atmosphere' in the literal sense as the Urban Gothic – especially when set in London – emphasizes fog and rain.[7]

Allan Pritchard makes a similar and even more forceful argument in relation to Dickens as the inventor of the Urban Gothic genre and focuses on *Bleak House*, published serially between March 1852 and September 1853. According to Pritchard, *Bleak House* is a watershed text in the transformation of the Gothic genre – a text that has at its centre 'the unprecedented subject of the great modern city and its horrors'.[8] Pritchard explains that *Bleak House* is a 'radical' innovation in the history of the Gothic novel as it shifts the action away from 'the traditional remote rural setting to a contemporary urban setting'.[9] He continues,

> This is indeed a fundamental reshaping of tradition, since the romantically distant setting had usually been regarded as essential for Gothic fiction, whether it is an old manor house in an isolated rural part of Britain or a secluded castle in a distant part of some foreign land.[10]

Dickens's *Bleak House* resituates the space of horror as the 'great modern city: the Gothic horrors are here and now'.[11]

Kathleen L. Spencer pushes the clock forward rather than backwards and argues that the Urban Gothic emerges late in the nineteenth century. In her article on Bram Stoker's *Dracula* (1897), she considers the transformation of the romance genre through 'an infusion of modern perspectives'[12] that she sees beginning to occur in the 1880s. In a separate article on the rise of the Urban Gothic, which similarly situates its invention in the 1880s, she emphasizes that these Urban Gothic tales foreground the city experience of being surrounded by 'people who do not know or care about you and whose private lives are mysteries',[13] and adds that

Over and over again the tales of the urban gothic repeat this message: surface appearances cannot be trusted. The natural, reasonable, mundane world is only a thin film covering a realm of horrors which at any moment might break through to attack the unsuspecting, and it is the city, that indiscriminate, crowded, roiling mass of humanity, which creates a hospitable space in the modern world for such monsters, a place where they can hide unsuspected.[14]

Moving backwards and to the American side of the Atlantic, Heyward Ehrlich rightly foregrounds the significance of George Lippard's sensationalistic *The Quaker City or, The Monks of Monk Hall* (1844–5) both as being indebted to French novelist Joseph Marie Eugène Sue's *Les Mystères de Paris* (1842–3) – a novel first published serially that depicts a crime- and poverty-ridden Paris – and as a watershed moment in the development of the Urban Gothic.[15]

The problem with these claims by Mighall, Pritchard, Spencer and, to a lesser extent, Ehrlich concerning the origins of the Urban Gothic is that a full forty years earlier than Dickens and Lippard there was Brown – an author who clearly exercised influence on both Poe and Lippard, and arguably on Dickens as well. In Brown's second and third novels, *Ormond* and *Arthur Mervyn*, Philadelphia is presented as a site of both literal and figurative disease – a home to criminality and contagion. In these two novels, Brown essentially performs the Gothicization of the city discussed by Mighall and Pritchard in relation to Dickens roughly fifty years before *Oliver Twist* and *Bleak House*. Brown, influential as he was upon Poe and Lippard, clearly should be recognized as the inventor at least of the American version of Urban Gothic, if not the Urban Gothic in general; and a line can be drawn directly from Brown's plague- and crime-ridden Philadelphia through 1940s film noir to modern visions of the city as an uncanny, unsettling labyrinth of vice and decay such as *Blade Runner*'s Los Angeles of the future and *Batman*'s Gotham city.

The feverish city

Before we can turn to Brown's novels, however, there is a bit more setting of the stage that must be performed. In chapter 1, I suggested that Brown's creation of the Frontier Gothic would have been influenced both by the existing literary traditions with which he was familiar (captivity narratives; historical accounts of American settlement; religious discourse that allegorized the wilderness as a Godless desert and place of temptation, torment and vice) and Brown's own interest in geography and personal experiences of exploring the Pennsylvania countryside and travelling back and forth between Philadelphia and New York. In a similar way, his authorial decisions in *Ormond* and *Arthur Mervyn* to foreground the City of Brotherly Love as a space of deception and depravity would have been influenced by his personal experiences and the general zeitgeist – notably plague and the growth of the city – during his lifetime.

At the centre of both *Ormond* and *Arthur Mervyn* is yellow fever, a disease that routinely ravaged East-Coast and southern American cities into the early part of the twentieth century. As Norman Grabo details in the 'Historical essay' included with the authoritative Kent State Bicentennial Edition of Brown's *Arthur Mervyn*, as well as in his book-length study of Brown, *The Coincidental Art of Charles Brockden Brown*, 1793 – the year in which both *Ormond* and *Arthur Mervyn* are set – was an especially bad plague year.[16] Philadelphia in 1793 was the site of a deadly outbreak of yellow fever. 2,500 people died over the course of a six-week period and over 5,000 died – more than a tenth of the city's population of 45,000 – over the course of the outbreak that lasted from mid-August until cold weather killed off the mosquitoes in October.[17] At first, death knells rang from church steeples, but as the death rate rose exponentially, this practice ceased so as not to increase the panic.[18] Neither the United States Congress (then situated in Philadelphia) nor the city governors were present during the epidemic and a group of businessmen eventually appointed themselves guardians of the city, but only after many had died and it was clear that some centre of authority needed to be established.[19] A Philadelphia mansion known as the Bush Hill mansion was appropriated to serve as a 140-bed hospital, but quickly proved to be entirely inadequate; and as Gregory Eiselein remarks, the medical practices of Dr Benjamin Rush and others, which included bleedings, induced vomiting and cold baths, probably hastened the deaths of more patients than they helped.[20]

Those who could flee the city – those who had the means to leave and somewhere to go – did, leaving behind primarily the sick, minorities and the indigent. As panic concerning the plague spread, ports, roads and bridges into and out of the city were blocked and those living in surrounding areas closed their doors to Philadelphians attempting to escape.[21] Rumour inflated the terrors of the plague still further throughout the surrounding countryside, with one newspaper reporting that 15,000 were dead.[22] In the absence of authority figures, the rule of law broke down and looters and vandals roamed the streets, necessitating the appointment of a civil guard to protect property. Men – particularly African Americans, who were considered to be less vulnerable to the disease – were hired to cart away the dead.

As David Axelrod observes, plague was a direct part of Brown's experience as he lived through four major yellow fever outbreaks: two in Philadelphia, including the 1793 outbreak (although Brown himself was not personally present in the city for this one), and two in New York.[23] The fourth one in New York in 1798 almost killed him: Brown became dangerously ill but recovered; his close friend Elihu Hubbard Smith, with whom he lived, was not so lucky.[24] Brown's biographer, Harry R. Warfel, comments concerning *Arthur Mervyn* that of Brown's four 'major' novels, this is the one that comes closest to reflecting real life. Warfel's vivid description of the cultural context informing Brown's novel here is useful:

> The background – the devastating yellow fever epidemic of 1793 – was fresh in the minds of most people in the Philadelphia area. The scenes of 1798 had not been so terrifying or gruesome, but the fear brought to mind vivid recollections of death symbols chalked on row after row of houses, of the frantic enmity to impromptu hospitals, of mass emigrations to rural homes, of hysteria causing suicide, of death by the thousands, of the tinkling bell announcing the death cart, and of the pillage of the deserted city by thieves.[25]

Warfel reminds us that during the 1793 yellow fever outbreak Brown was visiting Elihu Hubbard Smith in Wethersfield, Connecticut, so his memorable descriptions of the decimated plague-ridden city are reported at second hand. Brown's family and friends, however, were mostly based in Philadelphia, so he would have received numerous reports and descriptions of the outbreak, both during and after its destructive reign.

Perhaps not surprisingly given the threat of disease in the late eighteenth century, plague was a popular subject in literary and philosophical life. Almost immediately following the conclusion of the 1793 epidemic in Philadelphia, Matthew Carey, an author, publisher and bookseller, wrote and published his account of the plague, *A Short Account of the Malignant Fever* (1793), which as James Dawes notes was a 'wild success' and rapidly went through several editions.[26] Carey's account was immediately followed by numerous other reports, including William Currie's *A Description of the Malignant Infectious Fever* (1793), Benjamin Rush's *An Enquiry into the Origins of the Late Epidemic Fever in Philadelphia* (1793), and Absalom Jones and Richard Allen's *A Narrative of the Proceedings of the Black People, during the Late Awful Calamity in Philadelphia. In the Year 1793* (1793) – this last work a rejoinder to Carey's version, which had asserted that African Americans had looted and vandalized Philadelphia during the plague.[27] While these narratives and others purported to offer historical accounts of the plague and its aftermath, they also participated to varying extents in commonplace rhetoric (both in the eighteenth century and today) linking physical disease with socio-cultural concerns. That is, in the absence of any definitive scientific explanation for the plague, various causes were conjectured, often connecting outbreaks of illness to social conditions such as immigration and urbanization. This observation requires us to attend briefly to shifting socio-economic conditions in Philadelphia in the 1790s because, as numerous commentators have pointed out, Brown engages with plague in *Ormond* and *Arthur Mervyn* both in terms of its literal and figurative connotations. In these works yellow fever afflicts the city literally speaking; at the same time, however, Brown uses plague as a metaphor for the diseased state of the city's soul.

In Brown's two Urban Gothic novels, he taps into significant social anxieties related particularly to urbanization and the expansion of capitalism. As Carl Ostrowski observes, since Brown's brothers were businessmen and merchants in Philadelphia he would have had the opportunity to observe their successes and failures and would have taken an interest in business practices more generally.[28] Of particular note to him would have been the growing practice of 'speculation'

– trading in stocks and bonds. By the time Brown was writing *Arthur Mervyn*, speculation had become, according to Ostrowski, a 'byword for the unprincipled pursuit of wealth' and represented a 'degradation of public morality'.[29] Ostrowski adds that, set in 1793, the events depicted in *Arthur Mervyn* are connected to a financial crisis that occurred in the government bond market in 1791–2 and led to a panic in the securities markets of major American cities.[30] Ostrowski thus concludes that Brown employs yellow fever in his Urban Gothics as a 'symbol of rampant economic opportunism'.[31] The practice of speculation during the period is figured as a type of disease and greed is presented as contagious. For Ostrowski,

> the spread of habits of gambling, licentiousness, and greed that began in major commercial centers with the speculative crisis of the 1790s is figured as a serious threat to the continued prosperity of the United States. Brown's harrowing accounts of the yellow fever epidemic serve the purposes of both a gritty realism and a kind of allegory on the subject of political economy.[32]

Grabo contends, however, that even before the yellow fever epidemic of 1793 struck, Philadelphia was already in many ways 'feverish':

> Bank policies were erratic and unreliable. Merchants and businessmen were investing wildly in exotic financial schemes that burst with uncommon regularity. Prices – especially rents – sky-rocketed. And businesses failed in startling numbers with ruined bankrupts crowding the streets, the stock-piled wharves, the places of trade. It was a community demoralized, without confidence, without trust, and in no position to handle the stress of the epidemic that had descended upon it.[33]

What Grabo points out here is that economic anxieties in post-Revolutionary Philadelphia in the 1790s were connected to a variety of other social issues, including immigration and politics.

Philadelphia during this period was growing at a rapid clip, its population having increased from 23,700 in 1775[34] to 42,520 in 1790.[35] Of the city's population in 1790, over 10,000 were German, several thousand relatively recent French émigrés, and over 3,000 African American. Approximately 3,000 new Irish immigrants arrived annually.[36] As Levine notes, Philadelphia was the destination of choice for political refugees of varying stripes, especially displaced French escaping the French Revolution (it is one of the many provocative coincidences of history that the French Revolution's Reign of Terror was virtually concurrent with Philadelphia's own – the outbreak of plague in 1793).[37] Significantly, as the city of Philadelphia expanded rapidly in the final decades of the 1700s to accommodate the influx of new residents, it became a place in which 'strangers and newcomers were everywhere'.[38]

Confidence men

In Karen Halttunen's fascinating study of American culture in the nineteenth century, *Confidence Men and Painted Women*, she addresses the changes in social relations that nineteenth-century urbanization precipitated.[39] One central difference between living in a small town or village and living in a city of many thousands that she foregrounds is that one goes from knowing other people and being known by them to living among strangers. This key difference becomes a main source of anxiety in nineteenth-century narratives employing urban settings and revolving around the figure of the 'confidence man', a villain defined by his intense hypocrisy. Disguising his vice and greed with an outward facade of virtue, the confidence man seduced naïve and innocent young men – young men significantly distanced from traditional sources of patriarchal authority – off the path of righteousness and into the dens of depravity. Once the youth's witty, attractive and vastly more knowledgeable companion manipulated him into giving way on his moral principles, he was lost.

The figure of the urban confidence man condenses a variety of late eighteenth- and nineteenth-century anxieties into one supersaturated form. Not only is the confidence man connected to the establishment of large cities in which one cannot know all those whom one encounters, but the figure also reflects concerns about the shifting of related social patterns. As Halttunen observes, throughout the seventeenth and eighteenth centuries, the patriarchal structure of agrarian communities allowed fathers and the family to exercise a great deal of control over the lives of children. As farmers, however, become less able to provide farm holdings for their sons and new opportunities opened up elsewhere – especially in cities – the power of the patriarch and the associated familial structure began to wane. The conventional apprenticeship system also went into decline and those committed to traditional social values forecast grave consequences. Halttunen writes that

> The traditional master-servant relationship had stressed reciprocal obligations of moral watchfulness and deferential obedience, broad educational guidance and personal service but ... by the early nine-teenth century the entire system was breaking down under the impact of mercantile capitalism and the factory system.[40]

As a result, 'young men in the cities found themselves increasingly less inhibited by traditional restraints on the social conduct of single workingmen'.[41] Although both *Ormond* and *Arthur Mervyn* were written prior to the period addressed by Halttunen in her study, her representation of urban anxieties clearly resonates with the experi-ences of Brown's protagonists in navigating the city of Philadelphia. Both Ormond in *Ormond* and Welbeck in *Arthur Mervyn* are species of confidence men and Arthur Mervyn himself – at least one reading of him – exemplifies the pattern of the naïve young man who mi-grates from the country to the city and finds himself immediately preyed upon by a hypocritical villain, a figure that will emerge as central to literature later in the nineteenth century. Both, in short, are Urban Gothic tales establishing significant plot structures that ripple through subsequent nineteenth-century literary works. Here, as in so much else, Brown appears to have been uncannily prescient and to have been on the cusp of (if not influencing directly) new literary and social developments.

Conspiracy paranoia

One other factor related to urbanization and shifting social patterns that needs to be mentioned here as having clearly influenced Brown in his composition of *Ormond*, as well as the unfinished sequel to *Wieland* titled *Memoirs of Carwin the Biloquist*, was 1790s conspiracy paranoia, most importantly as related to the Illuminati – a secret society recently returned to the spotlight by *The Da Vinci Code* (2003) author Dan Brown's 2000 novel, *Angels and Demons*, and its 2009 cinematic adaptation staring Tom Hanks. As I mention in this book's Introduction, the 1790s was a period of considerable political tension in the United States as the Federalist-leaning administration of George Washington skirmished with Republicans led by Thomas Jefferson over how much power the American central government should possess. In 1793–4, Alexander Hamilton had encouraged Washington to consider pro-French Democratic-Republican societies that were organizing around the country as Jacobin clubs – essentially dangerous left-wing revolutionary organizations.[42] Federalists made nervous by the French Revolution and its aftermath insisted, as Levine observes, that the enthusiastic reception of French ambassador Edmond-Charles Genêt, the insurrectionary spirit of the Whiskey Rebellion and the increasingly strident opposition of the Jeffersonian Republicans 'were all secretly kindled and enflamed by Jacobin subversives'.[43] In contrast, Jeffersonian Republicans 'proclaimed that Federalist policies of economic centralization reflected the corruption of an oligarchical ministry deviously plotting to subvert the freedoms achieved by the American Revolution'.[44]

Nowhere did political tensions run higher in the 1790s than in Philadelphia, and Levine observes that because Philadelphia – as the United States's capital from 1790 until 1800 – was so politically factionalized, no city was more exposed to alarmist rhetoric.[45] The result was that conspiracy fears – concerning Jacobin Freemasons, deists and most of all the Bavarian Illuminati – were rampant, and repeated declarations of French, Illuminati, Federalist-aristocratic and even Irish conspiracy lead to a 'near panic' situation.[46] As detailed by Christophersen, the Order of the Illuminati was a fraternal society espousing rationalist ideas that was founded in 1776 by a law professor at the University of Ingolstadt in Germany to combat the powerful grip of the Bavarian Jesuits.[47] As Kafer explains, two books written independently of each other and published at about the same time touched off the Illuminati panic of 1798. Both French author Abbé Barruel's *Memoirs Illustrating the History of Jacobinism* (1797–8) and Scottish author John Robison's *Proofs of a Conspiracy against All the Religions and Governments of Europe, carried on in the Secret Meetings of the Free Masons, Illuminati, and Reading Societies* (1797) claimed that not only were the Illuminati opposed to both existing government and religion in general, but the Order now operated covertly across Europe and even in the United States.[48]

Within the United States, both Federalists and Congregationalist ministers blamed Jacobin plotting and the Illuminati for their diminishing cultural presence; and, unsettled by the rise of Unitarianism, a number of clergy pointed in their sermons of 1798 and 1799 to the influence of the Illuminati as the source of political turbulence both at home and abroad.[49] Exemplary here was Congregationalist minister Jedidiah Morse, who in May 1798 identified the major obstacle standing in the way of America achieving its divinely ordained greatness: the contagion of 'insidious French liberalism'. According to Morse, 'the Illuminati's ultimate aim . . . was to undermine America's civic and religious institutions. Hostile to true liberty and religion, the conspirators were ready to launch an all-out assault on the institutions the founding fathers had so painstakingly established'.[50] Morse's warning about the Illuminati conspiracy was, as Levine notes, quickly disseminated by the era's leading ministers, with the result was that by mid-1798 'Illuminati became a household word in America'.[51] In Philadelphia in 1798 and 1799, the Illuminati conspiracy was a frequent topic of discussion in newspapers and broadsides.[52]

A man perched on a fence at midnight: Ormond

Armed with this background knowledge about the contemporary ubiquity of the Urban Gothic, Philadelphia in the 1790s, yellow fever and the Illuminati, we are now in a position to consider Brown's achievement in *Ormond* and *Arthur Mervyn* as he adapted conventions of the Gothic novel to express contemporary anxieties. Greatly condensed, the plot of *Ormond* is as follows: narrated by Sophia Courtland as a letter to an individual named I. E. Rosenberg, *Ormond* is primarily the story of Constantia Dudley. After the bankrupting of her father's business by the unscrupulous confidence man Thomas Craig and her father's subsequent blindness as a result of cataracts, Constantia bravely attempts to care for him, assist others and retain her independence in Philadelphia amid the virulent yellow fever epidemic of

1793. The eponymous Ormond, who is not introduced into the work until more than a third of the way through, is initially presented as a thoroughgoing Godwinian rationalist who quickly becomes infatuated with Constantia but expresses a distaste for the institution of marriage. Despite being repulsed by Ormond's dispassionate rationalism and his heartless treatment of his mistress Helena who commits suicide after being cast off by him, Constantia nonetheless finds him intriguing (and, in an interesting side note, becomes equally intrigued with Martinette de Beauvais, Ormond's radical, cross-dressing sister). Ormond finally emerges as the villain of the work at the end when his rationalist mask is cast aside and he appears in his true form: a monomaniacal egotist – and secret society member – intent on consummating a sexual relationship with Constantia at all costs. Having used Craig to murder Constantia's father, Ormond seems poised to rape Constantia but she defends herself with a pen-knife and kills him. At the conclusion of the narrative, Constantia and Sophia relocate to Europe.

Ormond nicely condenses much of the discussion above about the Urban Gothic and late eighteenth-century American culture as it is a tale of urban anxiety and confidence men that features both literal plague and conspiracy paranoia. In attending to *Ormond*, however, I wish to start neither with Constantia, the tale's protagonist, navigating the city, nor with Ormond, the Illuminati member, nor even with Craig, the confidence man. I will begin instead by focusing on a subplot involving a minor character attempting to ferret out his neighbours' goings-on that, although mostly ancillary to the plot, nevertheless clearly captures the tenor of Brown's Urban Gothic.

If there are eight million stories in the naked city, Brown seems intent in his novels on interweaving them all and, characteristic of Brown's general tendency to introduce myriad narrative threads, the unhappy tale of Baxter is one of *Ormond*'s many apparent tangents. In the midst of the plague decimating Philadelphia, Constantia – herself newly recovered from illness – sets out to ascertain the condition of Sarah Baxter, a woman whose services as a laundress Constantia and her father have employed. Sarah had previously been regular in her visits to the Dudleys, but had abruptly ceased appearing. What Constantia discovers upon arriving at the laundress's home is a 'theatre of suffering'.[53] Sarah's two daughters have died from the disease and her husband, after an eleven-day struggle with illness, is on the verge of expiring as well – which he promptly does soon after Constantia's arrival. Constantia's weakened constitution is taxed by this experience and she suffers a relapse of sickness. Attended by Sarah, she learns the washerwoman's tragic tale.

As Sarah tells it (and it is worth bearing in mind that this is Sarah's husband's story, communicated by Sarah to Constantia, then by Constantia to Sophia and then by Sophia to us in her letter to the mysterious I. E. Rosenberg), the house next door to the Baxters' was inhabited by a Frenchman named Monrose and a younger woman named Ursula whom they presumed to be his daughter. Despite the fact that neither had been seen for several days, Baxter, who was 'deeply and rancorously prejudiced' against the French (p. 50), was initially disinclined to investigate, having 'too much regard for his own safety, and too little for that of a frog-eating Frenchman' (p. 51). Contemplation of the possible predicament of the daughter, however – contending with her father's and possibly her own sickness, 'without food, without physician or friends, ignorant of the language of the country, and thence unable to communicate their wants or solicit succour; fugitives from their native land, neglected, solitary, and poor' (p. 51) – eventually caused Baxter's heart to soften, and one evening while participating in the night watch he investigated, putting his eye to the keyhole of the dark, shuttered house. 'All was darksome and waste' (p. 51), so Baxter retired to his home.

Later that night he was awakened by his wife who directed his attention to the Monrose house and to that most Gothic of devices, a candle glimmering in the darkness. Baxter, suspecting that the Monrose house was being looted, investigated. He again peered through the keyhole of the house and again found the home appearing deserted and dark. The thought occurred to him to survey the rear of the house, so he proceeded around and took up a post allowing him to keep watch on the back door. Here Brown introduces a pithy comment that takes on increasing significance as the narrative progresses and to which I will return: 'Human life abounds with mysterious appearances. A man, perched on a fence, at midnight, mute and motionless, and gazing at a dark and dreary dwelling, was an object calculated to rouse curiosity' (p. 53).

Baxter's curiosity was rewarded with the appearance of Miss Monrose, 'pale, emaciated, and haggard' (p. 53), and the light of her candle revealed a shallow grave. When Miss Monrose next appeared, she was dragging a heavy bundle wrapped in a sheet – Baxter's paralysing fear 'instantly figured to itself a corpse, livid and contagious' (p. 54). His intuition was correct as the shroud slipped, revealing the 'pale and ghastly visage of the unhappy Monrose' (p. 54). The panicked Baxter retreated and the next day, despite not having come into close contact with either Ursula or the corpse, began to exhibit yellow fever symptoms that grew in intensity until his death eleven days later. On investigating the Monrose household, the authorities discovered neither proof that Monrose had succumbed to yellow fever nor any trace of Ursula Monrose. This mysterious interlude in Constantia's story then ends with the assertion that Baxter's case 'may be quoted as an example of the force of imagination. He had probably already received, through the medium of the air, or by contact of which he was not conscious, the seeds of this disease. They might perhaps have lain dormant, had not this panic occurred to endow them with activity' (p. 55).

Baxter's story is significant to the plot structure of *Ormond* only in introducing the reader to Ursula Monrose who is in reality Ormond's sister, Martinette de Beauvais. The account of Baxter, however, is thematically central in ways that are significant both to the novel as a whole and to this chapter's focus on the Urban Gothic. First, the interlude – featuring as it does a shuttered house, an exotic foreign woman and her father, candles moving in the darkness, a shallow grave, a shrouded corpse, paralysing fear and a mysterious disappearance – is a conventional Gothic plot in miniature. Second, the emphasis on voyeuristic curiosity and problematic perception is wholly in keeping with the prominence of the interrelated themes of vision and understanding that run throughout the narrative as a whole and are embodied in the novel's subtitle, 'The Secret Witness'. Third, the account brings together in the narrator's final comments literal and figurative understandings of plague that have the strange effect of both foregrounding and undercutting the affective machinery of the Gothic employed in the preceding account and in the text as a whole. In order to draw out these meanings, let us now return to the image of a man sitting alone on a fence at midnight.

In Christophersen's commentary on this image, he suggests that Baxter on the fence in the dark can be taken as Brown's figuration of the 'representative American' engaged in a 'precarious balancing act' between warring forces of the late eighteenth century, including Enlightenment optimism and Calvinist pessimism, Federalist cynicism and Republican faith in individual self-governance, and capitalist expansion and Christian morality.[54] All of this may indeed be embodied in the figure, but the potent symbol of Baxter perched on the fence at midnight peering at his neighbour's house seems to me to be more immediately connected to the interrelated themes in *Ormond* of urban anxiety and perceptual uncertainty. The simple fact of the matter is that Baxter lives next door – 'fifty paces', the reader is told (p. 52) – from people he does not know. In a scene that could just as easily have come from Alfred Hitchcock's *Rear Window* (1954), Baxter sees something suspicious going on in his neighbour's house from his window, and out of concern for their well-being (or so we are told) decides to investigate first by spying through the keyhole and then by keeping watch on their back door.

What Baxter's surveillance reveals to him and what the rest of the narrative unveils to the reader is the twofold essence of urban anxiety made manifest in *The Naked City*: that horrible things are going on in the house right across the way and that one's neighbours consequently are not at all what they seem. In Baxter's case, what his snooping uncovers is not murder – a device Brown saves for *Arthur Mervyn* – but rather sickness and death in the house next door leading to a hasty midnight interment in a shallow grave. What the reader later learns is that Ursula Monrose can be numbered with Craig and Ormond himself among the characters in *Ormond* who take advantage of the anonymity that the city provides to present themselves as something other than what they are. Ursula is not related to Monrose and is far from being the 'small and delicate' (p. 49) lady the Baxters describe. Baxter, perched on the fence at night trying to determine what is going on in his next-door neighbour's house and uncovering death and deceit, thus epitomizes the Gothicized urban experience of being surrounded by strangers.

The scene thereby clearly participates in the novel's thematic emphasis on vision and knowledge. As in all of Brown's works, among

---

the central questions of *Ormond*, in keeping with Gothic narratives in general, is the extent to which one can draw accurate conclusions from perceptual information – put another way, to what extent can one trust one's own eyes? As Julia Stern notes, *Ormond's* fascination with acts of perception is evident in virtually every important scene[55] and the novel raises questions of perceptual accuracy most explicitly in relation to appraisals of other people, thereby foregrounding the urban anxiety addressed by Halttunen in her study of nineteenth-century American culture: in a world of strangers and in the absence of reliable information about or character references for those one meets, how can one accurately determine their disposition and intentions? If we can't trust a book by its cover but we have nothing else to go on, then on what basis can we make any assumptions about it at all?

Indeed, the related themes of disguise and forgery are insistently foregrounded in *Ormond*. The villainous Thomas Craig initially presents himself as frank, modest and forthright, and is welcomed into Mr Dudley's home and business where he embezzles funds and ruins the Dudleys' name and fortune. The background he has provided is revealed to be as false as the forged bills he later gives to Constantia and the forged letters he shows Ormond that cast aspersions on Constantia's character. Although actuated by the love of liberty rather than the desire for personal gain, Martinette de Beauvais, the cross-dressing freedom fighter masquerading as Ursula Monrose, presents an equally false front to the world. And the true master of disguise and obfuscation is revealed to be none other than Ormond himself, who at one point even visits the Dudley home disguised as an African American chimney sweep! Ormond, like Craig and like his own sister Martinette, presents himself as the opposite of what he really is. The face he shows to the world is one governed solely by dispassionate reason. In the end, though, he is revealed to be an egomaniacal criminal, governed by lust and the desire for power. Even the virtuous Mr Dudley himself is revealed to have changed his name upon his removal from New York to Philadelphia 'to obliterate the memory of his former condition and conceal his poverty from the world' (p. 80). The unfortunate Baxter, sitting on a fence at midnight trying to draw some conclusions about what is taking place in the house next door is thus symbolic of the city-dweller in general, placed in the precarious position of trying to make determinations about strangers based on appearances.

Most significant about the Baxter episode is the unsettling conclusion to the event in which Baxter's assumptions – suppositions called into question by the narrative voice – have dramatic consequences and in a remarkable way turn the text back upon itself and make for an unsettling reading experience. Baxter succumbs to plague, believing himself infected as a result of spying on the nocturnal interment of his neighbour. The narrative voice, however – which here seems to be much more Brown himself than Sophia – questions whether his death was inevitable and suggests that the force of Baxter's imagination activated the 'seeds' of disease that might otherwise have 'lain dormant'. That is, in this instance the true disease might have been panic over the possibility of infection rather than the infection itself. This possibility succinctly links the two reciprocating 'levels' of plague, the literal and the symbolic, which organize *Ormond* and *Arthur Mervyn* as well.

Ormond is set in the context of the 1793 yellow fever outbreak in Philadelphia and literal contagion looms large, especially in the first half of the narrative. Many critics have echoed R. W. B. Lewis's assertion in *The American Adam* that 'the clear superiority of the plague scenes [both in *Ormond* and *Arthur Mervyn*] is a mark of Brown's deepest preoccupation and the area of his genuine talent; for the world that he could quite artfully bring into being and explore with the greatest assurance was the land of the dead'.[56] It is hard to contest Lewis's assertion that the decidedly Gothic scenes of plague and of a decimated Philadelphia are among the most horrific and haunting in the text; and in very interesting ways, the step from Brown's descriptions of disease-stricken individuals in mortal agony and empty city streets in his late eighteenth-century novel to contemporary horror thrillers similarly featuring gruesome images of contagion and deserted diseased-ravaged cities, like *28 Days Later* (2002) and *I Am Legend* (2007), is a surprisingly short one. The essence of Brown's Urban Gothic in *Ormond* and *Arthur Mervyn* is to turn Philadelphia into a city of the dying and the dead. As in a contemporary horror film, Brown is not above going for the 'gross out'. Consider, for example, Brown's description of the condition of Mary Whiston, an acquaintance of Constantia's whom she unsuccessfully tries to nurse back to health. When Constantia discovers Mary, who has been abandoned by her brother, 'her face was flushed and swelled, her eyes closed and some power appeared to have laid a leaden hand upon her faculties. The floor was moistened and stained by the effusion from her stomach' (p. 36). Alas, there is not much Constantia can do for Mary: 'Mary's condition hourly grew worse. A corroded and gangrenous stomach was quickly testified by the dark hue and poisonous malignity of the matter which was frequently ejected from it . . . On the succeeding night, the sufferings of the patient terminated in death' (p. 39).

Less immediately horrific and more eerily atmospheric is Brown's masterful and unsettling portrayal of a major city silenced by disease. Allow me to quote at some length the first paragraph of Chapter VI:

> Constantia had now leisure to ruminate upon her own condition. Every day added to the devastation and confusion of the city. The most populous streets were deserted and silent. The greater number of inhabitants had fled, and those who remained were occupied with no cares but those which related to their own safety. The labours of the artizan and the speculations of the merchant were suspended. All shops, but those of the apothecaries were shut. No carriage but the herse was seen, and this was employed, night and day, in the removal of the dead. The customary sources of subsistence were cut off. Those, whose fortunes enabled them to leave the city, but who had deferred till now their retreat, were denied an asylum by the terror which pervaded the adjacent country, and by the cruel prohibitions which the neighbouring towns and cities thought it necessary to adopt. Those who lived by the fruits of their daily labour were subjected, in this total inactivity, to the alternative of starving, or of subsisting upon public charity. (p. 42)

This powerful passage is amplified later in the same chapter by the observation that

> The shrieks and laments of survivors, who could not be prevented from attending the remains of an husband or child to the place of interment, frequently struck [Constantia's] senses. Sometimes urged by a furious delirium, the sick would break from their attendants, rush into the streets, and expire on the pavement, amidst frantic outcries and gestures. (p. 45)

These descriptions function in several capacities in *Ormond*. First, they paint an uncanny picture of a once populous city transformed into a city of death – work and commerce have ceased, except for commerce in the dead. Second, they reflect actual responses to the plague of 1793 during which the affluent fled the city, leaving behind primarily the impoverished underclass without the means to relocate, and during which the surrounding countryside, panicked by actual and inflated reports of the progress of the disease, refused to offer assistance or succour. Finally, they initiate the thematic paralleling of actual disease with the metaphoric diseases of greed, heartlessness and subversive radicalism that will be developed as the narrative progresses.

In relation to this last point, a number of critics have noted the ways in which literal contagion in *Ormond* and *Arthur Mervyn* parallels, reflects and expresses the figurative diseases of 'greed, lust, fraud, debauchery, cowardice, poverty . . . [and] violence'.[57] With this in mind, Kafer argues that *Ormond* is not really about the 1793 yellow fever outbreak, but rather about the heartlessness and hypocrisy of post-Revolutionary Philadelphia.[58] Christophersen observes that yellow fever in *Ormond* is both a real contagion and a 'correlative for generalized evil':[59] 'The yellow fever symbol signifies the danger of unregulated passion, both private and public'.[60] Linking disease in the novel specifically to greed, Ostrowski contends that 'the yellow fever epidemic may be seen as a judgment on economic liberalism, a vindictive invisible hand that punishes the people of Philadelphia for their habit of conspicuous consumption'.[61]

In the novel, it is clear that the virulence of the pestilence is matched by the heartlessness of Philadelphia's citizenry. In addition to the duplicity of Craig, the Dudleys are forced to contend with the avaricious landlord M'Crea who demands his due even in the midst of the height of the plague when no sources of income are available. Two men attempt to rape Constantia as she is making her way home one evening (pp. 62–3), and later her name is slandered by the petulant and petty sister of Balfour, the man whose offer of marriage Constantia refuses (p. 67). While there are kind citizens as well who recognize and reward virtue – notably Mr Melbourne and his wife who intervene on behalf of the Dudleys after Constantia innocently pays the rent with forged bills provided by Craig – the plague-ridden city is presented as infested not just by literal disease but by vice and heartlessness, and this Gothicization of the city finds its fullest expression in Ormond himself, the master criminal.

In Christophersen's estimation, Ormond essentially personifies plague. 'Ormond is, like the fever, a prototype of evil: insidious, virtually invisible . . . seemingly omnipresent, he penetrates people's thoughts the way the fever penetrates their bodily defenses. The plague incarnate, Ormond is an indiscriminate killer.'[62] Ormond is the apotheosis of the urban confidence man. He presents himself as being above all things *sincere*. The reader is informed, however, that 'a somewhat different conclusion would be suggested by a survey of his actions' (p. 86). Sophia explains that Ormond discovered early in himself remarkable talents of imitation that he routinely employs to gather information about others surreptitiously.

> [Ormond] was delighted with the power it conferred. It enabled him to gain access, as if by supernatural means, to the privacy of others, and baffle their profoundest contrivances to hide themselves from his view. It flattered him with the possession of something like Omniscience. (p. 87)

Far from being sincere, Ormond is the essence of duplicity. Indeed, in a story prominently emphasizing the theme of forgery, Ormond himself is a forgery of a human being; he is a monster, wearing a human face.

It is important to add here that Ormond also represents late eighteenth-century anxieties about the contagion of revolutionary and subversive ideology. Brown, capitalizing on the Illuminati scare of 1798, makes sure to identify Ormond as both a radical Godwinian and a member of an Illuminati-like secret society. Echoing the Godwinian rejection of social formalities such as marriage as artificial and constraining bonds, Ormond systematically ignores entrenched rules of social decorum, including those governing social intercourse between members of different classes (p. 86), and rejects marriage as being a 'hateful and absurd' (p. 132) restriction on liberty as likely to produce misery as happiness (p. 94). Further, Sophia later reveals Ormond to be 'engaged in schemes of an arduous and elevated nature' (p. 131). She continues:

These were the topics of epistolary discussion between him and a certain number of coadjutors, in different parts of the world. In general discourse, it was proper to maintain a uniform silence respecting these, not only because they involved principles and views, remote from vulgar apprehension, but because their success, in some measure, depended on their secrecy. (p. 130)

To a certain extent, Brown undercuts this critique of Godwinian rationalism and secret societies dedicated to progressive ideals by revealing that Ormond – unlike his sister Martinette – only dallies with revolutionary politics as a means through which to obtain influence over others. Ormond, we learn,

aspired to nothing more ardently than to hold the reins of opinion. To exercise absolute power over the conduct of others, not by constraining their limbs, or by exacting obedience to his authority, but in a way of which his subjects should be scarcely conscious. He desired that his guidance should controul their steps, but that his agency, when most effectual, should be least suspected. (p. 131)

Ormond quickly abandons his allegiance to rationalism and proposes marriage to Constantia when she rejects his attempts at seduction. Indeed, he is ultimately revealed to be consumed by lust to such an extent that he is willing to rape and murder to achieve his objective – which is to say that he is actuated by no principles apart from personal satisfaction and self-aggrandizement. Ormond is not a revolutionary but an egomaniac. Nevertheless, by associating Ormond with late eighteenth-century radical politics Brown was able to capitalize on conspiracy paranoia and helped to fuel the suspicion that Godwinians, Jacobins and Illuminati of all stripes were in reality committed to no principles apart from anarchy and hedonism.

Ormond is ultimately the perfection of that most urban of villains, the confidence man. Together with Craig and Martinette and even Mr Dudley, he takes advantage of the cover the city affords to obscure his true face, name and motivations. He feigns sincerity while seeking to extend the sphere of his influence and to capitalize on the misery of others. And he can get away with it – at least until Constantia's penknife punctuates his lustful pursuit – because the city allows him to invent and reinvent himself. What Brown gives us in *Ormond* in the end is a tale of urban anxiety – the invention of the Urban Gothic – in which the city is both literally and figuratively a place of disease and anxiety.

And this returns us to Baxter, seated on his fence at midnight, trying to draw some conclusions about what is taking place next door. He catches the plague, but the narrator suggests that he might just have imagined the disease into being. Brown himself can be likened to Baxter, trying to determine what is real and what is imaginary. In the course of his ruminations, however, Brown in *Ormond* imagines the Urban Gothic into being.

In a dark closet: Arthur Mervyn

In *Arthur Mervyn or, Memoirs of the Year 1793* – Part I of which was published immediately after *Ormond* in 1799 and Part II followed *Edgar Huntly* in 1800 – Brown again presents to the reader an image of a Philadelphia devastated by plague and rife with corruption. In *Arthur Mervyn*, however, the question of the reliability of perceptions thematized in *Ormond* becomes all-encompassing. The accuracy of assumptions made about everything and everyone in *Arthur Mervyn*, including those made by the reader about the eponymous protagonist himself, is repeatedly called into question and, as in *Ormond*, this epistemological uncertainty is echoed and magnified by the psychological distortions and confusion of the urban environment.

To summarize briefly (or as briefly as one can, given the convoluted nature of the story), the tale begins with a Philadelphia physician named Stevens discovering young Arthur Mervyn sick with yellow fever in front of his home. Stevens takes pity on Arthur and invites him into his home where he and his wife care for him. A visit from Stevens's friend Wortley raises questions, however, about Arthur's character, and Arthur narrates his story to Stevens and his wife in the attempt to clear his name. He explains that he was forced to leave his father's farm outside Philadelphia after his father married Betty, a much younger family domestic; not only was Arthur concerned that Betty had seduced his father for his property, but there were rumours (unfounded ones, claims Arthur) that Arthur himself had been intimate with Betty. Arthur reached the city penniless, having been cheated out of his meagre savings on the way. There he met a young man named Wallace who bought him a meal and offered him a place to sleep, but then promptly played a trick on Arthur and locked him in a pitch-black room in a strange house. Arthur managed to escape, leaving his shoes behind.

Penniless and shoeless, Arthur lacked the resources even to pay the bridge toll that would have allowed him to return home to his father's farm. His luck seemed to take a turn for the better, however, when he was hired to be an amanuensis to a man named Welbeck living in a sumptuous home with his daughter Clemenza. Welbeck, of course, turns out to be a thief and a forger and the pregnant Clemenza is revealed to be not his daughter, but rather his mistress and essentially his captive. Arthur recounts that he soon found himself helping Welbeck bury a murdered man named Watson in the basement and assisting Welbeck in fleeing the city – where it appeared that Welbeck committed suicide by jumping into the middle of the Delaware River. Arthur, disconcerted by everything that had transpired, then fled the city himself and ended up taking refuge on a farm owned by a family named Hadwin.

Plague now struck Philadelphia and Arthur explains to Stevens that Susan Hadwin, one of the two Hadwin daughters, was so concerned about her fiancé Wallace – who it turns out is the same Wallace who had played a prank on Arthur at the start – that Arthur took it upon himself to go and seek him out in the city. There he discovered chaos and death everywhere. He did find Wallace, who had contracted yellow fever, and put him into a carriage to be transported to the Hadwins' farm, but Wallace never made it (and Brown leaves Wallace's fate uncertain). Arthur himself now began to sicken and, terrified of being transported to the Bush Hill hospital – which he considered essentially a death trap – he decided instead to seek refuge in Welbeck's mansion. Here he was stunned to discover none other than Welbeck himself, whom Arthur had presumed dead. Welbeck had snuck back into the city to reclaim a large sum of ill-gotten money he had hidden in the house – money that Arthur had already found and intended to return to its rightful owner, Welbeck's mistress Clemenza Lodi. In an especially comic turn, Arthur explains to Dr Stevens that Welbeck told him the money was forged, Arthur burned it and Welbeck then became angry, revealing that he had lied about the money being forged and that Arthur had just burned 20,000 British pounds. Welbeck then abandoned Arthur again and Arthur eventually wandered out of the house with the idea of returning to the country, only to collapse outside Dr Stevens's home.

So ends the first part of Arthur's incredible narrative. Arthur rallies and insists on going to the Hadwin farm to make sure everyone is safe. When he does not return for several weeks, Dr Stevens, who has become suspicious that he has been 'played' by a con man, is summoned to the Philadelphia debtors' prison. Here he discovers Arthur, who has summoned him to attend to the dying Welbeck. Welbeck does die, but not before entrusting Arthur with another large sum of money taken from the body of Watson, the murdered man buried in the mansion's basement.

Arthur now continues his narrative, explaining what has happened to him since he left Dr Stevens's home. Arthur returned to the Hadwin farm to discover that only the two daughters, Eliza and Susan, remained alive; Susan died soon after. Eliza petitioned vigorously to be taken with Arthur back to the city, but he refused and instead placed her with the kindly Curling family, who agreed to care for her until a better situation could be found and the details of her inheritance worked out. Arthur also discovered that Clemenza Lodi was now residing in the home of Mrs Villars, madam of the local brothel. To wrap things up, after getting Dr Stevens up to speed, Arthur forces his way into the Villars home and discovers Clemenza with her dying baby, as well as a widow named Achsa Fielding who apparently has no idea that the Villars are prostitutes. Arthur enlightens Achsa, finds a better situation for Clemenza (with a woman named Wentworth), returns Watson's money to the Maurice family to whom it belongs, brings Eliza from the country to the city to live with Achsa, agrees to apprentice with Dr Stevens, and – in a shocking plot development – rejects the young and attractive Eliza Hadwin for the more experienced, older and Jewish Achsa Fielding.

As even this condensed summation of the convoluted plot of *Arthur Mervyn* suggests, confusion and mistaken assumptions reign supreme in the novel. Arthur's father is tragically misled by Betty; Arthur is misled first by Wallace and then repeatedly by the master deceiver Welbeck, who tricks and takes advantage of just about everyone he encounters; Arthur's sister, we learn, was misled and seduced by a teacher named Colvill, precipitating her suicide; Achsa Fielding is deceived by the Villars; a whole cast of minor characters react based upon mistaken assumptions, often having to do with Arthur's appearance and his uncanny resemblance to seemingly every third character in the book; and questions are ultimately raised even about Arthur himself: as I will discuss below, the reader is given cause to wonder whether he is the naïve and sincere narrator he presents himself as being or if he might not instead be the story's supreme confidence man. What is important to emphasize here, however, is the extent to which problems of perception and anxiety over interpretive accuracy are tied in *Arthur Mervyn*, as in *Ormond*, specifically to the urban environment. Even more so than *Ormond*, *Arthur Mervyn* is an Urban Gothic, a tale of the city itself as a centre of mystery and corruption.

In Norman Grabo's 'Historical essay' in the Bicentennial Edition of *Arthur Mervyn*, he asserts that in the novel, 'the city itself takes on nearly the aspect of a character whose conditions generate the actions of most of the other characters, and whose contagions infect all'.[63] To this, Kafer adds that what is 'aesthetically vital' in the novel, particularly in its opening sections, is the Gothicized '*feel* of the place Brockden Brown conjures'.[64] The Gothic 'feel' and ominous atmosphere Brown creates in *Arthur Mervyn*, as in *Ormond*, is certainly connected to his powerful representations of the plague-ridden city. As Arthur returns to Philadelphia in search of Wallace, he runs counter to a 'tide of emigration' and observes that 'families of weeping mothers, and dismayed children, attended with a few pieces of indispensible furniture, were carried in vehicles of every form'.[65] Entering the city, the few people he sees are 'ghost-like, wrapt in cloaks, from behind which they cast upon [him] glances of wonder and suspicion' (p. 108). Surveying the homes themselves, which formerly at this hour would have been 'brilliant with lights, resounding with lively voices, and thronged with busy faces' (p. 108), he now discovers them 'closed, above and below; dark, and without tokens of being inhabited' (p. 108). An occasional beam of light from a window contradicts the impression that all the homes are empty, indicating instead that the tenants are 'secluded or disabled' (p. 108).

As in *Ormond*, the primary street traffic observed in *Arthur Mervyn* consists of hearses conveying the dead, and here Brown adds – or, more properly, reintroduces – the especially Gothic device of premature burial. The possibility of overly hasty interment occurs three times in *Arthur Mervyn*. The first instance takes place when Arthur and Welbeck are burying Watson in the basement and, although Arthur admits that his 'imagination was distempered by terror', he nevertheless reports seeing Watson's eyes open (p. 85). Significantly here, Arthur meditates that death is perhaps naturally abhorrent to man 'until tutored into indifference by habit' (p. 86). In the second instance, as Arthur is searching for the financier Thetford's house believing Wallace to reside there, he observes two men removing a coffin from a home, their features 'marked by ferocious indifference to danger or pity' (p. 108). As they load the coffin into the hearse, he overhears them comment on the condition of the coffin's occupant: 'I'll be damned', says the first, 'if I think the poor dog was quite dead' (p. 108), to which the second responds, 'Pshaw! He could not live. The sooner dead the better for him; as well as for us' (p. 108). The suggestion here is precisely that these callous men have been 'tutored into indifference' towards the living as a result of their frequent communion with the dead and dying. The final reference to the possibility of premature burial occurs while Arthur is looking for Wallace in the wrong house and is knocked unconscious by an 'apparition', a figure he sees briefly in a mirror. When Arthur comes to, he finds himself companioned by three undertakers, one 'with hammer and nails in his hand, as ready to replace and fasten the lid of the coffin, as soon as its burthen should be received' (p. 114). Arthur has gone from possibly participating in a premature burial to overhearing a conversation about it to being on the verge of being buried alive himself.

The Gothic device of premature burial is accentuated by the eeriness of the setting. The apparition that Arthur sees in the mirror before being struck down both echoes the 'ghost-like' shrouded figures that move through the streets and foreshadows the next ghost that will confront Arthur as he moves though this city of haunted houses. Seeking Wallace in a deserted mansion in an abandoned city, Arthur's active imagination discovers

vestiges of that catastrophe which the past night had produced. The bed appeared as if some one had recently been dragged from it. The

sheets were tinged with yellow, and with that substance which is said
to be characteristic of the disease, the gangrenous or black vomit. The
floor exhibited similar stains. (p. 127)

Surveying this morbid setting, Arthur hears footsteps in what he
believes is a deserted house, footsteps characterized by 'ghost-like
solemnity and tardiness' (p. 127), and then his 'heart's-blood [is] chilled'
as Wallace makes his appearance:

If an apparition of the dead were possible, and that possibility I could
not deny, this was such an apparition. A hue, yellowish and livid; bones,
uncovered with flesh; eyes, ghastly, hollow, woebegone, and fixed in
an agony of wonder upon me; and locks, matted and negligent, constituted the image which I now beheld. (p. 128)

Wallace here is essentially a zombie, and the impression of Philadelphia that Brown creates in *Arthur Mervyn* is one in which the
line between life and death has dissolved. The living are buried too
soon and the dead – Wallace, Welbeck, even Arthur himself – keep
coming back.

Brown's creation of the Urban Gothic in *Arthur Mervyn*, however,
goes beyond painting Philadelphia with broad strokes as a necropolis, as a plague-ridden city populated only by the dying and the
dead. Rather, what complements and extends this uncanniness of
the urban environment is what we may refer to as the incoherence
of space in the novel: the paradoxical sense that the space of Philadelphia somehow is simultaneously constricting and large, fluid
and segmented. Brown essentially overlays two competing spatial-
ities on Philadelphia in *Arthur Mervyn*: Philadelphia as a space of
confinement and Philadelphia as a sprawling labyrinth. On the
one hand, Arthur repeatedly finds himself enclosed in constricting
spaces that highlight the city itself as a space of restriction and
concealment. Almost the first thing that happens to him when he
arrives in Philadelphia is that he innocently follows Wallace into a
strange house and is then locked in a dark, unfamiliar room. Afraid
of being discovered, Arthur then retreats into a closet, contemplating 'What a condition was mine? Immersed in palpable darkness!
shut up in this unknown recess! lurking like a robber!' (p. 30).[66]

In fact, Arthur is confined in a dark closet in a dark room in a strange house in an unfamiliar city and while his intent may not be robbery, he nevertheless becomes an 'Ormondian' secret witness to the dubious dealings of those around him.

Arthur's brief interment in Thetford's closet thereby functions as an apt initiation into urban life for him as he moves almost immediately from this house to Welbeck's mansion, a space as Gothic as any Italian castle when considered in light of its manifold locked doors, unreadable manuscripts, imprisoned maidens, buried corpses and hidden treasures. Welbeck is of course a villainous con man and criminal who lives with his pregnant mistress whom he represents to Arthur as his daughter. After Welbeck murders Watson and he and Arthur remove the corpse to the basement (the urban equivalent of a dungeon) for burial, Arthur again finds himself trapped in a dark, confined space – this time with a dead body. Trying to navigate the darkened space, Arthur crashes into the wall and, with blood 'gusting from [his] nostrils', reports that 'I had lost all distinct notions of my way. My motions were at random' (p. 86). He finds the stairs, only to discover the door at the top locked, and comes to the conclusion that Welbeck has trapped him with the intention of framing him for the murder of Watson. Arthur, however, is mistaken on all counts as it turns out that in the dark he stumbled across the wrong staircase and the wrong door, and Welbeck soon returns with a shovel. This instance of being trapped and finding doors locked will repeat as Arthur later seeks refuge in Welbeck's house in a locked room and still later conceals himself in a coffin-like attic space, 'musty, stagnant, and scorchingly hot' (p. 160). Arthur, it seems, is always on the verge of being buried alive.

When not being personally threatened with premature interment in a coffin or coffin-like space, what Arthur does is to transition from house to house, from confined space to confined space, serving as a sort of voyeur to the vice that he discovers. In Thetford's home, hiding in a closet, he learns of the substitution of a living child for a dead one and of a scheme to defraud someone, referred to mysteriously as the 'nabob' (who it turns out is Welbeck), of a substantial sum of money. In Welbeck's home, he discovers all manner of criminality, from the seduction of Clemenza to the murder of Watson. The Villars home – also a space defined by doors through which Arthur repeatedly passes uninvited – is revealed to be a space of 'licentious pleasures' (p. 240) concealing sickly Clemenza and her 'meager and cadaverous' child who promptly dies (p. 243). 'If I should escape undetected from this recess', thinks Arthur at the start of his story while trapped in Thetford's closet, 'it will be true that I never saw the face of either of these persons, and yet I am acquainted with the most secret transaction of their lives.' (p. 32) What Arthur quickly discovers and what is repeatedly emphasized over the course of his narrative is this paradoxical intimacy of urban existence: on one hand, the familiar facades of houses and buildings conceal all manner of vice and perversion; on the other, living in close proximity to many others, separated by thin doors and walls, one learns the routines and secrets of those one has never seen or only met in passing.

At the same time, however, that Arthur seems stuck in one confined space after another, he is also – like his country cousin, Edgar Huntly – constantly in motion. He moves from his father's farm to the city, from Thetford's house to Welbeck's, and from Welbeck's back to the country to the Hadwins' (at one point being in the middle of the Delaware River). From the Hadwins' he returns to the city and goes from house to house looking for Wallace until he ends up back again at Welbeck's and then at Dr Stevens's. From there, his dizzying itinerary takes him back to the Hadwins' in the country, to the Villars', to the debtors' prison, back to Dr Stevens's, and he ultimately ends up at the home of Achsa Fielding – his travels having also included stops at several other houses and a quick trip to Baltimore along the way. Arthur is somehow both constantly confined and constantly moving. Or, to put it another way, he is trapped by movement that somehow seems simultaneously directed and undirected, straight and circular. Arthur almost never quite knows where he is going and always seems to end up at his destination by accident. He is led to Thetford's house by Wallace, he flees from there and happens upon Welbeck, he arrives at the Hadwins' by chance, he stumbles into the wrong house looking for Wallace, he ends up on Dr Stevens's doorstep by happenstance, and so on.

This sense of haphazard movement (which I am tempted to call Brownian motion), however – like Freud recounting his experience of a certain European city in his now famous discussion of the uncanny – is undercut by the fact that Arthur can apparently never leave the same place only once and keeps circling back to the same houses – Thetford's house twice, Welbeck's house twice, the Hadwins' farm twice, Dr Stevens's house twice. Arthur thus wanders through a mazelike urban setting every bit as confusing and disconcerting as *Edgar Huntly*'s Norwalk and he always ends up circling even as he appears to be moving forward. It is doubtless this incoherence of urban space that leads Hinds to conclude that Philadelphia in *Arthur Mervyn* is a 'wilderness disguised as a city',[67] and Toles, attending to the 'special quality of terror' that Brown's novels generate,[68] observes that both forest and city in Brown's writing are characterized by what he refers to as 'inaccessible spaciousness' – the unsettling sense of being hedged in and confined even though one is aware of vast distances surrounding one.[69] It is ultimately difficult to decide in *Arthur Mervyn* whether Arthur's experience is of constant movement punctuated by periods of confinement or of constant confinement punctuated by periods of movement. The rhythm of the novel is one of insistent start and stop as the reader is led by Arthur's account from one incredible and surreal experience to the next. The Philadelphia through which Arthur wanders is finally both a tomb and a labyrinth.

What somehow holds together the centripetal and centrifugal trajectories of the novel – the movement inward towards the black heart of Philadelphia and the movement outward, away from the urban centre to the country – is the glue that pestilence provides. As in *Ormond*, disease in *Arthur Mervyn* operates on both literary and figurative levels as a unifying thematic. As Arthur wanders through the labyrinth of the necropolis, what he discovers is fraud and vice. According to Ostrowski, the

> multi-layered seediness and complexity of the financial dealings in the novel constitute Brown's extended critique of economic liberalism; the urban atmosphere in which a commercial economy thrives promotes speculation and fraud at the expense of productive labor and civic duty.[70]

But it is not just the merchants, landlords and financiers in the novel who are corrupt; from Wallace's prank at the beginning to the undertakers who would consign a still-living man to a coffin to the Villars bordello, Philadelphia is populated by villains of all stripes whose crimes range from playful mischief-making, heartlessness and greed to theft, adultery, prostitution and murder. As Christophersen notes concerning *Ormond*, yellow fever in *Arthur Mervyn* 'signifies the dangers of unregulated passion'[71] and Hedges adds that 'greed, lust, fraud, debauchery, cowardice, poverty, overt violence and finally the physical corruption of the plague transform Philadelphia into the moral equivalent of a waste land'.[72]

Finally, in *Arthur Mervyn*, nothing is what it seems to be:

> Appearances are almost always deceptive making it impossible in *Arthur Mervyn* to distinguish the sick from the dead, real money from counterfeit, friend from enemy, seduced from seducer, victim from criminal, or hero from villain. Survival depends on the ability to manipulate appearances rather than to be manipulated by them.[73]

The last question that the novel raises, then, is where to place Arthur himself on the continuum from hero to villain. Is Arthur passively manipulated by the social forces that engage him? Or is he instead a master manipulator, whose genius is marked by his successful facade of naïvety? As Elliott points out, there is no more contested issue in the body of criticism on Brown's fiction than how to regard Arthur: 'Some view him as the prototype of the successful American Adam – a young innocent who receives a just reward for a life of virtue – while others see him as a scoundrel, an opportunist, a "double-tongued deceiver"'.[74] Is Arthur what he seems or is he the ultimate confidence man? Michael Davitt Bell leans in the latter direction, writing that '[a]gainst Arthur's profession of virtuous intention stands his unacknowledged but persistent self-interestedness . . . Arthur's earnestness is never daunted, but it is, as Brown's irony makes clear, the earnestness of the confidence-man'.[75] Christophersen steers clear of taking a position by highlighting the difficulty of arriving at any firm conclusions about Arthur at all: 'Hayseed and hustler, novice and master of the pen, voyeur and accomplice, child and adult – Arthur Mervyn is a fictional palindrome, an enigma who reads true from opposite vantage points simultaneously'.[76]

This, finally, is Brown's achievement in *Ormond* and *Arthur Mervyn*: to emphasize the uncertainty of appearances and to root this anxiety

firmly in urban existence. The representative figure of urban existence in *Ormond* is a man on a fence at midnight trying to figure out
what is happening in his neighbour's house; in *Arthur Mervyn*, it is
a man trapped in a closet at night in a strange house in a strange city
overhearing the intimate details of the lives of people he has never
seen. What Brown highlights in both works is the fundamental strangeness of the 'naked city'. One lives in close proximity to hundreds
and thousands of people one does not know; apartments and houses
conceal vice and crime; streets that seem straight curve and lead in
unexpected directions; and finally, all assumptions based on appearances are suspect. Literally plagued by disease, figuratively infected
by greed, vice and fraud, the city is the congenial environment only
for the confidence man, the individual well versed in manipulating
appearances to his own benefit. In *Ormond* and *Arthur Mervyn*, Brown
updates the Gothic novel and gives it a modern urban twist. He
founds the Urban Gothic.

3

Charles Brockden Brown and the Psychological Gothic

෨ාඥ

Scooby Doo Ending: The stereotypical ending to a *Scooby Doo* cartoon, where having caught the bad guy who's diguised [*sic*] as a monster or ghost, and bound him up with rope, the four kids (Freddy, Velma, Daphne and Shaggy) and their anthropomorphic dog Scooby, describe the detective process that has led to the baddie's capture. After detailing all the clues, the masked villain is revealed . . . This ending is such a cliché that it's happily entered the zeitgeist and lodged itself there, and was famously lampooned in the film *Wayne's World*, which had three endings: the happy ending, the sad ending and the Scooby Doo ending.[1]

Connoisseurs of popular culture will be well versed in the now famous 'Scooby Doo' ending. For the uninitiated: at the end of each episode of the popular children's cartoon featuring a cowardly dog that somehow always manages to foil the villain's insidious plan, seemingly supernatural phenomena are revealed to be a combination of intentional deception and coincidence: there are never any actual ghosts, only smoke and mirrors. Connoisseurs of Gothic novels, however, will be very aware that *Scooby Doo* did not invent this formula and will probably agree that if eighteenth-century Gothic novelist Ann Radcliffe were to watch a few episodes of *Scooby Doo*, she might consider suing for plagiarism. After all, Radcliffe is famous for her use of the 'explained supernatural, where apparent mysteries are finally resolved into physical causes'.[2] The

'Scooby Doo' ending should more properly be referred to as the Radcliffean ending.

In contrast to the Scooby Doo ending which reconfirms our understanding of how the universe works, one can point to the common ending of another popular detective program, *The X-Files*. In *The X-Files*, which ran from 1992 until 2002, FBI agents Fox Mulder (David Duchovny) and Dana Scully (Gillian Anderson), like Scooby Doo and the gang, investigate 'X-Files' – unsolved cases involving apparently paranormal phenomena. Mulder is a believer in the existence of aliens and the paranormal, while Scully, a sceptic, is assigned to make scientific analyses of Mulder's discoveries. The endings of the majority of *X-Files* episodes vigorously reject the Scooby Doo conclusion and instead leave the existence of the paranormal an open question, more often than not leaning toward a supernatural explanation that would require a rethinking of natural laws. Contemporary paranormal detective programmes such as *Fringe*, *Medium* and *The Ghost Whisper* have done *The X-Files* one better by openly avowing the existence of the paranormal. This, of course, is not a contemporary innovation either. Aficionados of the Gothic novel will certainly be aware that, in contrast to Radcliffe and her Gothic novels of the 'explained supernatural', there was Matthew 'Monk' Lewis, the Gothic novel's *enfant terrible*. Inspired by Radcliffe's *The Mysteries of Udolpho* (1794), Lewis's notorious *The Monk, A Romance* (1796) features 'Incest and incestuous rape, murder, matricide and sororicide . . . together with a blasphemous identification of Satan and the Madonna, and of sexual temptation with religious devotion'.[3] Equally significant for our purposes, there is no Scooby Doo ending to *The Monk*. Actual ghosts wander in and out of the text, prophecies come true, and even the Wandering Jew puts in an appearance. The title character is led astray by a demon and ultimately Satan himself is revealed to be pulling the strings leading to the damnation of the lascivious monk Ambrosio.

These were the two models of the Gothic novel available to Charles Brockden Brown in the 1790s. Either the Scooby Doo ending or the X-Files ending; either the explained supernatural or the supernatural confirmed; either Radcliffean terror, in which anticipatory dread 'expands the soul and awakens the faculties to a high degree of life',[4] or Lewisean horror which curdles the blood and causes one to contract into oneself in revulsion; to shift the terms of this discussion somewhat, either what contemporary philosopher and literary theorist Tzvetan Todorov has famous defined as the 'fantastic uncanny', in which apparent violations of the natural order have real-world explanations, or the 'fantastic marvellous' in which we are forced to rethink the natural order itself.[5] The Gothic novel of the eighteenth century essentially established the parameters governing the response to seemingly supernatural phenomena that still resonates in today's literature and popular media; and, although broadly schematic, this is the Gothic dichotomy that Charles Brockden Brown – a reader of Radcliffe and Lewis and of German *schauerromane* (literally 'shudder-' or 'quiver-novels') – inherited and drew upon in his own writing: either the mind mistaken or the world reconfigured.

Part of Brown's brilliance, however, lies in the fact that he synthesized these options and invented a third possibility, a conclusion deconstructing the *Scooby Doo/X-Files* binary opposition. In Brown's first four novels, he essentially reconfigures the world in such a way that ghosts and hauntings are part of the order of things, thereby calling into question the 'naturalness' of the natural world. Rather than either ghosts *or* misperception, Brown chooses both and neither simultaneously. In order to develop this idea and to help make clear just what is so revolutionary about Brown's approach to the Gothic in his first four novels, let me jump ahead in time slightly from Brown to the middle of the nineteenth century and introduce some of the critical commentary about Brown's Gothic beneficiary and American compatriot, Edgar Allan Poe. In his overview of Poe's relation to the Gothic genre, Benjamin Franklin Fisher argues that Poe's 'greatest literary achievement' was 'his renovation of the terror tale from what had been its principal intent, to entertain by means of "curdling the blood" . . . into what have been recognized as some of the most sophisticated creations in psychological fiction in the English language'.[6] After surveying Poe's representations of deviant psychological states in several stories, Fisher concludes that Poe revolutionized the Gothic by presenting the reader not with haunted houses, but with haunted minds. Clive Bloom argues essentially the same point in his guide to the Gothic, making the case that Poe's fiction 'marks a decisive break' with the eighteenth-century Gothic and shifts the emphasis away from the threats of the external world and toward the dangers of the mind 'isolated with itself'.[7] Bloom concludes that 'whilst Poe's tales *invoke* the supernatural they never exploit it; rather Poe's tales were those of the irrational, concerned with perversity, monomania and obsession related to an ego-directed mysticism in which knowledge of the unknown coincides with knowledge of the self'.[8]

I am in full agreement with Fisher's and Bloom's characterizations of Poe's writing. I am forced, however, to take issue with their pronouncements concerning Poe's originality. The simple fact of the matter is that Brown did it first. In his fiction, Brown – over thirty years before Poe – powerfully developed a model of the haunted mind, of the human propensity for what Poe will later refer to as perverseness, of the human mind compelled by unconscious forces, and of the human mind not only unable to arrive at accurate inferences based upon sensory information but essentially dual in nature. There are no 'actual' ghosts haunting the forest in *Edgar Huntly* and apparitions in *Arthur Mervyn* invariably turn out to be sick or stealthy people; nevertheless, the worlds presented in these novels, as well as in *Wieland* and *Ormond*, are haunted ones. Undoing the opposition between Radcliffe's Scooby Doo endings and Lewis's tales of ghosts and demons – and pointing the way toward Poe's development of the Psychological Gothic later in the nineteenth century – are Brown's novels of the haunted psyche, of the mind haunted by itself and its expressionistic colouring of the world. In Brown's fiction, the most significant X-File investigates not extraterrestrials, but the alien within.

Hearing voices

Part of what is so significant about Brown and his writing – and, I would argue, why he merits this book – is that he acts as a kind of hinge between the Age of Enlightenment and nineteenth-century Romanticism. Brown, a child of the Enlightenment and early disciple of Godwin and Wollstonecraft, nevertheless repeatedly stages scenarios in his writing that call into question the abilities of human beings to understand not only the world but also themselves. In particular, in his novels, as any number of critics have pointed out, the reader can see a persistent troubling of Lockean sensationalist psychology.

Here a little background may be helpful in order to understand Brown's Gothic innovations. Among the most influential of Enlightenment philosophers was the English thinker and physician John Locke (1632–1704). Contrary to the philosophical ideas of Descartes and others, Locke proposed that individuals are born without innate ideas; rather, the mind begins as a blank slate or *tabula rasa* and knowledge is determined by reflection on experience derived from sense perception. That is, our understanding of the world begins with sensory perceptions that are then intellectually processed. These sense impressions may occasionally deceive but, on the whole, the act of perception can be trusted; and the reason for this, as Locke develops in his *An Essay Concerning Human Understanding* (1690), is essentially that man's ability to know anything at all is a gift from God. As summarized by John Dunn, 'a good Creator would not have endowed men with senses which systematically deceive them'.[9] For Locke, Dunn continues,

> Trust in the senses is so indispensable for practical life and so directly linked to the overwhelmingly powerful stimuli of pleasure and pain . . . that Locke cannot believe that any human being could sincerely doubt the validity of sense-experience, let alone live as though he supposed it illusory.[10]

Against Locke's optimistic empiricism, Brown in his first four novels introduces what one may arguably refer to as a form of radical scepticism. Repeatedly, Brown raises questions about the abilities of human beings to arrive at accurate inferences based on sensory information, and ultimately Brown undermines faith not only in the power of human beings to understand the world but also in the existence of a benevolent creator. Anxiety about the abilities of human beings to draw accurate inferences based upon sensory impressions is of course the central concern of Brown's first novel, *Wieland*, built as it is around the device of ventriloquism. As Baym suggests, the novel 'is experienced as a continuous sequence of mysterious events, systematically misread by a narrator motivated to make sense of her world'.[11] It is not just Clara, however, who is repeatedly mystified by surprising phenomena and who arrives at incorrect conclusions; rather, all the characters are confronted with inexplicable and confusing occurrences, only some of which are clarified by Carwin's confession. As Tompkins observes, it is never certain whether Carwin imitated the voice of God demanding that Wieland 'render' his family to God, whether it was the voice of God himself or whether Theodore is mad.[12] Further, the bizarre spontaneous combustion of Wieland Sr also remains unexplained at the end of the narrative.

Critical commentary on *Wieland* has emphasized the extent to which the novel calls into question Enlightenment rationalism and Lockean sensationalist psychology. Bradshaw, for example, argues that 'ambiguous events and incidences all throw into chaos the ordered, causal world postulated by the enlightened Wielands'.[13] Korobkin, who examines Brown's use of the novel to critique legal assumptions, comments that in *Wieland*

> There is evidence galore, but the normative relationships between evidence and inference, effect and cause, corroboration and truth, have broken down: identifiable voices do not belong to those who seem to be speaking; corroborated newspaper reports are false; sounds, lights, words all mislead. More frightening still, the instrument used to assess this evidence – the supposedly rational human mind – is shown to be warped, fragile, and malleable.[14]

And most insistent on this point is Hagenbüchle, who proposes that what *Wieland* demonstrates is the inaccessibility of truth to man. According to Hagenbüchle, what Clara discovers 'is the bleak truth that human nature and human relations are profoundly baffling and that dependable knowledge and secure happiness are unattainable in this world'.[15] The only truth therefore is that there is no truth and the implications of this are profound: 'If sense impressions are unreliable, then it follows that a deep and dangerous chasm divides the human mind from the world of objects it vainly seeks to apprehend'.[16] Brown is essentially calling into question the human ability to access truth or to be certain of anything at all.

Although *Wieland* has received the lion's share of critical commentary in relation to Brown's sceptical stance on the abilities of human beings to reach accurate conclusions on the basis of sensory information, this is one of the most significant recurring Gothic themes in his fiction. As noted in the last chapter, in both *Ormond* and *Arthur Mervyn* the protagonists are continually misled by antagonists who are other than what they seem to be. In *Ormond,* Craig and Ormond are confidence men and libertines, Martinette is a French radical in disguise, and even the virtuous Mr Dudley is living under an assumed name; here again, we are back to the prevailing metaphor of a man sitting on a fence at midnight trying to make inferences about what is going on next door on the basis of limited information and hindered by darkness. In *Arthur Mervyn*, plague-ridden Philadelphia is a cauldron of vice and deceit in which shady financial dealings and underhanded schemes are the order of the day and, rather than a man on a fence, the operative metaphor is a man stuck in a dark closet in a dark room in a strange house in a diseased city. Scheick, taking note of the characters' persistent misperceptions and inaccurate conclusions in *Ormond*, asserts that 'Brown's romance fails to provide any norm, any middle ground between perverse motive and inscrutable causality; it merely portrays human experience as a harrowing event in a world devoid of perceptible design'.[17] Christophersen, attending to *Arthur Mervyn*, maintains that the novel 'candidly and implicitly acknowledges the deceptiveness of appearances, the indeterminacy of truth, and the unreliability of fiction as a truth-telling instrument'.[18] In each novel, sensory perceptions are uncertain and the conclusions drawn from them therefore suspect.

This theme of the deceptiveness of appearances – or, more properly, the inability of human beings to arrive at accurate conclusions based on sensory perceptions – receives perhaps its fullest expression in *Edgar Huntly*. The simple fact of the matter is that, more so than Clara, Constantia or Arthur, poor Edgar always draws the wrong conclusions. Indeed, Edgar is so often off base in his assessment of what is taking place that the reader can't trust a thing he says. Because he discovers Clithero digging a hole at night in his sleep, he concludes erroneously that Clithero is the murderer of his friend Waldegrave; at almost the same instant he decides that he is the first human being to survey a sublime Norwalk vista, he spots Clithero; he wrongly conjectures that he has been kidnapped by Indians when he ends up in the cave; because he finds his gun in Indian hands, he incorrectly determines that his uncle and sisters are dead; the 'Indians' he shoots at turn out to be Sarsefield and men who are looking for him; he mistakenly assumes that someone has stolen his cache of Waldegrave's letters; he believes that learning that Mrs Lorimer is still alive will cure Clithero and the latter instead sets off to kill her; and this list could be expanded still further. Again and again, Edgar just cannot figure out what is going on. He immediately jumps to the wrong conclusion on the basis of limited information and his decision-making is further compromised by his agitated emotional state and sleep deprivation.

Edgar in the cave, uncertain how he arrived there and uncertain how to get out, constitutes *Edgar Huntly*'s variant on the man on the fence at midnight or the man in the closet, and the grounds for accurate decision-making are even more unstable in Brown's last novel than in *Ormond* or *Arthur Mervyn*. In each, Baxter and Arthur respectively at least know where they are and how they came to be there. Edgar, in contrast, has both literally and figuratively had the ground give way beneath his feet in the dark. Edgar exemplifies the Brown protagonist described by Hedges who 'exists in a world in constant flux, a world of false appearances, disguises, mysteries, a world in which, though rude awakenings are commonplace, ultimate clarity or illumination is conspicuously lacking',[19] and his experience bears out Scheick's assertion that Brown in his romances 'fails to provide any norm, any middle ground between perverse motive and inscrutable causality'. Rather, his Gothic novels portray 'human experience as a harrowing event in a world devoid of perceptible design'.[20]

As Witherington observes, in *Edgar Huntly* – and, indeed, in his first four novels more generally – Brown appropriates and alters the Gothic tradition for his own purposes.[21] It needs to be acknowledged, however, that questioning the ability of human beings to draw accurate inferences based upon sensory information is a hallmark of the Gothic genre, not something introduced by Brown. Indeed, confronting the protagonist with seemingly supernatural phenomena that cannot immediately be reconciled with the natural order of things is the essence of the late eighteenth- and early nineteenth-century Gothic. With this in mind, Voloshin writes:

The insistence on unsettling the protagonist's assumptions about the orderliness of mind and nature with unusual sensations and appearances and speculations about whether it is the mind that is not apprehending nature properly or whether nature is unapprehensible: these are among the characteristics of gothic fiction. Gothic fiction tests and often undermines eighteenth-century notions of the interconnected orders of mind and nature, which had their most influential early exposition in Locke's *Essay Concerning Human Understanding*.[22]

In Radcliffe's Gothic novels (as in Scooby Doo's adventures), the protagonists encounter all manner of apparently supernatural phenomena, only in the end to find rational explanations for the strange happenings: Radcliffe's protagonists arrive at mistaken assumptions on the basis of questionable sensory information; in Lewis (and Walpole before him and Maturin and Stoker after him, and so on leading up to *The X-Files*), confirmation of the supernatural requires a rethinking of possibility itself.

If all Brown did in his novels was to confront his protagonists with strange happenings in order to explain them away or confirm that ghosts exist, his novels would still be important contributions to the development of the American Gothic, the Frontier Gothic, the Urban Gothic and, as we shall see, the Female Gothic. Brown, however, takes the Gothic novel of Radcliffe and Lewis and puts a new spin on it by turning it inward. Human beings are haunted in Brown's novels, but not by ghosts in the conventional sense of spirits of the dead; rather, human beings are haunted by themselves, by the unconscious, by the unknowable other within. A good eight years before Poe was even born, Brown pioneered the Psychological Gothic in his novels about human beings impelled by internal forces that escape their conscious awareness and control. It is not the world that is haunted in Brown's fiction, but rather the mind.

The stranger within

Brown's most concise treatment of the theme of human beings as strangers to themselves appears in his short story, 'Somnambulism. A fragment'. As discussed in chapter 1, although 'Somnambulism' was not published until May 1805, many scholars believe the story to have been written between 1797 and 1799 during the period that Brown was at work on his lost first novel, *Sky-Walk; or, The Man Unknown to Himself.* The theme of unconscious motivations and human beings as strangers to themselves is apparent in the tale even from the headnote to the story, allegedly extracted from the *Vienna Gazette*, that details the strange case of a young man who shot dead the object of his affection while asleep. The rest of the story offers a dramatization of such an event.

What initially stands out about young Althorpe's first-person narration is its interrogative structure and the foregrounding of the absence of self-understanding. In keeping with Brown's mode of narration in general, Althorpe strings together question after question, hypothesizing potential situations and attempting to justify the conclusions at which he has apparently already arrived. For example, Althorpe, who has become enamoured of the beautiful Constantia Davis, considers the possible consequences of her and her father being abruptly summoned away. All manner of questions about Constantia and what course of action he should take in relation to her occur to him, particularly once he gets it into his head that she has another suitor:

> But soft! is she not betrothed? If she be, what have I to dread? . . . But how shall I contend with this unknown admirer? . . . But is it true that such is my forlorn condition? What is it that irrecoverably binds me to this spot? . . . Shall I want a motive or excuse for paying her a visit? . . . But why should I delay my visit? Why not immediately attend them on their way? If not on their whole journey, at least for a part of it?[23]

What Althorpe demonstrates here (and elsewhere) is logical reasoning run amuck. He begins with a questionable premise – that based on Constantia's 'expressions', her 'choice was fixed upon another' (p. 246) – and upon this shaky foundation he conjectures a variety of possibilities, all of which lead him to the conclusion that he has seemingly drawn before starting this associative chain of inquiries: that he must not let the object of his affection out of his sight. What Brown immediately shows us through this string of interrogatives is that there is no unbiased or objective way to assess sensory impressions. Althorpe interprets Constantia's expressions

– visual stimuli – in light of his own desires and anxieties. And, what is more, Brown emphasizes that Althorpe himself is not always – or even most of the time – aware of what motivates him. He reacts to his own responses as if they were coming from someone or somewhere else and, in a way, they are: some part of him in- accessible to consciousness in an uncanny way already seems to be leading him both figuratively and literally towards a particular course of action. In a sense, he is already sleepwalking even though he is still awake.

That Althorpe is moved by forces he does not understand and cannot control is also indicated on the very first page of the story when he admits to being surprised by the force of his response to the news of Constantia's departure: 'The shock that it produced in me was, to my own apprehension, a subject of surprise. I could not help perceiving that it was greater than the occasion would justify' (p. 246). After arguing that the Davises should delay their journey, he admits that 'I am unable to explain why I conceived this journey to be attended with uncommon danger' (p. 247); and in considering his 'terror' (p. 248) over the prospect of their imminent departure, he explains, 'all men are, at times, influenced by inexplicable senti- ments. Ideas haunt them in spite of all their efforts to discard them. Prepossessions are entertained, for which their reason is unable to discover any adequate cause' (p. 248). Althorpe here generalizes from his specific response to this particular situation to 'all men'. In contra- distinction to Enlightenment emphases on the judicious application of reason and logical thinking, Althorpe, extrapolating from his own affective response to Constantia, maintains that all human beings are prone at various times to irrational thought processes. Developing this idea further, he adds,

> The strength of a belief, when it is destitute of any rational foundation, seems, of itself, to furnish a new ground for credulity. We first admit a powerful persuasion, and then, from reflecting on the insufficiency of the ground on which it is built, instead of being prompted to dismiss it, we become more forcibly attached to it. (p. 248)

What Brown, through Althorpe, develops here is essentially a variant on what Edgar Allan Poe some forty-five years later will refer to as 'perverseness', defined in Poe's 'The Black Cat' (1843) as the desire to perform an action for no other reason than that we know we shouldn't do it. 'All men', according to Althorpe, at least occasionally feel irrational and potentially destructive impulses and desires – and we cling to our beliefs all the more forcibly for their having no rational basis. Elaborating even more fully, Althorpe explains to the reader that 'my imagination was vivid. My passions, when I allowed them sway, were incontroullable. My conduct, as my feelings, was characterized by precipitation and headlong energy' (p. 248). Althorpe, in short, is a man not in control of himself. His imaginative nature and lack of self-discipline compel him to act in ways that are counter-productive and, as the story bears out, deadly and destructive.

If Althorpe is impulsive and prone to irrational thinking by day, by night he surrenders entirely to unconscious motivations. Brown's most radical gesture of undermining assertions of human identity and self-presence in the story is of course the device of sleepwalking. Althorpe, as I have suggested above, seems motivated – and interest-ingly aware of the fact – by unconscious forces even while awake. But it is while asleep that the most fundamental and unsettling break occurs. After Constantia and her father depart, Althorpe, overwhelmed by 'a sort of persuasion that destiny had irreversibly decreed that [he] should never see [Constantia] again' (p. 250), falls into a 'profound slumber' (p. 250), but one in which his 'fancy was incessantly em-ployed in calling up the forms, into new combinations, which had constituted [his] waking reveries' (p. 250). The next morning he learns the tragic news: Constantia has been shot on the road. Piecing together the story from different 'witnesses', Althorpe presents the tale: Constantia and her father set out on their journey through the dark forest at night and felt themselves to be observed and followed. They first assumed their night stalker to be Althorpe, subsequently thought it was the mentally challenged Nick Handyside, and then were attacked.

The language of the Davises' journey through the woods is clearly Gothicized through and through. They are travelling across the 'rude, sterile, and lonely' wilderness of Norwood at night and feel them-selves watched in the darkness. '[T]hat thing, whatever it be, haunts us', exclaims Mr Davis (p. 253). And there is indeed a monster haunt-ing the forest. Nick Handyside 'merited the name of monster, if a projecting breast, a mis-shapen head, features horrid and distorted, and a voice that resembled nothing that was ever before heard, could entitle him to that appellation' (p. 255). But 'Somnambulism' is not a conventional monster tale. The headnote to the story, as well as the details about Althorpe's lack of self-awareness, all lead the reader to conclude that the culprit in the case is not Nick Handyside at all, the ostensible monster, but rather Althorpe himself who – like the Polish youth detailed at the start – murders the object of his affection in his sleep. The implications here are profoundly disconcerting: the human condition, suggests Brown in this story written roughly a century before Sigmund Freud's pronouncements on the subject, is one in which we are motivated by unconscious impulses, anxieties and desires of which we can have no accurate knowledge and which we cannot control. At such moments, we are compelled by forces that seem to come from without, from someone else, but rather that emerge from within – there is, in essence, *someone else within us*, someone we do not know who causes us to do things and to act in ways that our conscious, wakeful mind would reject. Not only does 'Somnambulism' assert that all human beings at times are prone to irrational thoughts, but the realization at the core of Brown's Psychological Gothic is that the mind is a kind of haunted house. Lurking within all us, beneath the facade of rationality, is a monster. To be haunted by the monstrous other within is the essential human condition.

This Psychological Gothic realization of the bipartite division of the human mind – which receives its fullest expression in the Gothic device of the doppelgänger and will be developed later in the century in works like Poe's 'William Wilson' (1839), Stevenson's *The Strange Case of Dr Jekyll and Mr Hyde* (1886), and of course by Freud – is one that Brown incorporates to varying degrees in all four of his novels conventionally categorized as Gothic romances. In *Wieland*, the question of human motivations is raised most powerfully through the murders committed by Wieland Jr and more subtly by the narrator Clara herself. Wieland is eloquent and clear-headed at his trial: he believes that in destroying his wife and children he 'subdued the stubbornness of human passions',[24] that his intentions were pure, and that the deed 'was enjoined by heaven' (p. 134). His auditors, however, reach a different conclusion: Mr Cambridge states that 'there could be no doubt as to the cause of these excesses. They originated in sudden madness' (p. 135). The third possibility is that Carwin is at fault – that he counterfeited the voice of God and misled Wieland into killing his family. While Korobkin supports this last possibility and places the blame fully on Carwin's head, I feel this argument is complicated by the Wieland family's history of mental instability, by Wieland's tendency toward religious mania and – perhaps most compellingly – by Brown's tendency in his writing in general to emphasize the irrational core of human nature. Carwin's intervention may well have been a precipitating factor leading Wieland to act upon repressed desires, but the evidence seems to suggest that the voice of God heard by Wieland was neither God nor Carwin but rather the voice of the other *within*.

At the beginning of the story, the reader learns about Wieland Sr's own brand of religious zealotry. As Barnard and Shapiro observe, 'that the elder Wieland becomes a disciple of a sect that believes in apocalyptic, divine commandments received through ecstatic experiences of foreign and ancient languages foreshadows later events for his children'.[25] Wieland Sr migrates to the New World and builds himself an isolated temple at which he participates in solitary religious observance twice daily. Wieland Jr, we learn, inherits his father's propensity for zealotry and melancholy: Clara describes him as 'grave, considerate, and thoughtful' (p. 22), inclined to meditate on the future and death, and as characterized by a species of 'thrilling melancholy' (p. 22). After Wieland Jr has performed his bloody deeds, Clara learns that there is a family history of mental instability on her mother's side as well. Her uncle Mr Cambridge explains that his father committed suicide by jumping off a cliff after claiming to have received a command to do so from his dead brother (p. 136). Wieland, then, due both to personal disposition and a family history of mental instability – which includes hearing voices commanding violence – seems predisposed toward the kind of psychosis he displays. Carwin's ventriloquistic meddling may well have been the immediate precipitating factor, but Brown makes it clear through Clara's narration that Wieland has been heading in this direction all along.

More to the point, however, is the fact that Brown in his writing generally eschews simplistic explanations that either confirm supernatural intervention or present a character as innocently led contrary to his or her desires by a typical Gothic villain. What Brown stages instead are scenes in which psychologically complex protagonists interpret sensory data in light of their own biases and dispositions, which gives them licence to do what they already on some level want to do. This is clearly the case with Althorpe in 'Somnambulism'. Through a process of specious reasoning, he justifies his first impulse to follow the Davises and, when that impulse is frustrated, he does so anyway – in his sleep. My argument is that Althorpe's killing of Constantia while asleep and Wieland's killing of his family are manifestations of the same underlying psychological process: the emergence of monstrous unconscious desires. Ultimately, whether or not Carwin counterfeits the voice of God is immaterial, because Wieland is acting upon the command he has been waiting to receive, a bone-deep desire to believe that the world is governed by Providence and to demonstrate his obedience to God. Carwin may be the 'biloquist' of the tale, but the true ventriloquist in *Wieland* is Wieland himself, speaking to himself as from afar in the voice of God.

This is the sensational and hair-raising example of ventriloquism in the novel; however, in some ways the more interesting version is the one represented by the narrator, Clara. In a curious and provocative way, the critics have been less kind to Clara, who presents herself as a kind of innocent bystander, than to Wieland himself who murders his entire family, and a number of critics have focused on Clara's unconscious desires as implicating her in the story's traumatic events. Christophersen, for example, is particularly ungenerous to Clara, who at the end is ready to kill her brother if need be. According to Christophersen,

> The real evil in *Wieland* lies not merely with the atrocities committed by the deranged brother, but in the frightful, if unrealized, impulses that surface in the sister – impulses whose source, apparently, is human nature, the familiar bond, and innate psychosexual processes in which we all partake.[26]

Fiedler, Grabo, Looby and Samuels all interpret Clara as compelled by unacknowledged sexual desires, including a deeply repressed incestuous wish for her brother, that implicate her in the violent events of the story.[27] The effect of Clara's 'unrelieved state of sexual excitation', according to Looby, is that 'it is Clara whose understanding is depraved, whose misapprehensions lead to her making deductions that result in various ill consequences'.[28] Clara, like Althorpe in 'Somnambulism', 'sees what she wants to see, hears what she wants to hear; then she assembles from these putative sense impressions a narrative construction that strengthens her belief in what she wants to believe'.[29] *Wieland* thus functions as an anti-Enlightenment 'study in disjointed self-perception'[30] demonstrating the extent to which all human beings are essentially dual in nature and motivated by unconscious forces. From this, Christophersen concludes that

> By portraying [Clara's] potential for evil, Brown delivers a more damning indictment than Matthew Lewis, Ann Radcliffe, or even William Godwin dreamed of. Whereas these Gothicists indicted individuals or social institutions, Brown indicts mankind. Whereas they accused the aggressor, Brown incriminates the victim ... *Wieland*, then, negates the optimistic philosophy and psychology of the Enlightenment, presenting man as naturally depraved, prey to evils beyond his control.[31]

Similar arguments can be presented for the primary characters in Brown's other novels. Because of space limitations, however – and because *Edgar Huntly* provides such a spectacular and sustained demonstration of my thesis that Brown pioneers the Psychological Gothic well before Poe – I will attend only briefly to *Ormond* and *Arthur Mervyn* in order to give a sense of how these novels have been approached and to provide possibilities for future exploration, before attending to *Edgar Huntly* in more depth. Critics on the whole have been far kinder to Constantia in *Ormond* than to Clara in *Wieland*, choosing to approach her – as I shall explore in the next chapter – more in terms of her defiance of conventional gender expectations and the queer intensity of her relationship with Sophia, and as a revision of the conventional eighteenth-century sentimental heroine, than in terms of unconscious motivations. Nevertheless, Russel Nye observes that Constantia 'fails to recognize her own unconscious, powerful response to Ormond and thus incorrectly estimates both her vulnerability and the strength of his passion',[32] and Christophersen argues that Constantia's penchant for 'rationalizing problematic truths' connects her to the novel's blindness motif that 'implicates everyone for their [*sic*] unwillingness to look upon motives and desires'.[33] From a different perspective, Hinds argues that both Constantia's facade of rationality and the connected structure of the narrative itself come undone as the story progresses:

> As Constantia's reason disintegrates, so does the narrative voice of *Ormond*. It is often difficult to determine just who is actually narrating . . . Plot is replaced by seemingly inchoate, random and circuitous eventuation in the narrative; fixity gives way to flux in the narrative as a whole.[34]

The result of this disintegration of the narrative is a bewildering sense for the reader of a character and a narrative out of control.

The character most obviously out of control in *Ormond*, however, is Ormond himself; initially presenting himself as a dispassionate observer motivated solely by logic and reason, Ormond casts aside this Godwinian mask at the end to reveal himself as the 'archetypal villain of popular fiction' motivated wholly by lust and selfish desire.[35] Beneath his logic and persuasive rhetoric, asserts Kafer, 'is the reality of a self-obsessed monster'.[36] Christophersen reads Ormond as 'blind to his own susceptibility to passion – and therefore to the true main-springs of his reasoning',[37] and notes in support of this thesis Brown's observation concerning Ormond that 'his conclusions [regarding his mistress, Helena] were specious but delusive, and were not un-influenced by improper byasses; but of this he himself was scarcely conscious' (p. 92). Despite this comment by Constantia (as com-municated by Sophia), I am not fully persuaded that Ormond actually subscribes to rationalist principles and is unconscious of the under-lying lusts that compel him and of his own hypocrisy. On the contrary, I would argue that he is fully aware of the irrationality of his desires and prepared to do anything to obtain his objectives. His Godwinian critique of marriage from this perspective is merely convenient rhet-oric available to allow him to pursue sensual pleasures without the complication of a formal, legal attachment.

What is disconcerting about Ormond is from this perspective not his self-delusion, but rather his excessive desire which overrides all forms of constraint. He is Althorpe awake to his motivations and

Wieland recognizing the voice of God as his own – or rather believing that he has become God himself. That Ormond considers himself God is everywhere apparent in his actions and his discourse. He gives sight to the blind by facilitating Mr Dudley's recovery from cataracts and then dictates life and death when Mr Dudley stands in his way of Ormond achieving his objective of enjoying Constantia. As 'the secret witness', he acquires knowledge of those upon whom he spies for the purpose of controlling them and appearing omnipotent. And his desire as part of the Illuminati-like organization, as mentioned in chapter 2, is 'to exercise absolute power over the conduct of others' (p. 131). A compelling argument can be made for interpreting Ormond not as internally divided and unaware of the unconscious forces that compel him, but rather as uncannily *undivided*. He is pure Id, unconstrained by conventional morality or social expectations and undeviating from his course. 'Living or dead', he expresses to Constantia, 'the prize that I have in view shall be mine' (p. 216). Rape, murder and even necrophilia are all options Ormond is fully willing to pursue. In Brown's Psychological Gothic, Ormond is the monster that emerges when tabooed wishes and desires receive full and unhindered expression. From this perspective – as I shall develop in more detail below in my discussion of *Edgar Huntly* – what *Ormond* suggests is that knowing oneself is potentially more dangerous than repression.

Arthur Mervyn tells essentially the same story as *Ormond* as it pits a seemingly naïve protagonist, possibly motivated by unconscious impulses, against a master dissimulator who pursues his lustful objectives at any cost. Both Constantia and Arthur attempt to counter vice with virtue and deception with sincerity in a city plagued not only by yellow fever but by heartlessness and greed. Brown's presentation of Arthur, however, amplifies the questions raised everywhere in Brown's writing about the wisdom of reading books based on their covers and about the extent to which individuals can ever fully discern their own motivations. As noted in chapter 2, questions about how to interpret Arthur's character are hotly contested in Brown criticism. Among those raising questions about Arthur's motivations is Michael Davitt Bell, who notes an apparent inconsistency between Arthur's words and deeds:

Against Arthur's profession of virtuous intention stands his un-acknowledged but persistent self-interestedness. Against the novel's apparent vindication of narrative sincerity, of the rational eloquence of Arthur's 'words', stands the welter of suppressed motives and 'sentiments' revealed briefly in the final dream.[38]

Dreams, of course, are – as Freud famously puts it – the 'royal road to the unconscious', and in Arthur's dream near the end of the novel he is stabbed through the heart by Achsa Fielding's first husband, suggesting repressed guilt about his actions. Bell concludes that 'Arthur's earnestness is never daunted, but it is, as Brown's irony makes clear, the earnestness of the confidence-man'.[39]

Emory Elliott considers Arthur's surprising proposal to Achsa Fielding at the end of the novel in a somewhat different light. In keeping with critical assessments of the novel in general, Elliott notes that Arthur's rejection of the young, pretty, pure and strong-minded Eliza Hadwin in favour of the woman he calls his 'mama' – the older, Jewish, less attractive, and rich Achsa – is so surprising that it forces a reconsideration of everything Arthur has previously told us. Elliott concludes that Arthur's final decision shows that he 'cannot overcome his psychological limitations, his feelings of inadequacy, insecurity, and dependence. Thus, he retreats from America and from the vision of the future which it offers and seeks safety and comfort in the arms of his Judeo-European mother'.[40]

Grabo addresses Arthur's hypocrisy from still another perspective. Focusing on the moment when Arthur assists Welbeck in burying a murdered man in the basement, Grabo asserts that 'Arthur becomes progressively locked into Welbeck's will and plan as they lug Watson's body to the cellar, a body that will not keep its eyes closed. Or, to put it another way, Arthur in this scene surrenders completely to the Welbeckian element in himself'.[41] The 'Welbeckian element' is that part of him that resists the imposition of law, that – despite his pretentions to sincerity and virtue – desires to do harm, to do wrong. The point here is that, in keeping with the assertions made by Bell, Grabo, Elliott, Christophersen and others, Clara, Constantia, Arthur and, as we shall see, Edgar, 'their virtue not withstanding, all become implicated in crimes of mythic proportion, crimes that suggest their unawareness of the urges that govern them'.[42] What Brown stages for the reader again and again are scenes and situations in which the Gothic trope of haunting is reconfigured so that the ghost emerges from within: to be human, asserts Brown through his fiction, is to be haunted.

Project Mayhem

In the 1999 film adaptation of *Fight Club*, the 1996 novel by Chuck Palahniuk, the nameless narrator played by Edward Norton discovers that he can achieve emotional release through violence. Together with a soap salesman named Tyler Durden (played by Brad Pitt), he establishes 'fight clubs' across the country, which morph into an anti-corporate and anti-materialist movement called 'Project Mayhem'. When the narrator attempts to shut the movement down, he discovers that (spoiler warning!) he *is* Tyler Durden: they are dissociated personalities and Tyler controls the body when the narrator is asleep. *Fight Club* is a Psychological Gothic tale of the mind turned against itself. The narrator of the story literally discovers that he has a stranger within himself compelling him to do things of which he has no conscious recollection; further, the narrator discovers his own capacity for spectacular violence. The narrator in *Fight Club* is not given a name, so perhaps we should just call him William Wilson in as much as the story is a variation on the well-established Gothic trope of the doppelgänger – the double or alter ego.

Although the fiction of Edgar Allan Poe is filled with characters that either seem to be duplicates of one another or complementary aspects of a single identity, 'William Wilson' is arguably Poe's most explicit use of the doppelgänger theme. In this story, the narrator – who does not give the reader his real name, but goes by William Wilson – explains how he went from bad to worse in one fell swoop. It began when he entered school and encountered his double. This other William Wilson shared the same name, birthday and appearance, and had an annoying tendency to show up precisely when the narrator was in the midst of some dishonest action: if the narrator was cheating at cards, the other William Wilson appeared and foiled him; if the narrator was taking steps to seduce a married woman, William Wilson II showed up with the intention of thwarting him. Finally, the narrator confronted and stabbed his uncanny pursuer, only to be faced not with a corpse but rather with a mirror reflecting an image of himself all bloodied. The image addresses the narrator and the story ends with the pronouncement:

> You have conquered, and I yield. Yet, henceforward art thou also dead
> – dead to the World, to Heaven and to Hope! In me didst thou exist
> – and, in my death, see by this image, which is thine own, how utterly
> thou hast murdered thyself.[43]

The gist of the story is that the narrator has been pursued by and has murdered his own conscience. He has killed off that part of himself charged with countering selfish and dishonest behaviour.

As has been the case in the other chapters of this study, my argument here is that one can trace the path of the development of this Gothic subgenre, the Psychological Gothic, back from its contemporary manifestations to its literary origins and elaboration in the late eighteenth century in the works of Brown. The map here shows a trajectory backwards from *Fight Club* to Henry James's 'The Jolly Corner' (1908) and Stevenson's *The Strange Case of Dr Jekyll and Mr Hyde*, to Poe's 'William Wilson' and then to Brown's novels – most of all *Edgar Huntly*, which outdoes them all in terms of demonstrating the uncanny duality of the human psyche. Indeed, Brown's *Edgar Huntly* is arguably among the most spectacular demonstrations of what I am calling the Psychological Gothic theme of the haunted human mind anywhere in world literature – it is Brown's own Project Mayhem.

Edgar Huntly's insistent emphasis on the bifurcated nature of the mind is signalled immediately by the surreal impossibility of *Edgar Huntly*'s subtitle: 'Memoirs of a Sleep-Walker'. What is so fundamentally disconcerting about sleepwalking is that one is performing actions over which one has no conscious control and no conscious recollection. One can only learn of one's actions while sleepwalking after the fact from someone else. Disquietingly, one must be told what one did. The title of Brown's novel itself thus stages the confrontation between the waking and sleeping mind – Edgar cannot himself tell his own story because his waking self does not know it. His memoirs thus can only be vicarious retellings of information received at second hand or deduced after the fact.

Edgar raises a further complication in the telling of his tale early in the first chapter when he explains that 'in proportion as I gain power over words, shall I lose dominion over sentiments; in proportion as my tale is deliberate and slow, the incidents and motives which it is designed to exhibit will be imperfectly revived and obscurely pourtrayed'.[44] What Edgar is suggesting is that there is a fundamental disconnection between affect and understanding. To translate what he felt into words, to order his experience and convey it clearly to his correspondent, would circumscribe and delimit its emotional impact. He can either attempt to create an emotional response in his reader replicating his own – to share his uncertainty and terror and horror, and in essence turn the reader into his doppel-gänger – or he can attempt to produce intellectual understanding. The poles Edgar outlines at the start are either empathy or sympathy, the reader feeling what Edgar felt or feeling a different emotion – pity – for what he has been through. Brown, however, tries to have it both ways: to communicate what cannot be communicated, the memoirs of someone who is asleep. Edgar will attempt to explain his experience clearly to the reader; however, the structure of the narrative itself undoes his attempt at clarity.

Edgar Huntly is ostensibly a murder mystery as Edgar attempts to track down the killer of his friend Waldegrave. The problem is that, precisely as Korobkin comments in relation to *Wieland*,

> There is evidence galore, but the normative relationships between evidence and inference, effect and cause, corroboration and truth, have broken down ... More frightening still, the instrument used to assess this evidence – the supposedly rational human mind – is shown to be warped, fragile, and malleable.[45]

The disconnections between intention and action, evidence and inference, are evident almost immediately as Edgar happens on an unexpected sight: a man digging in the middle of the night in the woods by the scene of Waldegrave's murder. Stranger still, Edgar concludes that the man is asleep. Here, the novel offers its first pro-nouncement on the duality of the human psyche: 'The incapacity of sound sleep', explains Edgar, 'denotes a mind sorely wounded'. He continues,

---

It is thus that atrocious criminals denote the possession of some dreadful secret. The thoughts, which considerations of safety enables them to suppress or disguise during wakefulness, operate without impediment, and exhibit their genuine effects, when the notices of sense are partly excluded, and they are shut out from a knowledge of their intire condition. (p. 11)

This in a nutshell is the fundamental premise informing all of *Edgar Huntly*: that human beings are not always, or even most of the time, in control of themselves. Unconscious impulses and repressed desires and anxieties move us in ways of which we are not aware. Extrapolating from the actions of this man – who turns out to be Clithero Edny – Edgar concludes that this must be the murderer of his friend. After all, 'what but the murder of Waldegrave could direct his steps hither?' (p. 11). Later reflecting on the scene, he convinces himself even more firmly of Clithero's guilt: 'That Clithero was instrumental to the death of Waldegrave, that he could furnish the clue, explanatory of every bloody and mysterious event, that had hitherto occurred, there was no longer the possibility of doubting' (p. 24). Edgar, however, falls flat as an amateur psychoanalyst. Here, as in virtually everything else, Edgar is off base. In response to Edgar's accusations, Clithero responds: 'The inferences which you have drawn, with regard to my designs, and my conduct, are a tissue of destructive errors. You, like others, are blind to the most momentous consequences of your own actions' (p. 25). Despite the circumstantial evidence based on an understanding of the duality of the human mind linking Clithero to the death of Waldegrave, Clithero maintains his innocence. Not only has Edgar drawn an inaccurate conclusion, but his actions here precipitate an unpredictable sequence of events.

In Edgar's defence, he is not entirely wrong. Clithero does possess a mind sorely wounded and does believe himself guilty of a monstrous crime – but not the crime of which he is being accused. Edgar's charge prompts Clithero's narrative in which he details his accidental murder of Arthur Wiatte and his attempted murder of his benefactress and future mother-in-law Euphemia Lorimer. Clithero's story is of particular interest in this context because it combines the Gothic devices of madness and the doppelgänger. Arthur Wiatte and Euphemia

Lorimer, Clithero informs the reader, are twins. They are, however, distinguished by their disparate moral polarities. 'Perhaps the rudiments of their intellectual character as well as of their form, were the same', explains Clithero. '[B]ut the powers, that in one case, were exerted in the cause of virtue, were, in the other, misapplied to sordid and flagitious purposes' (p. 32). Mrs Lorimer is a paragon of virtue and untinctured goodness; her brother Arthur, on the other hand,

> exceeded in depravity all that has been imputed to the arch-foe of mankind. His wickedness was without any of those remorseful intermissions from which it has been supposed that the deepest guilt is not entirely exempt. He seemed to relish no food but pure unadulterated evil. He rejoiced in proportion to the depth of that distress of which he was the author. (p. 32)

The twins Arthur and Eugenia are doppelgängers for one another – they are essentially one human identity severed into two parts, good and evil – an idea that both Poe and Stevenson will appropriate later in the nineteenth century.

Clithero's downfall begins when he accidentally shoots and kills Arthur in self-defence. Aware that Mrs Lorimer superstitiously believes her destiny to be connected to that of her wicked brother, the idea occurs to Clithero that she may be right. While Clithero does not credit the belief that the lives of the brother and sister are supernaturally intertwined, he does acknowledge the power of the human mind to control the body. According to Clithero, her belief

> is nothing more, perhaps, than a fond imagination . . . It matters not. Who knows not the cogency of faith? That the pulses of life are at the command of the will? The bearer of these tidings [concerning her brother] will be the messenger of death. A fatal sympathy will seize her. She will shrink, and swoon, and perish at the news! (p. 54)

Clithero concludes that the news of her brother's death will be fatal to Mrs Lorimer. Once this thought takes hold of him, he cannot shake it. 'My fancy', he tells Edgar, 'began to be infected with the errors of my understanding' (p. 55). At this point, some other force – the stranger within – took control of him: 'Was it I that hurried to the deed? No. It was the daemon that possessed me. My limbs were guided to the bloody office by a power foreign and superior to mine' (p. 59). This, too, is Edgar's conclusion when he reflects: 'It must at least be said that his will was not concerned in this transaction. He acted in obedience to an impulse which he could not controul, nor resist' (p. 64).

In sum: it matters not whether Clithero is asleep or awake. In either state he is compelled to act by irresistible forces that seem to originate from somewhere else, from outside him. Clithero, however, is not the only sleepwalker and Euphemia and Arthur are not the only doppelgängers in *Edgar Huntly*. Weird things also keep happening to Edgar. Not only is Waldegrave murdered, but a packet of his letters entrusted to Edgar by Waldegrave disappears. Most dramatically, he wakes up in the dark in a pit of some kind. The letters he presumes must have been stolen – although why anyone would want them or how anyone could know where he kept them is a mystery. Their disappearance causes Edgar to be haunted by 'ominous terrors' related to 'a whispering intimation that a relique which [he] valued more than life was torn forever away by some malignant and inscrutable destiny' (p. 91). As for ending up in the pit, Edgar is baffled but concludes when he finds Indians in possession of his musket that he must have been knocked over the head, kidnapped by them and deposited there.

The truth the reader discovers at the end is that Edgar himself is the thief in the night who removed Waldegrave's letters and that Edgar is responsible for his own interment in the pit: Edgar, the reader learns, is a sleepwalker just like Clithero. That Edgar sleepwalks is attested to by his uncle, who saw him leave the house: 'None but a man, insane or asleep, would wander forth so slightly dressed, and none but a sleeper would have disregarded my calls', he reports to Sarsefield (p. 166). The question that this information raises for the reader is: if sleepwalking is a symptom of a mind sorely wounded, as Edgar avers and the novel seems to support, what has wounded Edgar's mind? The answer, I think, returns us to the initial mystery of the novel: who murdered Waldegrave? Brown, it should be pointed out, does answer this question: it was an Indian who killed Waldegrave as an act of vengeance against white settlers for violence against and mistreatment of the Native American population. Waldegrave was picked at random: he was the first white man this Indian saw. To say that this conclusion is anticlimactic is an understatement. Not only is the solution to this mystery one for which the reader is not adequately prepared (the cardinal sin of any mystery novel!), but it seems to violate the logic of the entire narrative – logic which repeatedly emphasizes that all individuals are prone to irrational thinking, that the veneer of civilization masks a savage heart and that human beings not only fail to recognize their own motivations but act in ways of which they are unaware. In contrast to this unsatisfying conclusion is the solution to the mystery that the narrative consciously disavows but on which it nevertheless everywhere insists – that, as both Grabo and Christophersen assert, Edgar himself is responsible for the death of Waldegrave.

Consider the clues: first, there is the uncanny doubling of Clithero and Edgar, who are essentially doppelgängers of each other. Both are orphans. Both sleepwalk. Both attempt to hide a manuscript of some kind in their sleep – Clithero attempts to bury the manuscript of the woman he tried to kill, Edgar hides Waldegrave's letters. Clithero devises puzzle boxes and Edgar is also a 'mechanist' having 'constructed a writing desk and cabinet' on which he had 'endeavoured to combine the properties of secrecy, security, and strength, in the highest possible degree' (p. 79). Both attempt to kill someone they love – Clithero intends to murder Mrs Lorimer while Edgar barely misses killing Sarsefield. And, perhaps most bizarrely, both share Sarsefield as a mentor and father figure. As Grabo develops at length in his monograph study of Brown, these patterns of doubled characters, actions and meanings are central to Brown's art.[46] As in Poe's 'William Wilson', there are simply too many similarities for them to be coincidental or accidental. When Edgar views Clithero, he is essentially viewing himself without recognizing it.

Second is the narrative's insistence that the self Edgar fails to recognize is savage and brutal. Edgar tries to convince the reader that he is mild-mannered and peace loving. He tells the reader that 'my temper never delighted in carnage and blood. I found no pleasure in plunging into bogs, wading through rivulets, and penetrating thickets, for the sake of dispatching wood-cocks and squirrels' (p. 84). In almost the next breath, however, Edgar explains that he is exceptionally proficient in using a weapon associated with the Native Americans in the novel, the 'tomahawk'. According to Edgar, 'with this I have often severed an oak branch and cut the sinews of a cat-o'mountain, at the distance of sixty feet' (p. 84). It also turns out that Edgar, our non-hunter, is a crack shot with a rifle who can gun down Indians with ease and almost takes out Sarsefield at night at a distance as well. Although he tells the reader that his 'aversion to bloodshed was not to be subdued but by the direst necessity' (p. 119), once that aversion is overcome he becomes a killing machine.

Edgar's reversion to savagery once he awakens in the cave has been one of the most discussed aspects of Brown's novel. This is the moment at which he kills and eats a panther, then goes on his Indian-killing rampage. The panther, according to Christophersen, represents the brute, savage part of the self[47] and when he consumes it, according to Grabo, 'he takes into himself the savageness that is Clithero – murderous, mad and driven – the savageness that is man in his essential nature'.[48] Edgar at this point in the novel essentially 'goes native'. Able to brain a panther at sixty paces in the dark with a tomahawk, he is more savage than the voiceless 'savages' that stalk through the pages of Brown's Gothic novel. The point, however, is that – to express it in the racist terms of the narrative – Edgar here allows the inner savage Indian that inhabits us all to emerge un-fettered. When the repressive veneer of civilization is stripped away, what is revealed is the underlying barbarity of 'civilized' men. Brown's point, says Grabo, is that 'the animal in us cannot be dismissed or plastered over'.[49]

That Edgar and Clithero are doppelgängers of one another and that it takes very little for Edgar to transform into a panther-eating killing machine both suggest that Edgar – at least symbolically – is the murderer of Waldegrave. Beyond this evidence, however, there is the narrative's repeated insistence that human beings are not in control of themselves and cannot foresee the consequences of their actions. Listening to Clithero's story of his misguided attempt on Mrs Lorimer's life, Edgar thinks to himself 'how imperfect are the grounds of all our decisions!' (p. 64) While Clithero's intention was kind, the premise informing his actions was highly suspect. Edgar again highlights the epistemological constraints on human actions – the fact that human beings can never be entirely certain of their own motivations, that we can never possess a 'God's-eye view' of things that would allow us perfect knowledge and that we can never entirely predict the consequences of our actions even in the near term – towards the end of his account when he considers all that has transpired. Just in case the reader has missed the uncanny resemblance between Clithero and Edgar, Edgar makes the parallels explicit: 'Clithero had buried his treasure with his own hands as mine had been secreted by myself, but both acts had been performed during sleep. The deed was neither prompted by the will, nor noticed by the senses of him, by whom it was done' (p. 185). This observation leads Edgar to pronounce: 'Disastrous and humiliating is the state of man! By his own hands, is constructed the mass of misery and error in which his steps are forever involved' (p. 185). To this conclusion about the uncomfortable condition of humanity, Edgar adds: 'How little cognizance have men over the actions and motives of each other? How total is our blindness with regard to our own performances!' (p. 185). And, as if to add an extra exclamation point to this revelation, Brown has Edgar not long after inform Clithero that Mrs Lorimer is still alive, mistakenly believing that this will cure his madness. Counter to Edgar's expectations, Clithero promptly sets off to finish the job of killing her.

In *Edgar Huntly*, Brown develops the Psychological Gothic theme of human beings as strangers to themselves to the fullest extent anywhere in American literature. And the real dilemma, suggests Brown, is that there is no way out of this predicament. Not knowing what is down there, lurking in the depths of the unconscious, is bad; knowing what is there, however, may be worse. 'Consciousness', asserts Sarsefield, 'itself is the malady; the pest; of which he only is cured who ceases to think' (p. 184) – a conclusion with which Edgar can only concur. In place of a man on a fence at midnight or a man in a locked closet, Brown gives us in *Edgar Huntly* a locked puzzle box as a symbol for the mind. The only way to determine its contents, suggests Brown, is to break it. According to Christophersen, Brown in *Edgar Huntly* 'shows us not only the ghouls that inhabit our souls, but the prohibitive consequences of looking at them'.[50]

This is ultimately the way in which *Edgar Huntly* undoes itself. At the start, Edgar asserts that he can either attempt to communicate affect or understanding, to produce an emotional response in his reader approximating what he himself experienced or to explain things in a way that attempts to make sense. Edgar arguably chooses the latter, but the telling of his tale – its gaps and dislocations, its tangents and meanderings – performs the former. According to Hinds, the 'narrative confusion' of *Edgar Huntly* mirrors the confusion of its protagonist: 'Digression at the narrative level acts to create gothic effect through discursive as well as psychological terror. Both the hero himself and the narrative voice of *Edgar Huntly* move through a labyrinth of experience without novelistic causality'.[51] Edgar tries to make sense of his experience for the reader, but the narrative itself, the telling of the tale, leads the reader into a labyrinth from which there is finally no escape. The only ending to a story that consistently undermines all conclusions is that the conclusion is not the end.

There are then two conclusions to *Edgar Huntly*: the Scooby Doo ending in which the crime of Waldegrave's murder was a random one committed by a vengeful Indian, which rings false; and the much more compelling and unsettling conclusion of which neither Edgar nor the narrative are consciously aware but that is everywhere suggested: that Edgar symbolically, if not in actuality, is the murderer. Grabo asserts that with Edgar, as well as Clara and Constantia – and I would add Arthur – we discover characters that manifest repressed aspects of themselves: 'Each of these fictions relates the discovery of what was either unknown or unknowable, or both'.[52] It is not a question of either real ghosts or the explained supernatural – Brown gives us neither the Radcliffe nor the Lewis ending. What Brown repeatedly develops in his Psychological Gothics is a sort of *Fight Club*-esque 'Project Mayhem' in which what is contested is the Enlightenment faith in human reason and our abilities to draw accurate inferences from sensory data. Well before Poe and Freud, what Brown gives us is a picture of a world in which we cannot be certain of anything and in which to be haunted is the essential human condition. The realization at the heart of Brown's Psychological Gothic is that we are all haunted by the stranger within.

4

Charles Brockden Brown and the Female Gothic

⌘

In the preceding three chapters, I have made the case that Charles Brockden Brown should be regarded as an innovator within three subgenres of the Gothic: the Frontier, the Urban and the Psychological. In each case, Brown helped to define and shift the parameters of horror fiction and crafted conventions that still influence these subgenres today. In this chapter, I will present the argument that Brown was influential on a fourth Gothic subgenre – what has come to be called the 'Female Gothic'. In order to develop this thesis, I will first offer a definition and brief overview of the development of the idea of the Female Gothic. Since the Female Gothic is that subcategory of the Gothic that deals with the experiences of female protagonists, I will then introduce a bit of historical context that helps to situate Brown's writing in light of conversations taking place about women's rights in the last decade or so of the eighteenth century. From there, I will give some consideration to Brown's unjustly neglected treatise on women's rights, his 1798 dialogue *Alcuin*, before then turning to his two primary examples of the Female Gothic, *Wieland* and *Ormond*. I will then conclude this chapter by offering some brief discussion of one of Brown's two 'sentimental' novels, *Clara Howard*. Although critics have generally failed to take note of Brown's contributions in this area – perhaps because the Female Gothic tends to be associated primarily with female authors – Brown nevertheless must be numbered among those late eighteenth-century

Gothic novelists who used the Gothic form as a means to dramatize and critique the cultural disempowerment of women. Indeed, in *Wieland* and most of all in *Ormond*, Brown arguably articulates a more explicitly feminist platform than most novels conventionally associated with the category of the Female Gothic.

Ghosts and patriarchy

The rubric 'Female Gothic' can be traced back to Ellen Moers's 1976 publication *Literary Women*, in which Moers proposes straightforwardly that the Female Gothic can be defined as 'the work that women writers have done in the literary mode that, since the eighteenth century, we have called the Gothic'.[1] In Moers's famous reading of Mary Shelley's *Frankenstein*, in which she characterizes the text as a *'woman's* mythmaking on the subject of birth',[2] Moers defines the Gothic as a genre that gives visible form to women's 'fear of self'.[3] Elaine Showalter observes that the Gothic, in Moers's view, concerns itself with female anxieties over birth and creation and articulates 'self-hatred and self-disgust directed towards the female body, sexuality, and reproduction'.[4]

Less frequently noted, but more radical in its assessment of the subversive potential of the Female Gothic, is Margaret Anne Doody's 1977 essay, 'Deserts, ruins and troubled waters: female dreams in fiction and the development of the Gothic novel'. In this essay, while Doody does not specifically name the category 'Female Gothic', she understands Gothic fiction by women as arising out of and responding to the historical disempowerment of women. In as much as it deals constantly with unbalanced power relations and the associated emotions of rage, fear, guilt and loneliness, the Gothic is well suited to the expression of female distress. She writes that 'it is in the Gothic novel that women writers could first accuse the "real world" of falsehood and disorder',[5] and concludes that 'it is not surprising that the English Gothic . . . should become, along one line of its evolution, the novel of feminine radical protest'.[6]

Critics have subsequently been divided over the political implications of this subgenre of Gothic fiction. Some critics including Kahane, Radway, DeLamotte and Kilgour read Female Gothic literature as generally conservative and expressive of internal female division or self-hatred.[7] For Kahane, for example, the Female Gothic stages a confrontation with the mother and, in Showalter's words, the 'reproduction of mothering'.[8] The fear located in the Female Gothic is revealed to be 'the fear of femaleness itself, perceived as threatening to one's wholeness, obliterating the very boundaries of self'.[9] For Radway, popular literature in general is inherently conservative and its primary function is to legitimate the existing social order.[10] Female Gothic literature participates in this reaffirmation of the status quo by first staging female dissent before reassuring readers that the heroine's discontentment was unwarranted.[11]

Radway's approach is essentially shared by DeLamotte and Kilgour. In DeLamotte's analysis of what she terms 'Women's Gothic', Gothic literature by women does open up a space for protest: it articulates the alienation of women from patriarchal culture;[12] it expresses their sense of 'entrapment by and subjection to patriarchal familial, legal, and class structures';[13] and it voices the 'hidden, unspeakable reality of women's lives'.[14] In DeLamotte's estimation, however, the female Gothicists ultimately evade the implications of their insights. The happy endings of these texts in which the heroines marry and discover safety in domestic settings reveal the Female Gothic to be deeply conservative.[15] DeLamotte's ironic conclusion is that the Female Gothic 'is a deeply subversive genre, but only to the extent that it subverts itself'.[16] Kilgour's argument follows a similar trajectory: while the Female Gothic presents the home as a prison in which the disempowered female is at the mercy of 'ominous patriarchal authorities',[17] the inevitable re-establishment of domestic life at the end reveals the genre to be simply reactionary rather than revolutionary. It is worth pointing out that all the critics in the conservative camp recognize in Female Gothic literature reflections on female concerns. For none of these critics, however, do these reflections rise to the level of explicit critique. Rather, female Gothicists are either demonstrating their internal self-division without calling into question the patriarchal culture that constructs it or are ultimately reifying the status quo through happy endings even as their narratives depict difficulties that women face in patriarchal culture.

Other critics including Leeuwen, Modleski, Restuccia, Ellis, Heller, Williams, Hoeveler and Becker interpret Female Gothic literature not as reinforcing conservative patriarchal values, but rather as revolutionary in its critique of the oppressiveness of patriarchal constraints and, in some cases, its fantasizing of a reordered, more egalitarian cultural distribution of power.[18] These critics downplay the conclusions to the novels and are more willing to accept that a conventional conclusion does not necessarily diminish the radical potential introduced earlier in the novel. Such critics, working from the literary models provided by Gilbert and Gubar, Showalter and Harris among others, present the argument that a formulaic covering or 'overplot' allows the female author to express discontent without ostensibly challenging or undermining social definitions of women's roles.[19] Writing in 1982, Leeuwen, for example, in asserting that Female Gothic novels of the late eighteenth and early nineteenth centuries 'read like [Simone de Beauvoir's] *The Second Sex* in novel form',[20] presents among the most vigorous arguments for the radicalness of Female Gothic fiction. According to Leeuwen, Gothic authors Clara Reeve, Sophia Lee, Charlotte Smith, Ann Radcliffe and others were all writing about the same thing: 'the oppression of women'.[21] They used the Gothic mode to 'reveal the terror, the isolation, and the oppression of their lives'.[22]

The other proponents of the Female Gothic as the genre of radical feminine protest all adopt a more or less similar position: that, in the hands of women, the genre was made to express the nightmares of women oppressed by patriarchal restrictions. For Heller, Gothic novels by women in the Radcliffean vein record female fear of male domination. Modleski argues that the Gothic novels by women express women's fears of fathers and husbands and explore female psychic conflicts in relation to 'a society that systematically oppresses women'.[23] Restuccia also examines Gothic articulations of anxiety concerning fathers and husbands and, contrasting Gothic novels by men and women, observes that what women fear is not the extraordinary, but the ordinary. In Ellis's oft-cited study, *The Contested Castle: Gothic Novels and the Subversion of Domestic Ideology* (1989), she locates the female Gothicists' preoccupation with the home as a site of imprisonment and of violence performed against women and, despite the happy resolutions of most Gothic novels by women, argues that Female Gothic novels present a deeply subversive impulse in the form of 'an increasingly insistent critique of the ideology of separate spheres'.[24]

The understanding of the Female Gothic that I will use to develop this chapter's argument concerning Brown falls on the 'radical feminine protest side' and is along the lines of that articulated by Alison Milbank in the 'Female Gothic' entry in the *The Handbook of the Gothic*. As schematically presented by Milbank, the difference between the Male Gothic and the Female Gothic is based on plot rather than the sex of the author. The 'Male Gothic' is characterized by 'transgression of social taboos by an excessive male will, and explorations of the imagination's battle against religion, law, limitation and contingency in novels such as Matthew Lewis's *The Monk* (1796), in which rape, murder, and mortgaging of the self to the devil are variously attempted'.[25] In contrast, in the Female Gothic, 'the male transgressor becomes the villain whose authoritative reach as patriarch, abbot or despot seeks to entrap the heroine, usurps the great house, and threatens death or rape'.[26] While, as the debate between critics outlined above suggests, this Female Gothic plot is not inherently conservative or progressive, in the hands of Brown – a committed feminist who read and discussed current women's rights proposals and explicitly introduced questions about women's rights into his fiction and non-fiction writing – the conventions of the Gothic became a useful means to extend this dialogue and promote his feminist agenda. Brown, in short, used the Gothic as a means to dramatize women's disempowerment in late eighteenth-century Euro-American culture, to highlight the forces of explicit and implicit violence used against women to coerce their submission, and to critique these forms of oppression.

The late eighteenth-century sex panic

But why was Brown interested in the issue of women's rights in the first place? One of the important premises of this study has been that no author – or artist of any kind, for that matter – ever creates in a vacuum. Artistic works are always products of their times and will invariably reflect anxieties and desires of their cultural contexts. In some cases, this engagement with social and political issues may be purposeful and explicit; in other instances, the work may instead reflect the shared understandings and attitudes – the zeitgeist – of a particular cultural moment. In the vast majority of instances, the work does both – that is, it critically engages with some issues, while unconsciously reflecting others. This is why some background in cultural context assists in critical interpretation. With regard to Brown, knowing a bit about his personal history as well as important issues of the day helps one to understand what shaped him and his works, where his inspiration came from and why certain issues crop up repeatedly in his novels.

As Russel Nye observes, the abilities, potential and rights of women were topics of intense interest in the 1780s and 1790s.[27] In response to the assertions made by Jean-Jacques Rousseau and others that women were destined by nature to serve as wives and mothers, early feminist activists including Catharine Macaulay, Nicolas de Condorcet, Olympe de Gouges, Mary Wollstonecraft and Judith Sargent Murray were beginning to articulate challenges to the cultural restrictions on women's autonomy. Central to this conversation and to the development of Brown's work was Wollstonecraft's *A Vindication of the Rights of Woman*, which was published in 1792. In this treatise, Wollstonecraft presents the argument that women are not naturally inferior to men; rather, they only appear this way due to inequalities in education. Educating men and women equally, asserts Wollstonecraft, would not only permit women to contribute more to society, but would also allow them to be companions and partners for their husbands, rather than inferior attachments.

When it was first published in 1792, the *Rights of Woman* became the subject of intense debate on both sides of the Atlantic; Kafer notes that American readers – at least those with Enlightenment sympathies – tended to be admirers of Wollstonecraft,[28] and her work initiated in America a 'serious public discussion of women's rights'.[29] Burrows and Wallace observe that not long after the publication of *Rights of Woman*, pamphlets both supporting and condemning it and its arguments began to appear in New York bookshops, and newspapers and magazines, hoping to attract female readers, reprinted excerpts from the work in their pages, along with lengthy exchanges between its critics and defenders:

Articulate and well-informed women sent in essays to local newspapers and magazines, disputing offensive characterizations of female
intelligence, attacking the sexual double standard, challenging legal
and political discrimination, and questioning the institution of
marriage.[30]

Women's rights were also high up on the list of popular subjects
debated by the New York intellectual society, the Friendly Club,
with which Brown was associated, and he was clearly familiar with
Wollstonecraft's polemic.

Responses to Wollstonecraft and her *Rights of Woman* were not
uniform in America, of course, and her liberal ideas, as Comment
observes, precipitated a conservative backlash fuelled by anxieties
about all kinds of 'sexual anarchy'.[31] Enthusiasm for Wollstonecraft's
ideas – associated by her critics with French revolutionary radicalism
– also began to wane in the mid-1790s as the French Revolution
morphed into the Reign of Terror and Americans began to become
increasingly concerned about Jacobin infiltration. What really touched
off what Burgett refers to as the 'first modern sex panic', however,
was the 1799 publication by William Godwin of *Memoirs of the Author
of A Vindication of the Rights of Woman*, a work detailing Wollstonecraft's
love affairs, illegitimate children and suicide attempts.[32] Godwin's
memoirs had a devastating effect on Wollstonecraft's reputation and,
as Kafer comments, after Godwin's publication, 'Godwinian' in
America 'was to carry the odor of atheism and sexual libertinism'.[33]

Despite this increasing suspicion of Wollstonecraft (discrediting
is perhaps more apt), Charles Brockden Brown, both before and
after Godwin's publication of the memoirs, participated vigorously
in the debate over female potential and oppression and arguably was
among America's most ardent supporters of women's rights. Repeatedly in his fiction, by making use of the familiar Gothic trope of
the 'damsel in distress', Brown dramatizes the forms of violence –
both explicit and implicit – to which women are exposed in patriarchal culture. These dramatizations in turn reflect and extend the
thinking on the subject that Brown had previously contemplated in
his earlier publication, *Alcuin*, a 'dialogue' on the subject of women's
rights.

Alcuin and the 'Paradise of Women'

> Brown took risks in his work – exploring potential roles for women beyond the wildest fantasies of his female contemporaries. One point is clear: if Brown's first name had been Charlotte, as the creator of the first utopian feminist dialogue and of fictions that explore the widest imaginable range of woman's lives and lifestyles, (s)he would now be the early American author most studied and revered by the canon revisers.[34]

For the purposes of this 'polemical introduction' to Charles Brockden Brown and his work, I have for pragmatic reasons until now re-stricted my attention almost exclusively to Brown's commercially available texts. In this chapter, however, I am going to expand my gaze a bit and offer some consideration of Brown's dialogue on women's rights, *Alcuin*, and of his female-centred epistolary novel, *Clara Howard*. Taking these works into consideration (especially *Alcuin*) further helps to establish Brown's extraordinarily progressive stance on women's rights. Brown, as Lewis provocatively asserts in the epigraph to this section, arguably went further than any of his contemporaries, male or female, in exploring and dramatizing constraints on women's liberty.

Fleischmann considers *Alcuin* a 'small masterpiece',[35] and while this may be slightly hyperbolic, the work is nevertheless, as Davidson puts it, 'one of the most eloquent of the late eighteenth-century American discussions on the rights of women' and among the most radical up to that point.[36] The first two parts of *Alcuin* – which, clearly with Wollstonecraft in mind, were originally titled 'The Rights of Women' – were published in 1798 in Philadelphia in the *Weekly Magazine*. The more radical Parts III and IV were not published until 1815, five years after Brown's death, in William Dunlap's *Life of Charles Brockden Brown* and, as Robert D. Arner notes in the 'Historical essay' attached to the Kent State Bicentennial Edition of Brown's *Alcuin*, a complete edition of *Alcuin* was not published until 1971.[37]

Alcuin is a dialogue on women's rights: it consists of a conversation between the eponymous Alcuin, a poor schoolteacher, and Mrs Carter, a wealthy widow who now oversees her brother's household at which she holds a kind of 'lyceum' or salon for intellectual conversation. In Parts I and II of *Alcuin*, Alcuin and Mrs Carter engage in a general conversation about women's rights; Parts III and IV detail Alcuin's visionary journey to the utopian 'Paradise of Women' and Mrs Carter's response, which allows the two to continue their discussion.

As Fleischmann observes, *Alcuin* is strongly imbued with Godwinian and Wollstonecraftian (or 'Woldwinite', as Barnard and Shapiro put it in their introductions to the Hackett editions of Brown's Gothic novels) rhetoric, and echoes Wollstonecraft's emphasis on the legal disempowerment of women and the damaging effect of women's education on female development.[38] With this in mind, in Part I, in which the subject of education is introduced, Mrs Carter notes that 'nothing has been more injurious than the separation of the sexes'.[39] Offering different systems of education for boys and girls results in a situation in which 'different systems of morality, different languages, or, at least, the same words with a different set of meanings, are adopted' (p. 18). Mrs Carter is then especially blunt as she considers the disempowerment of women by the legal institution of marriage:

> By marriage she loses all right to separate property. The will of her husband is the criterion of all her duties. All merit is comprised in unlimited obedience. She must not expostulate or rebel. In all contests with him, she must hope to prevail by blandishments and tears; not by appeals to justice, and addresses to reason. She will be most applauded when she smiles with most perseverance on her oppressor, and when, with the undistinguishing attachment of a dog, no caprice or cruelty shall be able to estrange her affection. (p. 18)

In Part II, Mrs Carter is particularly incensed by the exclusion of women from American political life. The American Constitution is deficient in not extending the vote to women according to Mrs Carter, and – again making use of the comparison of the treatment of women with that of animals – she heatedly maintains, 'I cannot celebrate the equity of that scheme of government which classes me with dogs and swine' (p. 25).

What is said in Parts I and II of *Alcuin* about the subjugation of women is, to borrow from Hedges, 'in advance of virtually everything previously written on the subject by an American'.[40] But then in

Parts III and IV Brown goes even further – into an alternative world in fact. In Part III, Alcuin returns to Mrs Carter to report his mystical journey to the 'Paradise of Women' (p. 34), a communistic utopian community in which no distinctions are made between men and women. Education is blind to gender, all occupations are open to both men and women and dress is dictated by the requirements of one's occupation rather than one's sex. Alcuin gets this far in his description of this radical gender-neutral society and then demurs, anxious that he is about to cross over into forbidden territory because the Paradise of Women lacks an equivalent of the legal institution of marriage. Mrs Carter, however, is no shrinking violet and is fully prepared to consider, if not to accept or sanction, alternative sexual configurations.

Marriage then becomes the central topic of Part IV of *Alcuin* and Mrs Carter essentially takes over the conversation. When asked about her objections to the existing system of matrimony, Mrs Carter presents two weighty criticisms: 'I disapprove of it', she says, 'in the first place, because it renders the female a slave to the man. It enjoins and enforces submission on her part to the will of her husband' (p. 54). In the second place, she continues, 'it leaves woman destitute of property. Whatever she previously possesses, belongs absolutely to the man' (p. 55). These conditions transform what should be a harmonious pact between two individuals into something 'flagitious and hateful' (p. 57). Mrs Carter's solution to this situation is the reformation of marriage: divorces should be made easier to obtain, property laws should be changed and vows of obedience should either be mutual or abolished (p. 66). It is important to emphasize that Mrs Carter is not an advocate of 'free love', open marriages or the eradication of marriage altogether. Although her reluctance on this point rings a bit hollow after her fierce denunciations of the current system of marriage, she is unwilling to take the plunge into radical Godwinianism. As Davidson observes, 'one can support the rights of women, she implies, without overthrowing American republicanism. One can be a reformer, she insists, without being a radical'.[41] Nevertheless, Mrs Carter *is* a radical and so is Brown, as he repeatedly foregrounds and critiques, both in *Alcuin* and his novels, the social conditions giving rise to women's disempowerment.

Alcuin in interesting ways thus sets the stage for the Female Gothic narratives Brown will subsequently develop. Through this explicit dialogue on women's subjugation in patriarchal culture, it acts as a kind of companion piece for or position statement accompanying Brown's later texts – especially *Wieland* and *Ormond* – that illustrate and extend *Alcuin*'s meditation on proper education for women, woman's disempowerment in marriage, the victimization of women at the hands of men and woman's role in society more generally. *Alcuin*, from this perspective, offers a critical gloss on themes Brown develops in his Gothic and sentimental fictions and provides a lens through which to appreciate Brown's insightfulness as a social commentator. In the novels that follow *Alcuin*, Brown will move from discussing the social construction of female oppression to illustrating it.

'Audacious acts, and unheard-of disasters': Clara Wieland

There is, it is worth noting, already a sort of 'Gothic edge' to *Alcuin*, in as much as Mrs Carter's rhetoric foregrounds the confinement and enforced servitude of women in patriarchal culture. Not a woman to mince words, Mrs Carter refers to the 'fetters' of marriage (p. 58) and calls it 'slavery' (p. 57). In addition, what Alcuin's visionary journey to the Paradise of Women makes clear is that this fantasy land of sexual egalitarianism exists nowhere in the 'real' world. Moving now from Brown's dialogue to his first two Gothic novels, what Brown gives the reader is arguably the nightmarish other side to Alcuin's fantasy – not a paradise of women but rather, anticipating Herman Melville's short story – their Tartarus.[42] As Paul Lewis contends, 'Brown's . . . plotlines center on a single issue defined by gender: the destructive working out of patriarchal authority, domination, observation, and control'.[43] This is clearly the case in Brown's first Gothic novel, *Wieland*, in which his protagonist, Clara, must contend with a missing father, a murderous brother, a faithless lover and a male villain whose acts of mischief repeatedly revolve around Clara's 'virtue': Carwin both claims that he has been foiled in his designs to ravish Clara and leads Pleyel to believe he has been successful in this, causing Pleyel to abandon Clara.

Wieland is a Gothic tale of victimization and murder, and Clara, as Christophersen notes, is a heroine undoubtedly indebted to Radcliffe and the Gothic tradition.[44] In the midst of a story replete with seemingly supernatural phenomena, Clara is repeatedly placed by Brown into situations in which first her virtue and subsequently her life are in danger. The incidents in Clara's room, for example – as Ringe observes – are clearly derived from Radcliffe.[45] It is midnight and Clara is alone in her room in a house occupied only by her female servant, Judith, when she hears a whisper apparently proceeding from 'lips that were laid close to my ear'.[46] Subsequently, she hears the voices of bandits in her closet contemplating her murder and flees the premises in the middle of the night, making it almost all the way to her brother's door before fainting.

In as much as the reader can believe anything Carwin says, Clara in the instance above was in no danger. Nevertheless, the incident is sufficient cause for Clara's equanimity to be disturbed and when she next hears sounds in her house at night, she tells the reader, 'images of violation and murder assailed me anew, and the terrors which succeeded almost incapacitated me from taking any measures for my defense' (p. 79). Like Constantia in *Ormond*, Clara grabs a handy penknife and is prepared to commit suicide rather than submit to rape. Clara is again wrong in her assumption and has no need for her penknife – the footsteps in the house turn out to be those of Pleyel, not Carwin – but her imagining of murder turns out to be prophetic and her penknife will be utilized in a very different fashion later in the novel when her brother, Wieland, uses it to kill himself.

Again and again, the intimate domestic space of Clara's bedroom transforms into a scene of horror as Clara is threatened by and confronts violence. It is in her house that Clara discovers her sister-in-law Catherine dead, murdered so brutally that 'not a *lineament remained!*' (p. 121).[47] And it is yet again in her house, in her bedroom, that her final confrontation with her brother takes place. Having murdered his wife and children, Wieland, who has a knack for escaping from prison, returns to complete his bloody work by murdering his sister. Clara initially takes steps to defend herself with her penknife, before rejecting the possibility of inflicting violence upon her brother. Wieland subsequently uses the same knife to kill himself at the moment he becomes convinced that he has been tricked into killing his family.

Although Clara is at the centre of a decidedly Gothic plot, it should be pointed out that, far from being a conventional Gothic heroine, she is, as Lewis observes, a 'model of female independence and strength'.[48] In contrast to her sister-in-law Catherine whom Clara describes as 'clay, moulded by the circumstances in which she happened to be placed' (p. 65), Clara is made of stronger stuff. Clara has her own house, her own thoughts and her own identity. She has received an unconventional education for a young woman of the time: seemingly in keeping with Wollstonecraft's recommend-ations in *The Rights of Woman*, Clara appears to have been educated together with her brother and participates in the intellectual life of the small Mettingen community – and, with admirable Age-of-Enlightenment clarity, investigates unusual circumstances to the best of her ability and inclines toward rejecting groundless conjecture or supernatural explanations. When she first hears voices in her closet, for example, she explains to the reader, 'I entertained no apprehensions of either ghosts or robbers. Our security had never been molested by either' (p. 50). Considering the situation logically, Clara explains to the reader that 'I had mistaken the sounds, and that my imagination had transformed some casual noise into the voice of a human creature' (p. 51). Rather than faint when scared or threatened, Clara bravely probes the source of her confusion or fright.

The dilemma Clara faces is that no amount of level-headed investi-gation or rational cogitation can penetrate or undo the irrational restrictions on female autonomy and potential in Clara's rigidly patriarchal culture. What Brown's novel ultimately reveals is that Clara's real problem is not Carwin or Pleyel or even her brother Wieland, but rather the all-encompassing and smothering patriarchal system their combination represents. Scheiber is explicit on this point, asserting that

> Clara is by virtue of her sex a second-class citizen whose identity is contingent on the support and corroboration of authoritarian, masculine-centered institutions of power: the patriarchal family, the life of the intellect, and the religion of her ancestors. The origin of Clara's difficulty is her ambiguous and precarious status with respect to these institutions which at once subsume and marginalize her identity as a woman.[49]

Carwin's role here is clearest: he is a sort of watered-down Gothic villain who, to the extent that we can believe anything he says, decides to sport with Clara a bit because she is vulnerable. What he brings to the fore through his actions is the threat of sexual violence against women that underlies and energizes both the conventional Gothic and sentimental romance plots.

The horror that confronts Clara is that by virtue of being a woman in a patriarchal culture, she is systematically disempowered and there is nowhere to turn to for help. Pleyel is not only the novel's representative Age-of-Enlightenment thinker, but – as Clara's lover – should also be her protector. Here, however, is where Brown undoes the conventional Gothic novel: Pleyel does not ride to Clara's rescue; rather, he participates in her distress and increases her vulnerability. As Fleischmann notes, Pleyel is a 'patriarch of the first order' and, despite his pretentions to Enlightenment rationality, is 'neither nice nor reasonable'.[50] So committed is he to conventional definitions of female 'purity' that, after overhearing a conversation in the dark between speakers he presumes to be Clara and Carwin, he drops Clara like a stone, ignoring entirely her dismay and protestations of innocence, and disregarding the other incidents of unexplained, disembodied voices that have plagued Mettingen. Pleyel, it turns out, is a hypocrite and a fool who turns his back on the woman he professes to love on the basis of erroneous conclusions drawn from suspect information and undergirded by misogynistic premises. So much for Enlightenment rationality.

Alas, to go from Pleyel to her brother Wieland is to go from bad to worse – or out of the frying pan into the fire. While Pleyel may be a 'patriarch of the first order', Wieland in his emulation of Abraham follows a model of patriarchy that is literally biblical. This is Scheiber's argument when he asserts that, in Wieland's final attack on Clara, 'the mask of masculine authority is stripped away, denuded of its pretensions of any inherent moral or natural basis, and revealed in the full horror of its raw, naked power'.[51] Clara depends for her support and protection, continues Scheiber, on a system of power and authority 'which views her existence as conditional, marginal, sacrificeable'.[52] And what is most frightening here is that Wieland's derangement is not idiosyncratic but symptomatic of deeply engrained cultural misogyny:

Theodore's moral derangement is not merely an individual psychological aberration, but an extreme instance of more general patterns
of male-identified pioneer values that characterized the America of
the author's time, and which are focused in the Wieland family history
itself.[53]

The beast in the closet, as Scheiber puts it,[54] therefore is not simply
Carwin – or Wieland or Pleyel – but rather 'the patriarchal family
environment, in which worship and terror, protector and destroyer,
lie enfolded within one another'.[55]

At the core of *Wieland* is the horrifying realization of Clara's impossible situation. In his Female Gothic novel, Brown takes a level-
headed, unconventional heroine and drops her into a chaotic whirl-
wind of irrational masculine forces which buffet her continually and
from which she cannot extricate herself. Sported with by Carwin,
disbelieved by Pleyel and threatened by her own brother, it is Clara
who is forced into the realization that there is no escape or succour
available. Indeed, only Carwin's intervention prevents her from martyr-
ing herself to Wieland's murderous rage. While it is true, as I discuss
in chapter 3, that Clara too may be motivated by irrational, unconscious impulses, writ large for the reader is her victimization by
irrational social forces that constrain and even arguably produce her
behaviour.

'Homely liberty vs splendid servitude': Constantia Dudley

If Clara in *Wieland* were actually to have used her penknife to fight
back against the patriarchal forces that assail her, then she would be
Constantia Dudley in *Ormond*. Brown's Wollstonecraftian feminism
arguably finds its fullest expression in his second Gothic novel, which
fuses the explicit meditation on women's rights initiated in *Alcuin*
with the Female Gothic plot derived from Radcliffe and others.
Brown's original spin on the Female Gothic plot is to make his
protagonist Constantia in *Ormond* an atypical and self-aware Gothic
heroine who consciously considers the ways in which both law and
custom conspire to disempower women. Indeed, at moments *Ormond*
almost rises to the level of a 'meta-Female Gothic' – that is, a self-

reflexive Female Gothic text that comments on the tradition of the Female Gothic.

Constantia's difference from the typical Gothic female heroine is made clear by the text's narrator, Sophia, upon Constantia's first introduction. In keeping with Brown's Wollstonecraft-inspired meditation on female education expressed in *Alcuin*, Constantia's father has seen fit to dispense with the conventional female education and have her study instead a more traditionally male-centred curriculum:

> Women are generally limited to what is sensual and ornamental: music and painting, and the Italian and French languages, are bounds which they seldom pass . . . The education of Constance had been regulated by the peculiar views of her father, who sought to make her, not alluring and voluptuous, but eloquent and wise. He therefore limited her studies to Latin and English. Instead of familiarizing her with the amorous effusions of Petrarch and Racine, he made her thoroughly conversant with Tacitus and Milton. Instead of making her a practical musician or pencilist, he conducted her to the school of Newton and Hartley, unveiled to her the mathematical properties of light and sound, taught her as a metaphysician and anatomist, the structure and power of the senses, and discussed with her the principles and progress of human society.[56]

As Paul Lewis notes, Constantia has a 'practical, secular education that prepares her for a life of hard work and strict domestic economy'.[57] The result of Constantia's unconventional education is succinctly expressed as follows: 'These accomplishments tended to render her superior to the rest of women' (p. 26).

In the same way that Clara's wilfulness in *Wieland* is contrasted by her sister-in-law Catherine's malleable nature, Constantia's foil in *Ormond* is Ormond's sensual mistress, Helena Cleves, 'the perfect result of the feminine upbringing that outraged Wollstonecraft'.[58] Helena is 'endowed with every feminine and fascinating quality' and her appearance is 'calculated to excite emotions more voluptuous than dignified' (p. 89), but – having been educated in the traditional way for a woman of the period – she offers little in the way of intellectual stimulation. In this, the text explicitly states, she is no different from the average woman of the time: 'To say that Helena Cleves was silly or ignorant would be hatefully unjust. Her understanding bore no disadvantageous comparison with that of the majority of her sex' (p. 89). And because Helena is no different from the average woman of her time, she does not interest Ormond who considers women silly and ignorant:

> [Ormond] had not hitherto met with a female worthy of his confidence. Their views were limited and superficial, or their understandings were betrayed by the tenderness of their hearts. He found in them no intellectual energy, no superiority to what he accounted vulgar prejudice, and no affinity with the sentiments which he cherished with most devotion. (p. 88)

Helena would like Ormond to marry her but, because of her intellectual vapidity and Ormond's own selfish disinclination to bind himself to anyone, Ormond has no interest in doing so. Unfortunately, because of Helena's faulty education and her sentimental nature, she is unable to appreciate Ormond's true designs: 'the combined influence of passion and unenlightened understanding hindered her from fully comprehending them' (p. 90). When she is inevitably abandoned by Ormond after he becomes obsessed with Constantia, Helena commits suicide.

In contrast to voluptuous and empty-headed Helena who considers marriage 'more conducive to happiness' (p. 91) than single life, Constantia is very alert to the potential complications marriage presents to an independent woman. When proposed to by the wealthy merchant Balfour (who has saved her from being raped), Constantia carefully weighs the pros and cons of marrying a man whom she does not love:

> Now she was at least mistress of the product of her own labour. Her tasks were toilsome, but the profits, though slender, were sure, and she administered her little property in what manner she pleased. Marriage would annihilate this power. Henceforth she would be bereft even of personal freedom. So far from possessing property, she herself would become the property of another. (p. 65)

Seemingly having read Brown's *Alcuin* and appreciated Mrs Carter's arguments, Constantia ends this rumination on marriage by concluding that 'homely liberty was better than splendid servitude' (p. 66).

The problem for Constantia – as it remains for women, perhaps to a somewhat lesser extent, today – is that it is hard to be a self-aware, independent woman in a world that preys on weakness and presumes women to be less competent and weaker than men. Constantia's is a world in which a woman goes from living in her father's household to her husband's – and by default shares the fortunes of both – and in which a woman without a male protector is a target. This is repeatedly made clear to Constantia over the course of the text. Because her father is tricked and defrauded by Craig, she is forced into poverty along with him. In Philadelphia, she is threatened with rape before being rescued by Balfour (pp. 62–3). Attempting to track down Craig, she is berated by a waiter in a tavern and the text resignedly comments that 'Constantia was not disconcerted at this address. She knew that females are subjected, through their own ignorance and cowardice, to a thousand mortifications' (p. 71). Constantia is again exposed to physical mortification – 'one more disaster', as Ormond puts it (p. 198) – at the end of the text when Ormond threatens Constantia with rape, and insists he will carry through with the act even if she takes her own life first: 'Living or dead', he asserts during the text's most salacious moment, 'the prize that I have in view shall be mine' (p. 216).

Reprising Clara's confrontation with Wieland in her bedroom, the ending of *Ormond* in which Constantia is confronted by a murderous maniac in an empty house is the moment at which the Female Gothic plot of the novel becomes most insistent. 'The mansion', the reader is told, 'was desolate and lonely. It was night.' Constantia 'was immersed in darkness. She had not the means, and was unaccustomed to the office, of repelling personal injuries' (p. 208). Moving through the house with a lantern in her hand, she discovers what appears to be a corpse on the floor and then is confronted by the master villain himself, the dissembler Ormond, who finally throws off his mask of Enlightenment rationalist to reveal both his designs upon her person and his orchestration of her father's murder. Krause observes that the seduction plot of the novel blends the 'established Richardsonian and gothic seduction motifs of the desperate pursuit of the virtuous maiden'[59] and adds that, as concerns this culminating confrontation between Constantia and Ormond, 'only in [Matthew Lewis's]

The Monk do we find a situation that at least for directness is comparable to the one in *Ormond*.[60] Alone and trapped, Constantia is threatened by a murderous rapist intent on achieving his objective no matter what. The difference between *Ormond* and *The Monk*, however, is that Constantia is not raped and murdered as Lewis's pure and virginal Antonia is (or killed, as is Isabella in Walpole's *The Castle of Otranto* [1764] or the virtuous Lilla in Charlotte Dacre's *Zofloya; or, the Moor* [1806]). Neither is Constantia rescued or assisted in escaping as is Emily in Radcliffe's *The Mysteries of Udolpho* (1794). Instead, Constantia fends off her attacker and kills him using her penknife – here accomplishing the act that Clara in *Wieland* contemplates but rejects.

Constantia's rescuing herself from her attacker rather than being rescued is a significant revision of the conventional Gothic plot, but it is not Brown's only one; equally provocative is the narrative's conclusion in which any possibility of heterosexual union is rejected in favour of homosocial bonding. Noting that the narrator, Sophia, departs from Europe the day after her wedding to find Constantia and vows either to convince her to return to Europe with her or to 'live and die with her' in America, Kristin Comment interprets the text as not merely introducing lesbianism as a viable alternative to heterosexuality, but in fact privileging it. Observing that the text contains 'the first extended fictional portrayal in America of what the novelist calls 'romantic passion' between women,[61] Fleischmann concludes that in *Ormond*, 'communities of women offer the only escape from the mad world of men'.[62] Grabo, too, notes the 'queer intensity' of the affection between Sophia and Constantia, characterizing it as 'friendly', 'sisterly' and 'above all . . . passionate'.[63] Lewis also considers that Sophia offers to Constantia an attractive alternative to 'the necessarily confining bounds of heterosexual love'.[64]

The conclusion to *Ormond* thus essentially 'queers' the Female Gothic, foregrounding in a provocative way the social construction of gender roles that results in the subjugation of women. Constantia, who has received an unorthodox education, who actively contemplates the disempowerment attendant upon marriage and who ends up killing her attacker with a knife, chooses to exit the novel arm in arm with her friend Sophia. As was the case in *Alcuin*, however, it is important to note that Brown in *Ormond* waters down the provocative implications of this conclusion by refusing to sanction revolutionary politics. In *Ormond*, this stepping back from the brink is accomplished through the juxtaposition of Constantia with the cross-dressing freedom fighter, Martinette. Just as Constantia and Helena are foils, Constantia and Ormond's sister, Martinette, are foils as well. Martinette, aka Ursula Monrose, has received a non-traditional education similar to Constantia's own: '[Martinette's] education seemed not widely different from that which Constantia had received. It was classical and mathematical' (p. 141).[65] Martinette, however, exhibits a 'wild spirit of adventure' (p. 154) and has imbibed the 'political enthusiasm' – the freedom-fighting spirit – of her husband, Wentworth. She explains to Constantia that she 'delighted to assume the male dress, to acquire skill at the sword, and dexterity in every boisterous exercise' (p. 154). As Martinette continues her story, it becomes clear that in the context of Brown's meditation on gender roles, she has essentially surrendered her femininity. When questioned by Constantia concerning how 'the heart of a woman' can be 'inured to the shedding of blood' (p. 158), she responds: 'Have women, I beseech thee, no capacity to reason and infer? Are they less open than men to the influence of habit? My hand never faultered when liberty demanded the victim' (p. 158).

Martinette and Ormond, brother and sister, are cut from the same cloth. Neither has any compunction about using disguise and violence to achieve their ends. The difference between them is that Martinette is sincere in her revolutionary politics, while Ormond only plays at being the radical; in reality, his only concern is extending his power over others. Despite this difference, both are rendered monstrous by virtue of their shared lack of sympathy. Martinette recounts that among the men she has slain were two whom she had known and loved, but the cause they espoused 'cancelled their claims to mercy' (p. 158). Ormond is similarly willing to use people as pawns, notably Craig and Mr Dudley, to achieve his ends. Neither as a result is fully human, but while this kind of duplicity and violence seems to come naturally to men in the world of Brown's fiction, it is presented as a perversion of feminine nature. Martinette has shed not only female clothing, but the essential qualities that made her a woman.

Constantia in the end is the ideal synthesis of Helena's attractiveness and sympathetic nature and Martinette's self-sufficiency. When she needs to, Constantia has the constitutional fortitude to rescue herself, but she acts in self-defence and shrinks at the idea of committing violence at all. She is a self-possessed and self-sufficient woman who retains the essential 'feminine' qualities of sympathy and mercy. The fact that Brown does not marry her off, but rather removes her to Europe with her female friend Sophia at the end, is then all the more telling. *Ormond*, pronounces Ringe, 'is a strongly feminist work'[66] – one that illustrates 'Brown's attitude toward women's rights: their need for a sounder education, their right to be treated as free individuals, and their ability, once properly trained, to act in the practical world'.[67] But, as in *Wieland*, the men that surround Constantia – her father, Craig, Balfour, Ormond and so on – make abundantly clear that the 'practical world' is governed by irrational rules manipulated by men that objectify and disempower women. Fleischmann's description of *Ormond* is especially apt here:

> In *Ormond*, paternal failure starts a young woman's initiation into a world of men where women are objects, where utopian 'alternatives' are constructed by misogynists, and where the only happiness comes from the company of other women. Themes from *Wieland* are continued: masculine failure and hubris; a young woman's survival of the 'complicated havock' created by men; the possibilities of an independent existence for women; the support from women's friendships.[68]

One could be forgiven for missing the fact that at the end of *Wieland*, Clara, now living in Europe, actually marries Pleyel, because the narration glosses over the revival of their intimacy and wedlock in a paragraph. At the end of *Ormond*, however, there is not a viable suitor anywhere on the scene for Constantia's hand. She has left America and seemingly has turned her back on men in general. I therefore agree with the first part of Fleischmann's observation that

> Brown's repeated pleas to improve women's education mention the need of spinsters and widows to be self-supportive. His stories of husbands, fathers, or brothers failing in business emphasize, on the one hand, the linkage between male support and social status, and on the other, the new roles that women would have to assume to escape this trap.[69]

139

Nye says something similar when he writes that

> a significant portion of the discussion in *Ormond* concerns education, and whether or not a woman can successfully cope with the world, Brown suggests, is chiefly a matter of educational preparation. Women must be trained as men are to compete in the world, defend themselves from it, and live full and happy lives.[70]

Brown clearly develops in his two Female Gothic novels, *Wieland* and *Ormond*, the Wollstonecraftian line of thinking introduced in *Alcuin* that emphasizes the need for women and men to have commensurate educations and that demonstrates the ways in which women in patriarchal culture are dependent upon men for support and status. But the only answer Brown seems able to provide concerning how to escape the 'trap' of patriarchal oppression is a problematic rejection of men altogether. Both Clara and Constantia have unorthodox educations, both are self-sufficient and both are repeatedly threatened or victimized by the men around them. Presumably in order to find 'full and happy lives', both leave America altogether at the end – Clara to marry the man who treated her appallingly and married someone else first, and Constantia to remain single without a suitor in sight. The effect of education on both Clara and Constantia is arguably not to make them content, but rather to give them a clearer sense of their own disempowerment. In keeping with contemporary critical approaches to the Female Gothic in general, what Brown educates his heroines and his readers about in *Wieland* and *Ormond* is what we may refer to as the 'Gothicization of everyday life' for women: that is, the ways in which more frightening for women than ghosts and monsters are men – husbands, brothers, fathers, lovers and strangers. It may be that awareness is the first step toward overcoming, but the endings of *Wieland* and *Ormond* are far from joyous or hopeful.

Arthur and Edgar

In *Arthur Mervyn* and *Edgar Huntly*, Brown switches his attention from the psyches of female protagonists to male protagonists and, as a result, these works offer the reader less developed representations of female characters. Nevertheless, visible in both works – although to differing extents – is the continuation of Brown's meditations on the social status of women. *Arthur Mervyn* in fact offers a broad range of female characters, from naïve to experienced and from virtuous to criminal. All of the important female characters in this work, however, are to varying degrees victimized as a result of their attachments to men who die, disappear or betray them. *Edgar Huntly* introduces far fewer female characters, but the message remains the same: the dependency of women upon men sets women up for disaster.

The most obvious example in *Arthur Mervyn* of the Richardsonian/ Gothic seduction plot is the sad story of Clemenza Lodi. Initially introduced to Arthur and the reader as Welbeck's daughter, Clemenza is revealed to be a young woman seduced by Welbeck and kept as his mistress. Since she does not speak English, she is unable to communicate her situation. When Arthur rediscovers her late in the text, she is more or less being held captive by brothel madam Mrs Villars and has just given birth to Welbeck's illegitimate child. 'The child, like its mother', comments Arthur, 'was meagre and cadaverous. Either it was dead, or could not be very distant from death'.[71] Arthur is right – the child promptly expires and Arthur eventually sets up the dishonoured Clemenza in a better situation with Dr Stevens and his wife.

Clemenza's situation, however, is only the most extreme example of what is the general case in the novel in which, again and again, women are betrayed or abandoned by men. Upon arriving in Philadelphia and being tricked by Wallace, Arthur observes a situation in which he concludes that a man (who it turns out is Walter Thetford) is substituting his bastard child for a legitimate one that has died (p. 31); the sister of Captain Amos Watson – the latter shot by Welbeck and buried with Arthur's help in the basement – was seduced, impregnated and ruined by Welbeck; and the reader learns that Arthur himself had a sister who committed suicide after being seduced and abandoned by the schoolteacher Colvill.

The pattern, indeed, is so insistent as to be unmistakable: after the death of her father, Eliza Hadwin must contend with her uncle Philip who is 'a noted brawler and bully, a tyrant to his children, a plague to his neighbors' and by whom 'there is no doubt that his niece's property would be embezzled, should it ever come into his hands, and any power which he might obtain over her person would be exercised to her destruction' (pp. 227–8); Miss Carlton is left unprotected and in need after her brother is imprisoned for having assumed a debt of their father's (p. 270); then there is the story of Achsa Fielding who has been doubly abandoned – first her father committed suicide after being bankrupted, then she was left by her husband for another woman. While there are occasional counter-examples of villainous women who take advantage of men (Betty Lawrence who seduces Arthur's father; Mrs Villars the brothel madam) and of happy marriages (notably Dr Stevens and his wife), what Brown dramatizes again and again in *Arthur Mervyn* are the ways in which women are disempowered by law and custom in patriarchal culture.

In *Edgar Huntly*, no women are represented at all who escape vic-timization at the hands of men. As a result of the intervention of her brother, Arthur Wiatte, Euphemia Lorimer 'was not only denied the husband of her choice, but another was imposed upon her';[72] when Mrs Lorimer at long last unites with her lover Sarsefield, their hopes for a child are 'blasted' when she miscarries after mistakenly inter-cepting a letter from Edgar to her husband apprising him of Clithero's intention to kill her (p. 194); Mrs Lorimer's niece Clarice is almost murdered by her fiancé Clithero, who then flees and abandons her. Edgar's sisters depend upon him and their uncle but will be out in the cold, explains Edgar, when their uncle dies and his son, who dislikes them, inherits the property; on his odyssey back home, Edgar discovers the abused wife and child of the drunkard Selby seeking refuge in the barn and lamenting their situation in pitiable tones: 'Ah! me, my babe! Canst thou not sleep and afford thy unhappy mother some peace? Thou art cold, and I have not sufficient warmth to cherish thee! What will become of us? Thy deluded father cares not if we both perish' (p. 152). Not far from the Selbys' door, Edgar discovers the 'corse [*sic*] of a girl, mangled by an hatchet' who has been killed and scalped by Indians (p. 152). While decidedly less sympathy is extended in *Edgar Huntly* to the Indians, one could also argue that Old Deb, the crazy old Indian woman displaced from tribal land and suffered by the white population to live on the out-skirts of civilization with her dogs, should be included in this list of victimized women.

The slain girl that Edgar discovers near the Selbys' house of course reprises the most vivid and developed example of the victimization of women in *Edgar Huntly* – the captive woman that Edgar discovers and rescues as he attempts to exit the cave. As discussed in chapter 1 on Brown's Frontier Gothic, at the centre of *Edgar Huntly* is a Native American captivity narrative, which is part of Brown's conscious effort to Americanize the European Gothic novel. In place of an invidious aristocratic seducer or urbane confidence man, in *Edgar Huntly* Brown presents male power in its starkest form: the brutal kidnapping of a woman who will be used 'for torment or servitude' (p. 117). What Brown's narrative suggests, however, is that the deplorable situation of this captive is only a literalization of the condition of all the women in the story who, to varying extents, are captives of men – figuratively bound and literally dependent upon fathers, husbands and brothers for their survival.

This, finally, might be a useful way to think about *Alcuin* and Brown's four Gothic novels: as captivity narratives. Brown, as Lewis observes, was fascinated by 'melodramas of beset womanhood'[73] and repeatedly, in both explicit and implicit ways, uses the conventions of the Gothic to foreground and critique the forms of violence and control to which women must submit in patriarchal culture. Virtually all his female characters, major and minor, from Clara to Constantia to Clemenza to the woman Edgar rescues, are figuratively and at times literally captives. Trapped by a sexual double standard and legal restrictions that render them dependent upon men for their well-being and survival, these female characters make explicit the Female Gothic theme of the terror of the everyday. Taken together, Brown's Female Gothic novels, participating as they did in the late eighteenth-century discussion of women's rights, paint a horrifying picture of the forms of violence to which women are subject in patriarchal culture.

The Iron Maiden: Clara Howard

I would like to round out this chapter with some brief discussion of Brown's late 'sentimental' novel, *Clara Howard* (1801), because although Brown clearly shifts both tone and genre in this epistolary work, his interest in the situation of women in American culture in the late eighteenth century remains central. While this work (as well as his other late sentimental novel, *Jane Talbot*) has seldom been judged as favourably as his Gothic novels, one can clearly see Brown's interest in the social construction of gender roles being developed in a new direction. In *Clara Howard*, Brown reverses conventional gender expectations by making the eponymous protagonist eminently reasonable while her lover, Edward Hartley, is moved by sentiment.

The plot of *Clara Howard* is relatively simple. As revealed to the reader through the exchange of letters between Clara Howard and Edward Hartley, Edward loves Clara and wishes to marry her, but has previously proposed marriage to a woman named Mary Wilmot who loves him but whose affection he does not reciprocate in kind. The ethical dilemma at the heart of the novel is that Clara will only consider Edward honourable and hence marriageable if he keeps his pledge to Mary. Mary, however, does not want Edward if he loves someone else. Edward is thus placed in a paralysing situation which is only resolved when Mary conveniently falls in love with someone else.

As Michelle Burnham summarizes, beginning with Mary Shelley who remarked in 1814 that *Clara Howard* is 'very stupid', readers and critics have 'virtually delighted in condemning the book'.[74] Grabo has even gone so far as to hypothesize, not in an especially convincing way, that *Clara Howard* was a kind of 'pilot study' written before the Gothic novels although published after them.[75] More recently, a handful of defenders have stepped forward to present arguments as to why *Clara Howard* has been unjustly despised and should hold our interest. Jared Gardner, for example, reads the epistolary form of the novel as allowing Brown to present multiple points of view without conclusively determining that one is correct and the others wrong, thus developing an alternative form of citizenship that rejects the either/or of late eighteenth-century Republicanism or Federalism.[76] Sydney Krause interprets both *Clara Howard* and *Jane Talbot* as novels of ideas that put Godwin's ideas 'on trial'.[77] And Michelle Burnham focuses on the peculiar temporality of the novel that she sees as being not about events and occurrences but delays, deferrals and anticipation of the future, which she connects to 'America's incomplete revolution'.[78]

While the recent critical reconsideration of *Clara Howard* offers interesting perspectives that enrich our understanding of the novel, what is most notable about *Clara Howard* for our purposes here – and what links it to his Female Gothic plots in the four Gothic novels – is Brown's reversal of conventional gender expectations. As Bruce Burgett observes, inverting the conventional gendered dichotomy, the 'battle' in *Clara Howard* is between Edward's sentiment and Clara's reason.[79] Edward occupies the conventional female role in the novel, that of being swayed by sentiment. He first proposes marriage to a woman he does not love out of compassion for her situation and then seeks to dissolve that obligation when he falls in love with Clara. In one of Clara's letters to him, she describes him as 'fiery and impetuous'. She continues: 'Thy spirit is not curbed by reason. There is no outrage on discretion; no crime against thyself, into which they headlong spirit may not hurry thee'.[80]

Clara, occupying the conventional masculine role in the novel, is Edward's foil, and she is very clear that she is wholly willing to sacrifice her own personal happiness on the altar of disinterested justice:

> I never will be yours, while Mary's condition is unknown. I never will be yours while she is single; unmarried to another and unhappy. I will have no intercourse with you. I will not grant you even my esteem, unless you search for her; find her; and oblige her to accept your vows. (p. 7)

Clara will not be moved by Edward's pleas, telling him, 'I shall never so little consult my own dignity and yours, as to accept your hand *through compassion*' (p. 21). Clara's inflexibility leads Krause to characterize her, rather dismissively, as the 'original Iron Maiden of American Literature'.[81]

But the fact of the matter is that Clara, the 'Iron Maiden', not only wins in the end but occupies the moral high ground in the novel, and one is forced to wonder to what extent the negative appraisals of the novel – and derogatory characterizations of Clara – in fact stem from Brown's inversion of conventional gender expectations. What Brown gives us in *Clara Howard* is a picture of a disciplined and forceful woman who lives by a rigid ethical code that demands that her happiness should not result from or rest upon someone else's misery. In keeping with Brown's presentation of unorthodox heroines in *Wieland* and *Ormond* and his implicit and explicit commentaries on the situation of women in American culture in *Alcuin, Arthur Mervyn* and *Edgar Huntly*, what Brown thus performs in *Clara Howard* is a tacit interrogation of conventional gender expectations.

Conclusion: Brown and the Female Gothic

Throughout his body of work, Brown repeatedly explored and called attention to the social construction of gender roles and the cultural forces that disempower women. In keeping with the conclusions of commentators on the Female Gothic, what Brown discusses in *Alcuin* and then demonstrates in *Wieland, Ormond, Arthur Mervyn* and *Edgar Huntly* are the Gothicized conditions of female existence in which what women have to fear most are those closest to them: fathers, brothers and husbands. The real world, Brown shows us, is no 'paradise of women'. Instead, it is a world in which women – dependent first upon fathers and then husbands for support – are subject to varying forms of abuse and are always only one step away from disaster. As Fleischmann observes, Brown's stories of men who fail in business and drag the women dependent upon them into poverty emphasize both the connections between male support and social status and the new roles women must assume to escape this trap.[82] Brown's works insistently foreground the need to educate women equally and to revise property and marriage laws. Through *Alcuin*'s Mrs Carter, *Wieland*'s Clara Wieland, *Ormond*'s Constantia Dudley, Sophia Courtland and Martinette de Beauvais, *Arthur Mervyn*'s Achsa Fielding and *Clara Howard*'s Clara, Brown presents to the reader a range of intelligent, self-sufficient and assertive female characters who defy late eighteenth- and early nineteenth-century stereotypes and testify to Brown's early American feminism. In his four Gothic novels – as well as to a lesser extent in *Alcuin* and his sentimental novels – Brown appropriates the tradition of the Female Gothic from Radcliffe and rearticulates it as an even more explicit conversation about the roots of female oppression. Brown thus needs to be recognized as the founder of the American version of the Female Gothic.

Conclusion: The Legacy of Charles Brockden Brown's Four Gothics

ಬಂಡ

My argument in this 'polemical introduction' to the work of Charles Brockden Brown has been that he must be considered a central figure in the development of four subgenres of the Gothic: the Frontier Gothic, the Urban Gothic, the Psychological Gothic and the Female Gothic. In Brown's four Gothic novels, *Wieland, Ormond, Arthur Mervyn* and *Edgar Huntly* – as well as to lesser extents in his dialogue on women's rights, *Alcuin,* his sentimental novels, *Clara Howard* and *Jane Talbot* and his other writings including his unfinished *Memoirs of Carwin the Biloquist* and *Stephen Calvert* – Brown consciously appropriated elements of the existing Gothic novel tradition associated with Ann Radcliffe and Matthew Lewis, and rescripted them better to reflect his own insights and experiences in a newly established country attempting to chart its path forward on the cusp of the nineteenth century. In his novels, Brown gives us the dark underside to Enlightenment optimism as he repeatedly questions the extent to which human beings can draw accurate inferences from sensory data and foresee the outcome of their actions. In advance of Washington Irving, James Fenimore Cooper and Ambrose Bierce, he depicts the American frontier as a liminal zone fraught with danger. Looking forward to Charles Dickens, George Lippard and even twentieth-century film noir, Brown establishes the city as itself a sort of labyrinthine wilderness populated by insidious confidence men. Setting the stage for Edgar

Allan Poe's fiction and later Sigmund Freud's psychology, Brown powerfully represents the mind as inherently haunted as the unconscious, the stranger within, compels irrational and 'perverse' behaviour. And well before Harriet Prescott Spofford, Charlotte Perkins Gilman and contemporary authors such as Margaret Atwood and Angela Carter, Brown in his Female Gothic narratives vividly demonstrates the forms of violence and victimization to which women are exposed in patriarchal culture. Brown, my argument has been, was instrumental in developing and defining the Frontier Gothic, the Urban Gothic, the Psychological Gothic and the Female Gothic.

The question, however, remains: whatever his innovations, did anyone read Brown? He may have had brilliant and original insights but, especially given Brown's relative obscurity today, to what extent can he in fact be considered to have influenced anyone? It may be the case that, as Michael Davitt Bell asserts, 'the real history of American fiction, the history of its development as a serious form of literary art, begins with the six romances of Brown',[1] but did this history then come to a screeching halt when Brown turned away from novelistic endeavours, only to restart some fifty years later? Or is there a continuous line running from Brown to the great American romancers, Irving, Cooper, Poe, Hawthorne and Melville? And, beyond American shores, did Brown exercise any influence on the European novelistic tradition? The question finally is of how far one can go in making claims for Brown's significance. Is it simply a matter of having an accurate understanding of the chronologies of American and Gothic literatures in which Brown, like some kind of evolutionary anomaly, briefly surfaced only then to sink out of sight without having impacted on the course of things? Or do we need to revise our understanding of these traditions to accommodate Brown and his achievements? The evidence, I think, points to the latter.

This at least is the impression that Cathy Davidson creates in *Revolution and the Word* when she discusses Brown's reputation during his lifetime. According to Davidson, Brown liked to consider himself as 'the best American novelist of his generation'. On this score, she continues, 'his peers agreed'.[2] *Ormond* was the first American novel to be published in England. *Edgar Huntly* received a second printing during Brown's lifetime – unusual for a period during which second printings were rare. John Allen's biography of Brown's life was published only five years after Brown's death and, thanks in large measure to author John Neal's efforts, 'by 1830, Charles Brockden Brown became the first American novelist to be cast, in the best Romantic tradition, as the moody iconoclast, appreciated by the "intelligent, the cultivated, and the reflecting classes of society" but, of course, spurned by the philistine masses'.[3] According to Davidson, Brown is in fact unique in his time for the amount of discussion elicited by his literary productions: 'No other novelist of the early national period has been accorded such an extensive body of response'.[4] Davidson continues, citing Parker, by observing that there were forty-three published assessments of Brown produced between 1798 and 1820.[5]

So it seems clear that Brown attracted the attention at least of the literary establishment, if not the masses, during his lifetime and for some time afterward. In Europe, as mentioned in the introduction to this volume, Mary Shelley – although she had dismissed Brown's *Clara Howard* as 'very stupid' in 1814[6] – apparently read and enjoyed *Wieland* just prior to beginning work on *Frankenstein* in 1816,[7] and Brown was allegedly admired by European authors including Mary's husband Percy, who was 'captivated' by Brown's fiction,[8] and fellow Romanticists John Keats, William Hazlitt and Thomas Peacock.[9] In American literature, claims have been made for Brown's influence on writers as diverse as Poe, John Greenleaf Whittier and Margaret Fuller – the last of whom wrote concerning the republication of Brown's *Wieland* and *Ormond* in 1846:

> We rejoice to see these reprints of Brown's novels, as we have long been ashamed that one who ought to be the pride of our country, and who is, in the hither qualities of mind, so far in advance of our other novelists, should have become almost inaccessible to the public.[10]

It is clear that almost all of the major male writers of the American Romantic tradition knew of Brown – although it is unclear just how much. As Axelrod notes, both James Fenimore Cooper and Nathaniel Hawthorne mention Brown twice in their writings.[11] Leslie Fiedler asserts that Cooper borrowed 'shamelessly' from Brown[12] and Hawthorne interestingly includes Brown – referred to as 'the author of *Arthur Mervyn*' – in his 'Hall of Fantasy', a sketch included in his 1846 *Mosses from the Old Manse* in which the narrator discovers himself in a place of the imagination where 'all who have affairs in that mystic region, which lies above, below, or beyond the Actual, may here meet, and talk over the business of their dreams'.[13] Brown is the only American author included in this pantheon of literary demigods that also includes Homer, Dante, Rabelais, Shakespeare, Spenser and Milton. Kafer adds that Hawthorne must have had Brown in mind when he wrote his short story, 'My Kinsman, Major Molineux', and that Brown 'hovers' all around Hawthorne's 'Roger Malvin's Burial'.[14]

Not surprisingly, however, the most attention has been paid to Brown's influence on Edgar Allan Poe – and here the evidence for Brown's impact on the development of Gothic literature is unambiguous. Poe not only mentions Brown five times in his writings, but promised an essay on Brown and American literature (which he never produced).[15] There have been a number of critical studies exploring Brown's importance as an inspiration for Poe. Kafer comments wryly that Poe 'paid Brown the high Poeian compliment of plagiarizing from him, directly in "A Tale of the Ragged Mountains", and indirectly in numerous wilderness scenes and perhaps in selective renditions of the insane imagination'.[16] Neil Fitzgerald, curator of the 'Philadelphia Gothic' exhibit, contends that Poe's 'Masque of the Red Death' is indebted to Brown's *Arthur Mervyn*.[17] Several critics including Carter, Clark and Hirsch have emphasized Poe's borrowing from the cave scene in *Edgar Huntly* for his 'The Pit and the Pendulum',[18] and Axelrod extends this conversation by suggesting that the cave scene also centrally informs Poe's only attempt at a novel, *The Narrative of Arthur Gordon Pym* (1837).[19] Axelrod concludes in fact that 'Poe's borrowing from *Edgar Huntly* amounts to a reading of Brown'[20] – that is, Poe, according to Axelrod, interpreted Brown 'intellectually';[21] he appreciated and drew out from Brown's work the underlying anxieties about epistemological certainty, 'basic questions about the nature and perception of reality' that inform the 'Great Tradition of American fiction' in general.[22]

Axelrod, in this analysis of Brown's influence upon Poe, emphasizes – as does Kafer to a lesser extent – the central role of the frontier as a 'metaphor of the confrontation between subject and object',[23] and this observation allows Axelrod to link Brown's *Edgar Huntly* not just to Poe and *Pym*, but to Hawthorne, Thoreau, Melville, Whitman, Twain and even James. I agree, of course, that in Brown's fiction the frontier – as developed in chapter 1 – certainly plays a key role. Equally, if not more important, however, is what I would refer to as the 'internal frontier' – the confrontation with the unknowable other within that I discuss in chapter 3. Bringing together these ideas of external and internal frontiers and inflecting them through the idea of the urban wilderness introduced in chapter 2, I would like to close this introduction to Charles Brockden Brown by arguing for Poe's channelling of Brown not just in his representations of the actual wilderness in *Pym* and 'Ragged Mountains', but also in his representation of what – to borrow from Elizabeth Hinds – we may wish to refer to as the 'frontier of discourse' in his Urban Gothic tale, 'The Man of the Crowd' (1840).[24] While Brown's influence is arguably stamped all over Poe's fiction, this story seems to offer a concise representation of several of Brown's favourite themes: the resistance of the world to rational interpretation, the mysteries of the city, the double and the bifurcation of the self.

Poe's story begins with an epigraph attributed to the French essayist Jean de La Bruyère commenting on the 'great misfortune' of being unable to be alone, and then the story proper begins with an observation that acquires increasing force as it progresses: 'It was well said of a certain German book that "*es lässt sich nicht lesen*" – it does not permit itself to be read. There are some secrets which do not permit themselves to be told'.[25] In order to illustrate this maxim, the anonymous narrator then recounts his strange story. The narrator, who significantly was recovering from a fever, was seated in a London coffee house one afternoon amusing himself by exercising his remarkable ability to classify individuals based on their appearances. Attentive to detail, he 'regarded with minute interest the innumerable varieties of detail, dress, air, gait, visage, and expression of countenance' of those passing outside the window and, through this process of differentiation, was able to impose order on the fluid mass of life. Drawing inferences from sensory data, the narrator confidently was able to impose order upon the unruly spectacle of the world – that is, until the idiosyncratic visage of an old man presented itself, throwing a spanner into the narrator's interpretive machine. The old man could not be easily 'typed' or fit into a category. He embodied a variety of contradictory characteristics: 'there arose confusedly and paradoxically within my mind, the ideas of vast mental power, of caution, of penuriousness, of avarice, of coolness, of malice, of blood-thirstiness, of triumph, of merriment, of excessive terror, of intense – of extreme despair'. Confronted by this resistant figure, the narrator was compelled out of his seat and began to follow the man around the city.

The narrator explains that he followed the old man for twenty-four hours in a loop around London as the man in turn followed the life of the city from place to place, seeking out crowds wherever he went. But all the narrator's attempts to make sense of this old man, to categorize him and understand him, were thwarted. At the end of the story, the narrator reveals that he was forced to resign the chase after confronting the old man and being ignored: 'I gazed at him steadfastly in the face. He noticed me not, but resumed his solemn walk, while I, ceasing to follow, remained absorbed in contemplation'. The man will not surrender his secrets, will not allow himself to be known and understood. '"This old man", I said at length, "is the type and the genius of deep crime".' Invoking both the opening epigraph to the story and the story's initial observation, the narrator continues concerning the old man,

> He refuses to be alone. *He is the man of the crowd*. It will be in vain to follow; for I shall learn no more of him, nor of his deeds. The worst heart of the world is a grosser book than the *Hortulus Animae*, and perhaps it is but one of the great mercies of God that *es lässt sich nicht lesen*.

The story then closes on this note of resignation.

What the narrator of Poe's story realizes through his inability to reconcile appearances with the 'truth' is the lesson Brown's novels insistently and repeatedly make – that the human ability to draw accurate inferences from sensory data is always tenuous. To borrow a metaphor from Brown's *Ormond*, the narrator of 'The Man of the Crowd' sitting in the coffee-house window and staring out at the world through the smoky panes is like a man sitting on a fence at midnight peering at his neighbour's house in the dark and attempting to understand what is going on inside. The world for both Brown and Poe is a book that refuses to be read, that resists any final, conclusive determination of the truth. This is the frontier of discourse – the limits of what can be said. The narrator at the end of 'The Man of the Crowd' is poised on the edge of a momentous revelation concerning the limitations of human knowledge. Only his faith in God prevents him from reaching the unsettling conclusion that the world may not be a rational place at all.

Beyond this shared anti-Enlightenment theme of calling into question the human ability to make sense of the world, Poe's story also arguably demonstrates a provocative anti-humanist thread that seems tugged directly from Brown's literary tapestry. It is not just the world that cannot be definitively interpreted, the story seems to indicate, but also the self. While the mystery of the old man of the crowd goes unrevealed, a lot of evidence in the story suggests that he should be considered a projection or doppelgänger of the narrator himself. We learn that the narrator is recovering from illness and there is the 'lurking of an old fever' still in his system. The narrator first spies the old man as it is getting dark, when lights in the coffee house would turn the windows into reflective surfaces – which would suggest that the narrator sees himself. And perhaps most compellingly, the manic old man's behaviour and the responses (or rather non-responses) to him by others suggest that he is unreal – he moves ceaselessly without ever resting and apparently goes unseen by anyone else but the narrator. Here, Poe (who also powerfully develops the device of the double in his 'William Wilson') arguably outdoes Edgar following his double Clithero in *Edgar Huntly* by suggesting that the narrator is following a part of himself around the city – that is, he is attempting to confront a resistant part of himself.[26]

In both these respects, Poe's story seems indebted to Brown's recurring themes and concerns. What really cements the connection, however, is the development of these themes in relation to an urban setting and in the aftermath of illness. 'The Man of the Crowd' is set in London; however, at the time that Poe wrote 'The Man of the Crowd', he was living in Philadelphia – the plague-stricken venue for Brown's *Ormond* and *Arthur Mervyn*. With this in mind, it seems telling that the narrator of 'The Man of the

Crowd' reveals as he stalks through the city streets that there is the remnant of an old fever still lurking in his system. Beyond even this, however, is the simple fact of Poe's Urban Gothic setting. As noted in chapter 2, Brown was substantially ahead of the curve in developing the idea of city as itself a sort of bewildering frontier full of secrets and untrustworthy appearances. In both *Ormond* and *Arthur Mervyn*, the dissimulators, the confidence men, the urban villains, seek to disguise their true intentions and prey upon the young and the naïve. Poe's story, too, is an Urban Gothic tale – the story of a bewildering city filled with strangers and vice and mystery. Among those the narrator initially observes are gamblers, shifty 'Jew pedlars', beggars and prostitutes and, as the narrator trails the old man through the city, he ends up outside 'one of the huge suburban temples of Intemperance – one of the palaces of the fiend, Gin'. In both Brown's Urban Gothic novels and Poe's story, disease is both literal and figurative. In Brown, as yellow fever ravages the city, Philadelphia is simultaneously burning with the fevers of corruption, greed and callousness. And in Poe's story, the remnants of the narrator's fever correspond to a city similarly infected with poverty and addiction.

Because of Poe's centrality to the Gothic literary tradition, Brown's influence on him and his writing as suggested by 'The Man of the Crowd' offers us a useful and compelling place to conclude this study. Poe, it turns out – for all his genius and originality – is essentially 'Brownian' in his sympathies. Like Brown's *Edgar Huntly*, 'The Man of the Crowd' is a kind of anti-detective story in which the detective is unable to read the clues and seems to avoid the profound implications of his own discoveries. In its meditation on the inability of human beings to be alone, Poe's story seems indebted to Brown's development of the idea of the bifurcated human psyche – we are never alone because we are always in the company of the unknowable other within; in its consideration of the unreadability of certain books, 'The Man of the Crowd' develops Brown's characteristic interrogation of the limitations on the human ability to arrive at accurate conclusions based on sensory information; and in its foregrounding of the city as an irrational space of concealment, Poe is indebted to Brown's own elaboration on the same themes some forty years before. In tracing the American

Gothic genealogy back from King to Lovecraft to Poe, we must now extend the roots back one step further – to Brown and his creation of the American Frontier, Urban, Psychological and Female Gothics.

Notes

ഇൻരാ

Introduction

[1] Bernard Rosenthal, 'Introduction', in B. Rosenthal (ed.), *Critical Essays on Charles Brockden Brown* (Boston: G. K. Hall, 1981), p. 1.
[2] Paul Lewis, 'Charles Brockden Brown and the gendered canon of early American fiction', *Early American Literature*, 31/2 (1996), 167–88, 167.
[3] Michael Davitt Bell, *The Development of the American Romance: The Sacrifice of Relation* (Chicago: University of Chicago Press, 1980), pp. 41–2.
[4] Robert S. Levine, *Conspiracy and Romance: Studies in Brockden Brown, Cooper, Hawthorne, and Melville* (Cambridge: Cambridge University Press, 1989), p. 29.
[5] W. M. Verhoeven, 'Displacing the discontinuous; or, the labyrinths of reason: fictional design and eighteenth-century thought in Charles Brockden Brown's *Ormond*', in W. M. Verhoeven (ed.), *Rewriting the Dream: Reflections on the Changing American Literary Canon* (Amsterdam: Rodopi, 1992), pp. 202–29, p. 203.
[6] Leslie Fiedler, *Love and Death in the American Novel* (New York: Anchor Books, 1992 [1960]), p. 145.
[7] Peter Kafer, *Charles Brockden Brown's Revolution and the Birth of the American Gothic* (Philadelphia: University of Philadelphia Press, 2004), xi–xxi.
[8] William Hedges, 'Charles Brockden Brown and the culture of contradictions', *Early American Literature*, 9/2 (1974), 107–42, 109.

9   Charles A. Carpenter, 'Selective bibliography of writings about Charles Brockden Brown', in Rosenthal, *Critical Essays* , pp. 224–39, p. 231.

10   Roland Hagenbüchle, 'American literature and the nineteenth-century crisis in epistemology: the example of Charles Brockden Brown', *Early American Literature*, 23/2 (1988), 121–51, 133.

11   Kristin M. Comment, 'Charles Brockden Brown's *Ormond* and lesbian possibility in the early Republic', *Early American Literature*, 40/1 (2005), 57–78, 57.

12   Bill Christophersen, *The Apparition in the Glass: Charles Brockden Brown's American Gothic* (Athens, GA: The University of Georgia Press, 1993), p. 56.

13   Hedges, 'Culture of contradictions', 122.

14   Myra Jehlen, 'The literature of colonization', in Sacvan Bercovitch (ed.), *The Cambridge History of American Literature, vol. 1: 1590–1820* (Cambridge: Cambridge University Press, 1994), pp. 13–168, p. 161.

15   Dennis Berthold, 'Charles Brockden Brown, *Edgar Huntly*, and the origins of the American picturesque', *The William and Mary Quarterly*, 41/1 (1984), 62–84, 63; Beth L. Lueck, 'Charles Brockden Brown's *Edgar Huntly*: the picturesque traveler as sleepwalker', *Studies in American Fiction*, 15/1 (1987), 25–42.

16   Hagenbüchle, 'American literature and the nineteenth-century crisis', 132.

17   John Seelye, 'Charles Brockden Brown and early American fiction', in Emory Elliott (ed.), *Columbia Literary History of the United States* (New York: Columbia University Press, 1988), pp. 168–86, p. 184.

18   Hagenbüchle, 'American literature and the nineteenth-century crisis', 137.

19   Peter Kafer, 'Charles Brockden Brown and the pleasures of "unsanctified imagination", 1787–93', *The William and Mary Quarterly*, 57/3 (2000), 543–68, 567.

20   Verhoeven, 'Displacing the discontinuous', p. 203.

21   Ibid., p. 203.

22   Ibid., pp. 202–3.

23   Pamela Clemit, *The Godwinian Novel: The Rational Fictions of Godwin, Brockden Brown, Mary Shelley* (Oxford: Clarendon Press, 1993), p. 106.

24   Ibid., p. 106.

25   Donald A. Ringe, *Charles Brockden Brown* (Boston: Twayne Publishers, 1991 [1966]), p. 2.

26   Berthold, 'American picturesque', 72.

27   Fiedler, *Love and Death*, p. 154.

28   Ibid., p. 154.

29   Ibid., p. 145.
30   Ibid., p. 149.
31   Hedges, 'Culture of contradictions', 109.
32   Emory Elliott, 'Narrative unity and moral resolution in *Arthur Mervyn*', in Rosenthal, *Critical Essays*, pp. 142–63, p. 142.
33   Rosenthal, *Critical Essays*, p. 4.
34   Fiedler, *Love and Death*, p. 155.
35   Norman S. Grabo, *The Coincidental Art of Charles Brockden Brown* (Chapel Hill, NC: The University of North Carolina Press, 1981), p. 183.
36   Nina Baym, 'A minority reading of *Wieland*', in Rosenthal, *Critical Essays*, pp. 87–103, p. 87.
37   Christopher Looby, *Voicing America: Language, Literary Form, and the Origins of the United States* (Chicago: University of Chicago Press, 1996), p. 146.
38   David Kazanjian, 'Charles Brockden Brown's biloquial nation: national culture and white settler colonialism in *Memoirs of Carwin the Biloquist*', *American Literature*, 73/3 (2001), 459–96, 461.
39   Cathy N. Davidson, *Revolution and the Word: The Rise of the Novel in America* (New York: Oxford University Press, 1986), p. 203.
40   David M. Larsson, 'Arthur Mervyn, Edgar Huntly, and the critics', *Essays in Literature*, 15 (1988), 207–19, 207.
41   Jane Tompkins, *Sensational Designs: The Cultural Work of American Fiction 1790–1860* (Oxford: Oxford University Press, 1985), pp. 44–61.
42   Kazanjian, 'Charles Brockden Brown's biloquial nation', p. 464.
43   Fiedler, *Love and Death*, p. 153.
44   Kafer, *Charles Brockden Brown's Revolution*, p. 34. The Stamp Act of 1765 was a tax imposed by the British Parliament on the North American colonies that required many printed materials to be produced on stamped paper produced in London. The Stamp Act was met with great resistance in the colonies and added impetus to the growing movement for independence.
45   Ed White, 'Carwin the peasant rebel', in Philip Barnard, Mark L. Kamrath and Stephen Shapiro (eds), *Revising Charles Brockden Brown: Culture, Politics, and Sexuality in the Early Republic* (Knoxville, TN: The University of Tennessee Press, 2004), pp. 41–59, p. 43.
46   White, 'Carwin the peasant rebel'.
47   Brown quoted in Kafer, *Charles Brockden Brown's Revolution*, p. 49.
48   Mary Chapman, 'Introduction', in Charles Brockden Brown, *Ormond; or, The Secret Witness*, ed. M. Chapman (Ontario: Broadview Press, 1999), pp. 9–31, p. 17.

49   See for example Laura H. Korobkin, 'Murder by madman: criminal
      responsibility, law, and judgment in *Wieland*', *American Literature*, 72/4
      (2000), 721–50; Paul Witherington, 'Charles Brockden Brown's *Ormond*:
      the American artist and his masquerades', *Studies in American Fiction*, 4
      (1976), 111–19.
50   Brown quoted in Harry R. Warfel, *Charles Brockden Brown: American
      Gothic Novelist* (Gainesville, FL: University of Florida Press, 1949),
      p. 29.
51   Emory Elliott, *Revolutionary Writers: Literature and Authority in the New
      Republic 1725–1810* (New York: Oxford University Press, 1982), p. 214.
      Ossian is the narrator of a cycle of poems published by Scottish poet
      James Macpherson in 1760. The poems, which Macpherson claimed
      he found and translated from old Gaelic, deal with a character, Oisín,
      from Irish myth and were an international success.
52   Charles Brockden Brown, *Ormond; or, The Secret Witness, with Related
      Texts*, ed. Philip Barnard and Stephen Shapiro (Indianapolis: Hackett
      Publishing Company, 2009 [1799]), p. 15. Future quotations from
      Ormond will be from this edition and page numbers will be indicated
      parenthetically within the text. Exactly when Brown dissolved his
      association with Wilcocks is disputed. Kafer writes that it was the
      summer of 1793: see *Charles Brockden Brown's Revolution*, p. 72.
53   Korobkin, 'Murder by madman', 723–4.
54   See Barnard and Shapiro's introduction to Charles Brockden Brown,
      Edgar Huntly; or, Memoirs of a Sleep-Walker, with Related Texts, ed. Philip
      Barnard and Stephen Shapiro (Indianapolis: Hackett Publishing Company,
      2006 [1799]), xii; as well as Mary Chapman's introduction to *Ormond*,
      p. 19. The Connecticut Wits were a group of American authors centred
      around Yale University in Connecticut in the 1780s and 1790s with
      interests in the creation of a national literature.
55   Kafer, *Charles Brockden Brown's Revolution*, p. 74.
56   Barnard and Shapiro, introduction to *Edgar Huntly*, xii.
57   Brown as quoted in David Lee Clark, *Charles Brockden Brown: Pioneer
      Voice of America* (Durham, NC: Duke University Press, 1952), x.
58   Robert A. Ferguson, 'Yellow fever and Charles Brockden Brown: the
      context of the emerging novelist', *Early American Literature*, 14 (1980),
      293–305, 302.
59   Brown as quoted in Alan Axelrod, *Charles Brockden Brown: An American
      Tale* (Austin: University of Texas Press, 1983), p. 126.
60   Kafer, *Charles Brockden Brown's Revolution*, p. 194.
61   As will be developed more fully in the chapters to follow, Brown repeat-
      edly questions in his fiction the premise articulated in philosopher

John Locke's influential *An Essay Concerning Human Understanding* (1690),
a seminal text for the philosophical school of thought known as empiricism which holds that accurate knowledge of the world is gained through
reflection on sensory information.

62   Linda K. Kerber, *Federalists in Dissent: Imagery and Ideology in Jeffersonian
      America* (Ithaca, NY: Cornell University Press, 1970), viii. See also Anita
      Vickers, 'Patriarchal and political authority in *Wieland*', *AUMLA: Journal
      of the Australasian Universities Modern Language Association*, 90 (1998),
      1–19, 3.

63   Douglas Anderson, 'Edgar Huntly's dark inheritance', *Philological Quarterly*,
      70/4 (1991), 453–73, 454.

64   Tompkins, *Sensational Designs*, p. 47.

65   Kafer, *Charles Brockden Brown's Revolution*, p. 59.

66   Christophersen, *Apparition in the Glass*, p. 106.

67   Sean X. Goudie, 'On the origin of American specie(s): the West Indies,
      classification, and the emergence of supremacist consciousness in *Arthur
      Mervyn*', in Barnard, Kamrath, and Shapiro, *Revising Charles Brockden
      Brown*, pp. 60–87, p. 62.

68   'Woldwinite' is the neologism formed through the combination of
      Wollstonecraft and Godwin, introduced by Barnard and Shapiro in
      their introductions to the Hackett Press editions of Brown's works to
      highlight the mutual contribution of Wollstonecraft and Godwin to
      1790s radical political theory. In their estimation, the more traditional
      term 'Godwinian' effaces the contributions of Wollstonecraft and other
      women. See Barnard and Shapiro, introduction to *Edgar Huntly*, xv.

69   Barnard and Shapiro, introduction to *Edgar Huntly*, xiv–xvii.

70   Both Wollstonecraft's reputation and Godwin's (Wollstonecraft and
      Godwin married in 1797 despite the latter's own critique of the insti-
      tution of marriage) were significantly damaged after the publication
      by Godwin of *Memoirs of the Author of A Vindication of the Rights of
      Woman* in 1798, one year after Wollstonecraft's death. The work was
      unusually frank for the time and includes among other details accounts
      of Wollstonecraft's love affairs, her illegitimate child and her suicide
      attempts – all of which made it easy for opponents of Godwin and
      Wollstonecraft's ideas to dismiss them as immoral.

71   According to Kafer, Philadelphia in 1790 was a city of approximately
      50,000 people, including over 10,000 Germans, several thousand recent
      French émigrés and approximately 3,000 African Americans. Over 3,000
      new Irish immigrants arrived each year. See Kafer, *Charles Brockden
      Brown's Revolution*, p. 107.

72   Ibid., p. 66.

73   Christophersen notes among other formative changes industrial and financial revolutions that were transforming the Northeast; cotton re-structuring agriculture in the South; 'an ascendant individualism that was making itself felt in everything from the breakdown of the patri-archal family and the relaxation of fornication laws to the burgeoning number of newspapers being published'; and 'the movement for women's rights that crested about the time Brown began writing novels'. See Christophersen, *Apparition in the Glass*, p. 7.

74   Clemit, *The Godwinian Novel*, p. 114.

75   Levine, *Conspiracy and Romance*, p. 17. Edmond-Charles Genêt was a French ambassador to the United States during the French Revo-lution. He was dispatched in 1793 during France's wars with England and Spain to garner support – and resources – for France, thereby endangering the United States's neutrality in the conflicts. He also encouraged Democratic-Republican societies, which was an implicit rebuke to the Federalist administration of George Washington. The Whiskey Rebellion was an insurrection that began in 1791 and culminated in a military conflict in 1794. During Washington's presidency, a tax was levied on alcohol producers primarily to pay the national debt but also justified by Secretary of the Treasury, Alexander Hamilton, as a means of social control that would advance the power of the federal government. Tensions crested in 1794 in Pennsylvania when social unrest became violent rebellion that was subsequently subdued by a militia led by Washington and Hamilton. Jacobins were supporters of the French Revolution.

76   Christophersen, *Apparition in the Glass*, p. 77.

77   Kafer, *Charles Brockden Brown's Revolution*, p. 142.

78   Charles C. Bradshaw, 'The New England Illuminati: conspiracy and causality in Charles Brockden Brown's *Wieland*', *The New England Quarterly*, 76/3 (2003), 356–77, 356.

79   Ibid., 357.

80   Buel quoted in Levine, *Conspiracy and Romance*, p. 22.

81   Levine, *Conspiracy and Romance*, p. 23.

82   Frank Shuffelton, 'Juries of the common reader: crime and judgment in the novels of Charles Brockden Brown', in Barnard, Kamrath and Shapiro, *Revising Charles Brockden Brown*, pp. 88–114, p. 97.

83   Christophersen, *Apparition in the Glass*, p. 170.

84   Gregory Eiselein, 'Humanitarianism and uncertainty in *Arthur Mervyn*', *Essays in Literature*, 22/2 (1995), 215–27. See also pp. 447–8 of Norman S. Grabo, 'Historical essay', in Brown's *Arthur Mervyn; or, Memoirs of the Year 1793, First and Second Parts*, in *The Novels and Related Works of*

Charles Brockden Brown: Bicentennial Edition, vol. 3 (Kent, OH: Kent State University Press, 1980), pp. 447–75.

85 In Richardson's *Pamela*, the beautiful and virtuous servant girl, Pamela Andrews, is preyed upon by her lascivious master, Mr B., who abducts her and attempts to seduce her. Pamela steadfastly refuses to become his mistress and Mr B. is eventually won over by Pamela's goodness. In 1774, Benjamin Franklin himself published a version of Richardson's *Pamela*, making it the first English novel to be reprinted on American shores.

86 Russel B. Nye, 'Historical essay', in Charles Brockden Brown, *Ormond; or, The Secret Witness*, in *The Novels and Related Works of Charles Brockden Brown: Bicentennial Edition*, vol. 2 (Kent, OH: Kent State University Press, 1982), pp. 295–341, p. 314.

87 Lulu Rumsey Wiley, *The Sources and Influence of the Novels of Charles Brockden Brown* (New York: Vantage Press, 1950), p. 59.

88 Nye, 'Historical essay', p. 314.

89 Harry R. Warfel, *Charles Brockden Brown: American Gothic Novelist* (New York: Octagon Books, 1974 [1949]), p. 11.

90 The *philosophes* were eighteenth-century intellectuals upholding Age of Enlightenment ideals including a distrust of organized religion and an emphasis on education.

91 Nye, 'Historical essay', pp. 317–18.

92 Sydney J. Krause, '*Clara Howard* and *Jane Talbot*: Godwin on trial', in Rosenthal, *Critical Essays*, pp. 184–211, p. 193.

93 Kafer, *Charles Brockden Brown's Revolution*, p. 52.

94 Ibid., p. 58.

95 Nye, 'Historical essay', p. 316.

96 Ibid., p. 302.

97 Ibid., p. 321.

98 Brown, *Edgar Huntly*, p. 4.

1 Charles Brockden Brown and the Frontier Gothic

1 Washington Irving, 'The Legend of Sleepy Hollow', in *The Sketch-Book of Geoffrey Crayon, Gent* (New York: G. P. Putnam's Sons, 1880 [1820]), pp. 382–419, p. 384.

2 David Mogen, Scott P. Sanders and Joanne B. Karpinski, 'Introduction', in D. Mogen, S. P. Sanders and J. B. Karpinski (eds), *Frontier Gothic: Terror and Wonder at the Frontier in American Literature* (Rutherford, NJ: Fairleigh Dickinson University Press, 1993), pp. 1–27, p. 15.

3   Ibid., p. 15.
4   Ibid., p. 22.
5   Irving, 'Sleepy Hollow', p. 383.
6   William Bradford, *Of Plymouth Plantation 1620–1647*, ed. Samuel Eliot Morison (New York: Alfred A. Knopf, 1953), p. 25.
7   Cotton Mather, *The Wonders of the Invisible World*, reprinted in Paul Lauter et al. (eds), *The Heath Anthology of American Literature*, third edn, vol. 1 (New York: Houghton Mifflin, 1998), pp. 421–5, p. 421.
8   Mary Rowlandson, *A Narrative of the Captivity and Restoration of Mrs Mary Rowlandson*, in Paul Lauter et al. (eds), *The Heath Anthology of American Literature*, third edn, vol. 1 (New York: Houghton Mifflin, 1998), pp. 343–65, p. 344.
9   J. Hector St John de Crèvecoeur, *Letters from an American Farmer* (New York: Fox, Duffield and Company, 1904 [1782]), p. 58.
10   Ibid., p. 59.
11   Ibid., p. 67.
12   Ibid., p. 59.
13   Ibid., p. 67.
14   Charles Brockden Brown, 'Somnambulism. A fragment', in *Edgar Huntly; or, Memoirs of a Sleep-Walker, with Related Texts*, ed. Philip Barnard and Stephen Shapiro (Indianapolis: Hackett Publishing Company, 2006 [1805]), pp. 244–58, p. 255. Subsequent references to this story will refer to this edition and will be indicated parenthetically within the text.
15   Philip Barnard and Stephen Shapiro, headnote to 'Somnambulism. A fragment', in *Edgar Huntly*, p. 244.
16   Ibid., p. 244.
17   Dennis Berthold, 'Desacralizing the American Gothic: an iconographic approach to *Edgar Huntly*', *Studies in American Fiction*, 14/2 (1986), 127–38, 127.
18   Elizabeth Jane Wall Hinds, 'Charles Brockden Brown and the frontiers of discourse', in Mogen, Sanders and Karpinski, *Frontier Gothic*, pp. 109–25, p. 109.
19   George Toles, 'Charting the hidden landscape: *Edgar Huntly*', *Early American Literature*, 16/2 (1981), 133–53, 146.
20   Peter Kafer, *Charles Brockden Brown's Revolution and the Birth of the American Gothic* (Philadelphia: University of Philadelphia Press, 2004), p. 132.
21   Charles Brockden Brown, *Wieland; or, The Transformation. An American Tale, with Related Texts*, ed. Philip Barnard and Stephen Shapiro (Indianapolis: Hackett Publishing Company, 2009 [1798]), p. 12. Subsequent

references to *Wieland* will be to this edition and will be indicated parenthetically within the text.

22 Pamela Clemit, *The Godwinian Novel: The Rational Fictions of Godwin,
    Brockden Brown, Mary Shelley* (Oxford: Clarendon Press, 1993), p. 127.

23 Shirley Samuels, '*Wieland*: alien and infidel', *Early American Literature*,
    25/1 (1990), 46–66, 60.

24 Leslie Fiedler, *Love and Death in the American Novel* (New York: Anchor
    Books, 1992 [1960]), p. 150.

25 Bill Christophersen, *The Apparition in the Glass: Charles Brockden Brown's
    American Gothic* (Athens, GA: The University of Georgia Press, 1993),
    p. 48.

26 Hinds, 'Charles Brockden Brown and the frontiers of discourse', p. 121.

27 Ibid., p. 116.

28 Ibid., p. 123.

29 Lisa West Norwood, '"I may be a stranger to the grounds of your belief":
    constructing sense of place in *Wieland*', *Early American Literature*, 38/1
    (2003), 89–122, 90.

30 Jane Tompkins, *Sensational Designs: The Cultural Work of American Fiction
    1790–1860* (Oxford: Oxford University Press, 1985), p. 49.

31 Ibid., p. 49.

32 Anita Vickers, 'Patriarchal and political authority in *Wieland*', *AUMLA:
    Journal of the Australasian Universities Modern Language Association*, 90
    (1998), 1–19, 1.

33 Tompkins, *Sensational Designs*, p. 44.

34 Ibid., p. 61.

35 Vickers, 'Patriarchal and political authority', 1.

36 Tompkins, *Sensational Designs*, p. 53.

37 Ibid., p. 54.

38 Roland Hagenbüchle, 'American literature and the nineteenth-century
    crisis in epistemology: the example of Charles Brockden Brown',
    Early American Literature, 23/2 (1988), 121–51, 25. See also Joseph V.
    Ridgely, 'The empty world of *Wieland*', in Kenneth H. Baldwin and
    David K. Kirby (eds), *Individual and Community: Variations on a Theme
    in American Fiction* (Durham, NC: Duke University Press, 1975),
    pp. 3–16.

39 Hagenbüchle, 'American literature and the nineteenth-century crisis',
    p. 125.

40 Christophersen, *Apparition in the Glass*, p. 51.

41 Cathy N. Davidson, *Revolution and the Word: The Rise of the Novel in
    America* (New York: Oxford University Press, 1986), p. 237.

42 Berthold, 'Desacralizing the American Gothic', 134.

43 Charles Brockden Brown, *Edgar Huntly; or, Memoirs of a Sleep-Walker, with Related Texts*, ed. Philip Barnard and Stephen Shapiro (Indianapolis: Hackett Publishing Company, 2006 [1799]), p. 134. Subsequent references to *Edgar Huntly* will be to this edition and will be indicated parenthetically within the text.

44 Harriet Hustis, 'Deliberate unknowing and strategic retelling: the ravages of cultural desire in Charles Brockden Brown's *Edgar Huntly*', *Studies in American Fiction*, 31/1 (2003), 101–20, 101.

45 Ibid., 101.

46 Berthold, 'Desacralizing the American Gothic', 127.

47 Kafer, *Charles Brockden Brown's Revoluion*, p. 167.

48 Christophersen, *Apparition in the Glass*, p. 11.

49 Sydney J. Krause, 'Penn's elm and *Edgar Huntly*: dark "instructions to the heart"', *American Literature*, 66/3 (1994), 463–84, 473.

50 Mabel Morris, 'Charles Brockden Brown and the American Indian', *American Literature*, 18/3 (1946), 244–7, 244.

51 Myra Jehlen, 'The literature of colonization', in Sacvan Bercovitch (ed.), *The Cambridge History of American Literature, vol. 1: 1590–1820* (Cambridge: Cambridge University Press, 1994), pp. 13–168, p. 163.

52 Hustis, 'Deliberate unknowing', 116.

53 Robert D. Newman, 'Indians and Indian-hating in *Edgar Huntly* and *The Confidence Man*', *MELUS*, 15/3 (1988), 65–74, 68.

54 Ibid., 73.

55 This is Brown's language in *Edgar Huntly*, p. 115.

56 Norman S. Grabo, *The Coincidental Art of Charles Brockden Brown* (Chapel Hill, NC: The University of North Carolina Press, 1981), p. 68.

57 Christophersen, *Apparition in the Glass*, p. 156.

58 Hinds, 'Charles Brockden Brown and the frontiers of discourse', p. 114.

59 Paul Downes, 'Constitutional secrets: "Memoirs of Carwin" and the politics of concealment', *Criticism*, 39/1 (1997), 89–117, 105.

60 Paul Downes, 'Sleep-walking out of the Revolution: Brown's *Edgar Huntly*', *Eighteenth-Century Studies*, 29/4 (1996), 413–31, 424.

61 Jehlen, 'The literature of colonization', p. 161.

62 Newman, 'Indians and Indian-hating', 66.

63 John Seelye, 'Charles Brockden Brown and early American fiction', in Emory Elliott (ed.), *Columbia Literary History of the United States* (New York: Columbia University Press, 1988), pp. 168–86, p. 184.

64 Hinds, 'Charles Brockden Brown and the frontiers of discourse', p. 110.

65 Ibid., p. 115.

66 Ibid., p. 123.

67 Toles, 'Charting the hidden landscape', 144.

68 Ibid., 145.
69 Seelye, 'Charles Brockden Brown and Early American Fiction', p. 185.
70 See Jeffrey Andrew Weinstock, 'Lostness (Blair Witch)', in Sarah L. Higley and Jeffrey Andrew Weinstock (eds), *Nothing That Is: Millennial Cinema and the* Blair Witch *Controversies* (Detroit: Wayne State University Press, 2004), pp. 229–44.
71 Seelye, 'Charles Brockden Brown and early American fiction', p. 184.
72 Steve Hamelman, 'Rhapsodist in the wilderness: Brown's Romantic quest in *Edgar Huntly*', *Studies in American Fiction*, 21/2 (1993), 171–91. Online: Gale Cengage Learning, *http://www.gale.cengage.com/*, accessed 28 September 2009, 4.
73 Ibid., 4.
74 Mogen, Sanders and Karpinski, 'Introduction', in *Frontier Gothic*, p. 15.

2 Charles Brockden Brown and the Urban Gothic

1 Brown's note immediately precedes the text of *Edgar Huntly*. See Charles Brockden Brown, *Edgar Huntly; or, Memoirs of a Sleep-Walker, with Related Texts*, ed. Philip Barnard and Stephen Shapiro (Indianapolis: Hackett Publishing Company, 2006 [1799]). See also Paul Downes, 'Sleep-walking out of the Revolution: Brown's *Edgar Huntly*', *Eighteenth-Century Studies*, 29/4 (1996), 413–31; Steve Hamelman, 'Rhapsodist in the wilderness: Brown's romantic quest in *Edgar Huntly*', *Studies in American Fiction*, 21/2 (1993), 171–91; Robert D. Newman, 'Indians and Indian-hating in *Edgar Huntly* and *The Confidence Man*', *MELUS*, 15/3 (1988), 65–74; and John Seelye, 'Charles Brockden Brown and early American fiction', in Emory Elliott (ed.), *Columbia Literary History of the United States* (New York: Columbia University Press, 1988), pp. 168–86.
2 Robert Mighall, *A Geography of Victorian Gothic Fiction: Mapping History's Nightmares* (Oxford: Oxford University Press, 1999), p. 30.
3 Ibid., p. 31.
4 Ibid., p. 34.
5 Ibid., p. 58.
6 Ibid., p. 65.
7 Robert Mighall, 'Gothic cities', in Catherine Spooner and Emma McEvoy (eds), *The Routledge Companion to the Gothic* (New York: Routledge, 2007), pp. 54–72, pp. 55–6.
8 Allan Pritchard, 'The Urban Gothic of *Bleak House*', *Nineteenth-Century Literature*, 45/4 (1991), 432–52, 433.
9 Ibid., 435.

10   Ibid., 435.

11   Ibid., 436.

12   Kathleen Spencer, 'Purity and danger: *Dracula*, the Urban Gothic, and the late Victorian degeneracy crisis', *ELH*, 59 (1992), 197–225, 203.

13   Kathleen Spencer, 'Victorian Urban Gothic: the first modern fantastic literature', in Eric S. Rabkin (ed.), *Intersections: Fantasy and Science Fiction* (Carbondale, IL: Southern Illinois University Press, 1987), pp. 87–96, p. 92.

14   Spencer, 'Victorian Urban Gothic', p. 92.

15   Heyward Ehrlich, 'The "Mysteries" of Philadelphia: Lippard's *Quaker City* and "Urban" Gothic', *ESQ*, 18/1 (1972), 50–65.

16   See Norman S. Grabo, 'Historical essay', in Charles Brockden Brown's *Arthur Mervyn; or, Memoirs of the Year 1793, First and Second Parts*, in *The Novels and Related Works of Charles Brockden Brown: Bicentennial Edition*, vol. 3 (Kent, OH: Kent State University Press, 1980), pp. 447–75; and Norman S. Grabo, *The Coincidental Art of Charles Brockden Brown* (Chapel Hill, NC: The University of North Carolina Press, 1981).

17   Gary B. Nash, *First City: Philadelphia and the Forging of Historical Memory* (Philadelphia: University of Pennsylvania Press, 2002), p. 127; see also Russell F. Weigley, *Philadelphia: A 300-Year History* (New York: W. W. Norton & Company, 1982), p. 188.

18   Grabo, 'Historical essay', p. 447.

19   Grabo, *Coincidental Art of Charles Brockden Brown*, p. 104.

20   Gregory Eiselein, 'Humanitarianism and uncertainty in *Arthur Mervyn*', *Essays in Literature*, 22/2 (1995), 215–27.

21   Grabo, *Coincidental Art of Charles Brockden Brown*, p. 105.

22   Grabo, 'Historical essay', p. 448.

23   Alan Axelrod, *Charles Brockden Brown: An American Tale* (Austin: University of Texas Press, 1983), p. 45.

24   Ibid., p. 117.

25   Harry R. Warfel, *Charles Brockden Brown: American Gothic Novelist* (Gainesville, FL: University of Florida Press, 1949), p. 144.

26   James Dawes, 'Fictional feeling: philosophy, cognitive science, and the American Gothic', *American Literature*, 76/3 (2004), 437–66, 441.

27   Peter Kafer, *Charles Brockden Brown's Revolution and the Birth of the American Gothic* (Philadelphia: University of Philadelphia Press, 2004), p. 164.

28   Carl Ostrowski, '"Fated to perish by consumption": the political economy of *Arthur Mervyn*', *Studies in American Fiction*, 32/1 (2004), 3–20, 3.

29   Ibid., 6.

30   Ibid., 5.

31   Ibid., 13.

32   Ibid., 14.

33   Grabo, 'Historical essay', p. 448.

34   Sam Bass Warner Jr, *The Private City: Philadelphia in Three Periods of its Growth*, second edn (Philadelphia: University of Pennsylvania Press, 1968), p. 5.

35   Richard G. Miller, 'The Federal city, 1783–1800' in Russell F. Weigley (ed.), *Philadelphia: A 300-Year History* (New York: W. W. Norton & Company, 1982), pp. 155–208, p. 172.

36   Kafer, *Charles Brockden Brown's Revolution*, p. 107.

37   Robert S. Levine, *Conspiracy and Romance: Studies in Brockden Brown, Cooper, Hawthorne, and Melville* (Cambridge: Cambridge University Press, 1989), p. 23.

38   Grabo, *Coincidental Art of Charles Brockden Brown*, p. 105.

39   Karen Halttunen, *Confidence Men and Painted Women: A Study of Middle-Class Culture in America, 1830–1870* (New Haven, CT: Yale University Press, 1982).

40   Ibid., p. 13.

41   Ibid., p. 13.

42   Kafer, *Charles Brockden Brown's Revolution*, p. 87.

43   Levine, *Conspiracy and Romance*, p. 17.

44   Ibid., p. 17.

45   Ibid., p. 23.

46   Ibid., p. 23.

47   Bill Christophersen, *The Apparition in the Glass: Charles Brockden Brown's American Gothic* (Athens, GA: The University of Georgia Press, 1993), p. 77.

48   Kafer, *Charles Brockden Brown's Revolution*, p. 142.

49   Levine, *Conspiracy and Romance*, p. 18.

50   Charles C. Bradshaw, 'The New England Illuminati: conspiracy and causality in Charles Brockden Brown's *Wieland*', *The New England Quarterly*, 76/3 (2003), 356–77, 356.

51   Buel quoted in Levine, *Conspiracy and Romance*, p. 22.

52   Levine, *Conspiracy and Romance*, p. 23.

53   Charles Brockden Brown, *Ormond; or, The Secret Witness, with Related Texts*, ed. Philip Barnard and Stephen Shapiro (Indianapolis: Hackett Publishing Company, 2009 [1799]), p. 47. Additional citations from *Ormond* will refer to this edition with page numbers indicated parenthetically within the text.

54   Christophersen, *Apparition in the Glass*, p. 171.

55   Julia Stern, 'The state of "women" in *Ormond*; or, patricide in the new nation' in Philip Barnard, Mark L. Kamrath and Stephen Shapiro (eds),

Revising Charles Brockden Brown: Culture, Politics, and Sexuality in the Early Republic (Knoxville, TN: The University of Tennessee Press, 2004), pp. 182–215, p. 186.

56   Lewis as quoted in William Hedges, 'Charles Brockden Brown and the culture of contradictions', *Early American Literature*, 9/2 (1974), 107–42, 108.

57   Ibid., 123.

58   Kafer, *Charles Brockden Brown's Revolution*, p. 164.

59   Christophersen, *Apparition in the Glass*, p. 61.

60   Ibid., p. 72.

61   Ostrowski, '"Fated to perish by consumption"', 4.

62   Christophersen, *Apparition in the Glass*, p. 68.

63   Grabo, 'Historical essay', p. 450.

64   Kafer, *Charles Brockden Brown's Revolution*, p. 138.

65   Charles Brockden Brown, *Arthur Mervyn; or, Memoirs of the Year 1793, with Related Texts*, ed. Philip Barnard and Stephen Shapiro (Indianapolis: Hackett Publishing Company, 2008 [Part I 1799; Part II 1800]), p. 107. Subsequent quotations from *Arthur Mervyn* will be from this edition and will be indicated parenthetically within the text.

66   The Kent State Press Bicentennial Edition of *Arthur Mervyn* follows Arthur's expression 'What a condition was mine' (pp. 37–8) with an exclamation point rather than the question mark used in the Hackett edition.

67   Elizabeth Jane Wall Hinds, 'Charles Brockden Brown and the frontiers of discourse', in David Mogen, Scott P. Sanders and Joanne B. Karpinski (eds), *Frontier Gothic: Terror and Wonder at the Frontier in American Literature* (Rutherford, NJ: Fairleigh Dickinson University Press, 1993), pp. 109–25, p. 115.

68   George Toles, 'Charting the hidden landscape: *Edgar Huntly*', *Early American Literature*, 16/2 (1981), 133–53, 138.

69   Ibid., 139.

70   Ostrowski, '"Fated to perish by consumption"', 10.

71   Christophersen, *Apparition in the Glass*, p. 72.

72   Hedges, 'Culture of contradictions', 123.

73   Eiselein, 'Humanitarianism and uncertainty in *Arthur Mervyn*'.

74   Emory Elliott, 'Narrative unity and moral resolution in *Arthur Mervyn*', in Bernard Rosenthal (ed.), *Critical Essays on Charles Brockden Brown* (Boston: G. K. Hall, 1981), pp. 142–63, p. 142.

75   Michael Davitt Bell, *The Development of the American Romance: The Sacrifice of Relation* (Chicago: University of Chicago Press, 1980), p. 59.

76   Christophersen, *Apparition in the Glass*, p. 91.

3 Charles Brockden Brown and the Psychological Gothic

1   *http://everything2.com/title/Scooby+Doo+ending.*
2   Marie Mulvey-Roberts (ed.), *The Handbook of the Gothic*, second edn (New York: New York University Press, 2009), p. 77.
3   Ibid., p. 66.
4   Ibid., p. 185.
5   Tzvetan Todorov, *The Fantastic: A Structural Approach to a Literary Genre*, trans. Richard Howard (Ithaca, NY: Cornell University Press, 1973).
6   Benjamin F. Fisher, 'Poe and the Gothic tradition', in Kevin J. Hayes (ed.), *The Cambridge Companion to Edgar Allan Poe* (Cambridge: Cambridge University Press, 2002), pp. 72–91, p. 78.
7   Clive Bloom (ed.), *Gothic Horror: A Guide for Students and Readers*, second edn (New York: Palgrave Macmillan, 2007), p. 3.
8   Ibid., p. 5.
9   John Dunn, *Locke: A Very Short Introduction* (Oxford: Oxford University Press, 1984), p. 81.
10 Ibid., p. 81.
11 Nina Baym, 'A minority reading of *Wieland*', in Bernard Rosenthal (ed.), *Critical Essays on Charles Brockden Brown* (Boston: G. K. Hall, 1981), pp. 87–103, p. 97.
12 Jane Tompkins, *Sensational Designs: The Cultural Work of American Fiction 1790–1860* (Oxford: Oxford University Press, 1985), p. 54.
13 Charles C. Bradshaw, 'The New England Illuminati: conspiracy and causality in Charles Brockden Brown's *Wieland*', *The New England Quarterly*, 76/3 (2003), 356–77, 376.
14 Laura H. Korobkin, 'Murder by madman: criminal responsibility, law, and judgment in *Wieland*', *American Literature*, 72/4 (2000), 721–50, 725.
15 Roland Hagenbüchle, 'American literature and the nineteenth-century crisis in epistemology: the example of Charles Brockden Brown', *Early American Literature*, 23/2 (1988), 121–51, 138.
16 Christopher Looby, *Voicing America: Language, Literary Form, and the Origins of the United States* (Chicago: University of Chicago Press, 1996), p. 192.
17 William J. Scheick, 'The problem of origination in Brown's *Ormond*', in Rosenthal, *Critical Essays*, pp. 126–41, p. 129.
18 Bill Christophersen, *The Apparition in the Glass: Charles Brockden Brown's American Gothic* (Athens, GA: The University of Georgia Press, 1993), pp. 89–90.
19 William Hedges, 'Charles Brockden Brown and the culture of contradictions', *Early American Literature*, 9/2 (1974), 107–42, 107.

20 Scheick, 'The problem of origination', p. 129.

21 Paul Witherington, '"Not my tongue only": form and language in Brown's *Edgar Huntly*', in Rosenthal, *Critical Essays* , pp. 164–83, p. 165.

22 Beverly R.Voloshin, '*Edgar Huntly* and the coherence of the self', *Early American Literature*, 23/3 (1988), 262–80, 263.

23 Charles Brockden Brown, 'Somnambulism. A fragment', in *Edgar Huntly; or, Memoirs of a Sleep-Walker, with Related Texts*, ed. Philip Barnard and Stephen Shapiro (Indianapolis: Hackett Publishing Company, 2006 [1805]), pp. 244–58, p. 247. Subsequent quotations from this story will be from this edition and page numbers will be indicated parenthetically within the text.

24 Charles Brockden Brown, *Wieland; or, The Transformation. An American Tale, with Related Texts*, ed. Philip Barnard and Stephen Shapiro (Indianapolis: Hackett Publishing Company, 2009 [1798]), p. 32. Subsequent quotations from *Wieland* will be from this edition and page numbers will be indicated parenthetically within the text.

25 Ibid., p. 9 n. 13.

26 Christophersen, *Apparition in the Glass*, p. 32.

27 See Leslie Fiedler, *Love and Death in the American Novel* (New York: Anchor Books, 1992 [1960]); Norman S. Grabo, *The Coincidental Art of Charles Brockden Brown* (Chapel Hill, NC: The University of North Carolina Press, 1981); Looby, *Voicing America*; and Shirley Samuels, '*Wieland*: alien and infidel', *Early American Literature*, 25/1 (1990), 46–66.

28 Looby, *Voicing America*, p. 191.

29 Ibid., p. 191.

30 Christophersen, *Apparition in the Glass*, p. 41.

31 Ibid., p. 32.

32 Russel B. Nye, 'Historical essay' in *Ormond; or, The Secret Witness*, in *The Novels and Related Works of Charles Brockden Brown: Bicentennial Edition*, vol. 2 (Kent, OH: Kent State University Press, 1982), pp. 295–341, p. 334.

33 Christophersen, *Apparition in the Glass*, p. 85.

34 Elizabeth Jane Wall Hinds, 'Charles Brockden Brown and the frontiers of discourse', in David Mogen, Scott P. Sanders and Joanne B. Karpinski (eds), *Frontier Gothic: Terror and Wonder at the Frontier in American Literature* (Rutherford, NJ: Fairleigh Dickinson University Press, 1993), pp. 109–25, p. 122.

35 Robert S. Levine, *Conspiracy and Romance: Studies in Brockden Brown, Cooper, Hawthorne, and Melville* (Cambridge: Cambridge University Press, 1989), p. 45.

36   Peter Kafer, *Charles Brockden Brown's Revolution and the Birth of the American Gothic* (Philadelphia: University of Philadelphia Press, 2004), p. 158.

37   Christophersen, *Apparition in the Glass*, p. 71.

38   Michael Davitt Bell, *The Development of the American Romance: The Sacrifice of Relation* (Chicago: University of Chicago Press, 1980), p. 59.

39   Ibid., p. 59.

40   Emory Elliott, 'Narrative unity and moral resolution in *Arthur Mervyn*', in Rosenthal, *Critical Essays*, pp. 142–63, p. 160.

41   Grabo, *Coincidental Art of Charles Brockden Brown*, p. 98.

42   Christophersen, *Apparition in the Glass*, p. 166.

43   Edgar Allan Poe, 'William Wilson. A Tale', *Burton's Gentleman's Magazine* (October 1839), 205–12, 212. Online, accessed 4 July 2010, *http://www.eapoe.org/works/tales/wilwilb.htm*.

44   Charles Brockden Brown, *Edgar Huntly; or, Memoirs of a Sleep-Walker, with Related Texts*, ed. Philip Barnard and Stephen Shapiro (Indianapolis: Hackett Publishing Company, 2006 [1799]), p. 5. Subsequent quotations from this story will be from this edition and page numbers will be indicated parenthetically within the text. There is a minor difference between the quotation provided here from the Hackett edition and the same text in the Kent State University Press Bicentennial Edition. In the latter, a full stop replaces the semicolon falling between 'sentiments' and 'in proportion'. 'In' is therefore capitalized in the Kent State edition.

45   Korobkin, 'Murder by madman', 725.

46   Grabo, *Coincidental Art of Charles Brockden Brown*, xi.

47   Christophersen, *Apparition in the Glass*, p. 144.

48   Grabo, *Coincidental Art of Charles Brockden Brown*, p. 65.

49   Ibid., p. 65.

50   Christophersen, *Apparition in the Class*, p. 127.

51   Hinds, *Charles Brockden Brown and the frontiers of discourse*, p. 113.

52   Grabo, *Coincidental Art of Charles Brockden Brown*, p. 86.

4 Charles Brockden Brown and the Female Gothic

1   Ellen Moers, *Literary Women* (Garden City, NY: Anchor Books, 1976), p. 138.

2   Moers, *Literary Women*, p. 142.

3   Eugenia C. DeLamotte, *Perils of the Night: A Feminist Study of Nineteenth-Century Gothic* (New York: Oxford University Press, 1990), p. 13.
4   Elaine Showalter, *Sister's Choice: Tradition and Change in American Women's Writing* (Oxford: Clarendon Press, 1991), p. 128.
5   Margaret Anne Doody, 'Deserts, ruins, and troubled waters: female dreams in fiction and the development of the Gothic novel', *Genre*, 10 (1977), 529–72, 560.
6   Doody, 'Deserts, ruins, and troubled waters', 562.
7   See Claire Kahane, 'The Gothic mirror', in Shirley Nelson Garner, Claire Kahane and Madelon Sprengnether (eds), *The (M)other Tongue: Essays in Feminist Psychoanalytic Interpretation* (Ithaca, NY: Cornell University Press, 1985), pp. 334–51; Janice Radway, 'The utopian impulse in popular literature: Gothic romances and "feminist" protest', *American Quarterly*, 33/2 (1981), 140–62; DeLamotte, *Perils of the Night*; and Maggie Kilgour, *The Rise of the Gothic Novel* (London: Routledge, 1982).
8   Showalter, *Sister's Choice*, p. 128.
9   Kahane, 'Gothic mirror', p. 347.
10 Radway, 'Utopian impulse', 140–1.
11 Ibid., 142.
12 DeLamotte, *Perils of the Night*, p. 151.
13 Ibid., p. 161.
14 Ibid., p. 165.
15 Ibid., p. 186.
16 Ibid., p. 188.
17 Kilgour, *Rise of the Gothic Novel*, p. 9.
18 See Frederike van Leeuwen, 'Female Gothic: the discourse of the Other', *Revista Canaria de Estudios Ingleses*, 14 (1982), 33–44; Tania Modleski, *Loving with a Vengeance: Mass-Produced Fantasies for Women* (Hamden, CT: Archon Books, 1982); Frances L. Restuccia, 'Female Gothic writing: "under cover to Alice"', *Genre*, 28 (1986), 346–66; Kate Ferguson Ellis, *The Contested Castle: Gothic Novels and the Subversion of Domestic Ideology* (Urbana: University of Illinois Press, 1989); Tamar Heller, *Dead Secrets: Wilkie Collins and the Female Gothic* (New Haven, CT: Yale University Press, 1992); Anne Williams, *Art of Darkness: A Poetics of Gothic* (Chicago: University of Chicago Press, 1995); Diane Long Hoeveler, *Gothic Feminism: The Professionalization of Gender from Charlotte Smith to the Brontës* (University Park, PA: Pennsylvania State University Press, 1998); Susanne Becker, *Gothic Forms of Feminine Fiction* (Manchester: Manchester University Press, 1999).
19 Susan K. Harris, *Nineteenth-Century American Women's Novels: Interpretive Strategies* (Cambridge: Cambridge University Press, 1990), p. 20. See

also Sandra M. Gilbert and Susan Gubar, *The Madwoman in the Attic: The Woman Writer and the Nineteenth-Century Literary Imagination* (New Haven, CT:Yale University Press, 1979); Elaine Showalter, *A Literature of their Own: British Women Novelists from Brontë to Lessing* (Princeton, NJ: Princeton University Press, 1977).

20 Leeuwen, 'Female Gothic', 43.
21 Ibid., 36.
22 Ibid., 37.
23 Modleski, *Loving With a Vengeance*, p. 83.
24 Ellis, *Contested Castle*, xv.
25 Alison Milbank, 'The Female Gothic', in Marie Mulvey-Roberts (ed.), *The Handbook of the Gothic*, second edn (New York: New York University Press, 2009), pp. 120–4, p. 121.
26 Milbank, 'Female Gothic', p. 121.
27 See Russel B. Nye, 'Historical essay' in *Ormond; or, The Secret Witness*, in *The Novels and Related Works of Charles Brockden Brown: Bicentennial Edition*, vol. 2 (Kent, OH: Kent State University Press, 1982), pp. 295–341.
28 Peter Kafer, *Charles Brockden Brown's Revolution and the Birth of the American Gothic* (Philadelphia: University of Philadelphia Press, 2004), p. 68.
29 Ibid., p. 94.
30 Edwin G. Burrows and Mike Wallace, *Gotham: A History of New York to 1898* (New York: Oxford University Press, 1998), p. 377.
31 Kristin M. Comment, 'Charles Brockden Brown's *Ormond* and lesbian possibility in the early Republic', *Early American Literature*, 40/1 (2005), 57–78, 58.
32 Bruce Burgett, 'Between speculation and population: the problem of "sex" in Thomas Malthus's *Essay on the Principle of Population* and Charles Brockden Brown's *Alcuin*', in Philip Barnard, Mark L. Kamrath and Stephen Shapiro (eds), *Revising Charles Brockden Brown: Culture, Politics, and Sexuality in the Early Republic* (Knoxville, TN: The University of Tennessee Press, 2004), pp. 122–48, p. 126.
33 Kafer, *Charles Brockden Brown's Revolution*, p. 68.
34 Paul Lewis, 'Charles Brockden Brown and the gendered canon of early American fiction', *Early American Literature*, 31/2 (1996), 167–88, 170.
35 Fritz Fleischmann, *A Right View of the Subject: Feminism in the Works of Charles Brockden Brown and John Neal* (Erlangen: Verlag Palm & Enke, 1983), p. 22.
36 Cathy N. Davidson, 'The matter and manner of Charles Brockden Brown's *Alcuin*', in Bernard Rosenthal (ed.), *Critical Essays on Charles Brockden Brown* (Boston: G. K. Hall, 1981), pp. 71–86, p. 72.

[37] Robert D. Arner, 'Historical essay', in *Alcuin: A Dialogue and Memoirs of Stephen Calvert*, in *The Novels and Related Works of Charles Brockden Brown: Bicentennial Edition*, ed. Sydney J. Krause and S. W. Reid, vol. 6 (Kent, OH: Kent State University Press, 1987 [1798]), pp. 273–312, p. 274.

[38] Fleischmann, *Right View of the Subject*, p. 25. Barnard and Shapiro's neologism, 'Woldwinite', appears in their introductions to each of the Hackett editions of Brown's four Gothic novels. See for example their introduction to Brown's *Wieland; or, The Transformation. An American Tale, with Related Texts*, ed. Philip Barnard and Stephen Shapiro (Indianapolis: Hackett Publishing Company, 2009 [1798]), xvii.

[39] Charles Brockden Brown, *Alcuin; A Dialogue and Memoirs of Stephen Calvert*, in *The Novels and Related Works of Charles Brockden Brown: Bicentennial Edition*, ed. Sydney J. Krause and S. W. Reid, vol. 6 (Kent, OH: Kent State University Press, 1987 [1798]), p. 18. Subsequent quotations from *Alcuin* will be from this edition and will be indicated parenthetically within the body of the text.

[40] William Hedges, 'Charles Brockden Brown and the culture of contradictions', *Early American Literature*, 9/2 (1974), 107–42, 115.

[41] Davidson, 'Matter and manner', p. 80.

[42] I am referring here to Herman Melville's two-part story, 'The Paradise of the Bachelors and the Tartarus of the Maids' in which the situation of unmarried men and women is starkly contrasted. The story is frequently anthologized and may be found in many places, including online at *http://etext.virginia.edu/toc/modeng/public/MelPara.html*.

[43] Lewis, 'Charles Brockden Brown and the gendered canon', 172.

[44] Bill Christophersen, *The Apparition in the Glass: Charles Brockden Brown's American Gothic* (Athens, GA: The University of Georgia Press, 1993), p. 127.

[45] Donald A. Ringe, *Charles Brockden Brown* (Boston: Twayne Publishers, 1991 [1966]), p. 11.

[46] Charles Brockden Brown, *Wieland; or, The Transformation. An American Tale, with Related Texts*, ed. Philip Barnard and Stephen Shapiro (Indianapolis: Hackett Publishing Company, 2009 [1798]), p. 50. Subsequent quotations from *Wieland* will be from this edition and will be indicated parenthetically within the text.

[47] In the Kent State Bicentennial Edition of *Wieland*, the entire phrase 'not a lineament remained' is italicized (p. 157).

[48] Lewis, 'Charles Brockden Brown and the gendered canon', 172.

[49] Andrew J. Scheiber, '"The arm lifted against me": love, terror, and the construction of gender in *Wieland*', *Early American Literature*, 26/2 (1991), 173–94, 174.

50 Fleischmann, *Right View of the Subject*, p. 46.

51 Scheiber, '"The arm lifted against me"', 184.

52 Ibid., 176.

53 Ibid., 184.

54 Ibid., 190.

55 Ibid., 176.

56 Charles Brockden Brown, *Ormond; or, The Secret Witness, with Related Texts*, ed. Philip Barnard and Stephen Shapiro (Indianapolis: Hackett Publishing Company, 2009 [1799]), pp. 25–6. Additional quotations from *Ormond* will be from this edition and will be indicated parenthetically within the text.

57 Lewis, 'Charles Brockden Brown and the gendered canon', 176.

58 Fleischmann, *Right View of the Subject*, p. 56.

59 Sydney J. Krause, '*Ormond*: seduction in a new key', *American Literature*, 44/4 (1973), 570–84, 571.

60 Krause, 'Seduction in a new key', 575.

61 Fleischmann, *Right View of the Subject*, p. 57.

62 Ibid., p. 59.

63 Norman S. Grabo, *The Coincidental Art of Charles Brockden Brown* (Chapel Hill, NC: The University of North Carolina Press, 1981), p. 47.

64 Lewis, 'Charles Brockden Brown and the gendered canon', 181.

65 The Kent State Bicentennial Edition includes a comma in this passage between 'different' and 'from': '[Martinette's] education seemed not widely different, from that which Constantia had received.'

66 Ringe, *Charles Brockden Brown*, p. 34.

67 Ibid., p. 34.

68 Fleischmann, *Right View of the Subject*, p. 54.

69 Ibid., p. 70.

70 Nye, 'Historical essay', p. 328.

71 Charles Brockden Brown, *Arthur Mervyn; or, Memoirs of the Year 1793, with Related Texts*, ed. Philip Barnard and Stephen Shapiro (Indianapolis: Hackett Publishing Company, 2008 [Part I 1799; Part II 1800]), p. 243. Subsequent quotations from *Arthur Mervyn* will be from this edition and will be indicated parenthetically within the text.

72 Charles Brockden Brown, *Edgar Huntly; or, Memoirs of a Sleep-Walker, with Related Texts*, ed. Philip Barnard and Stephen Shapiro (Indianapolis: Hackett Publishing Company, 2006 [1799]), p. 33. Subsequent quotations from *Edgar Huntly* will be from this edition and will be indicated parenthetically within the text.

73 Lewis, 'Charles Brockden Brown and the gendered canon', 170.

74   Michelle Burnham, 'Epistolarity, anticipation, and revolution in *Clara Howard*', in Philip Barnard, Mark L. Kamrath and Stephen Shapiro (eds), *Revising Charles Brockden Brown*, pp. 260–80, p. 260.

75   Grabo, *Coincidental Art of Charles Brockden Brown*, p. 131.

76   See Jared Gardner, 'Alien nation: Edgar Huntly's savage awakening', *American Literature*, 66/3 (1994), 429–61.

77   Sydney J. Krause, '*Clara Howard* and *Jane Talbot*: Godwin on trial', in Rosenthal, *Critical Essays*, pp. 184–211, p. 186.

78   Burnham, 'Epistolarity, anticipation, and revolution', p. 274.

79   Bruce Burgett, 'Masochism and male sentimentalism: Charles Brockden Brown's *Clara Howard*', *The Arizona Quarterly*, 52/1 (1996), 1–25, 7.

80   Charles Brockden Brown, *Clara Howard in a Series of Letters: Bicentennial Edition*, ed. Sydney J. Krause and S. W. Reid (Kent, OH: Kent State University Press, 1986 [1801]), p. 26. Subsequent quotations from *Clara Howard* will be from this edition and will be indicated parenthetically within the text.

81   Krause, '*Clara Howard* and *Jane Talbot*', p. 187.

82   Fleischmann, *Right View of the Subject*, p. 70.

Conclusion: The Legacy of Charles Brockden Brown's Four Gothics

1   Michael Davitt Bell, *The Development of the American Romance: The Sacrifice of Relation* (Chicago: University of Chicago Press, 1980), p. 41.

2   Cathy N. Davidson, *Revolution and the Word: The Rise of the Novel in America* (New York: Oxford University Press, 1986), p. 238.

3   Ibid., p. 238.

4   Ibid., p. 239.

5   Ibid., p. 238.

6   Michelle Burnham, 'Epistolarity, anticipation, and revolution in *Clara Howard*', in Philip Barnard, Mark L. Kamrath and Stephen Shapiro (eds), *Revising Charles Brockden Brown: Culture, Politics, and Sexuality in the Early Republic* (Knoxville, TN: The University of Tennessee Press, 2004), pp. 260–80, p. 260.

7   Pamela Clemit, *The Godwinian Novel: The Rational Fictions of Godwin, Brockden Brown, Mary Shelley* (Oxford: Clarendon Press, 1993), p. 106.

8   Peter Kafer, *Charles Brockden Brown's Revolution and the Birth of the American Gothic* (Philadelphia: University of Philadelphia Press, 2004), p. 198.

9   Clemit, *The Godwinian Novel*, p. 106.

10 Fuller quoted in Paul Lewis, 'Charles Brockden Brown and the gendered canon of early American fiction', *Early American Literature*, 31/2 (1996), 167–88, 167.

11 Alan Axelrod, *Charles Brockden Brown: An American Tale* (Austin: University of Texas Press, 1983), p. 36.

12 Leslie Fiedler, *Love and Death in the American Novel* (New York: Anchor Books, 1992 [1960]), p. 154.

13 Nathaniel Hawthorne, 'The Hall of Fantasy', in *Mosses from an Old Manse* [1846]. Online, accessed 5 July 2010, *http://www.ibiblio.org/eldritch/nh/hall.html*.

14 Kafer, *Charles Brockden Brown's Revolution*, p. 199.

15 Axelrod, *Charles Brockden Brown: An American Tale*, p. 36.

16 Kafer, *Charles Brockden Brown's Revolution*, p. 198.

17 Neil Fitzgerald, 'Philadelphia Gothic: Charles Brockden Brown'. Online, accessed 5 July 2010, *http://www.librarycompany.org/gothic/brown.htm*.

18 See Boyd Carter, 'Poe's debt to Charles Brockden Brown', *Prairie Schooner*, 27 (1953), 190–6; David Lee Clark, 'The sources of Poe's "The Pit and the Pendulum"', *Modern Language Notes*, 44/6 (1929), 349–56; and David H. Hirsch, 'Another source for "The Pit and the Pendulum"', *Mississippi Quarterly*, 23/1 (1969–70), 35–43.

19 Axelrod, *Charles Brockden Brown: An American Tale*, pp. 36–43.

20 Ibid., p. 46.

21 Ibid., p. 46.

22 Ibid., p. 46.

23 Ibid., p. 47.

24 On the 'frontiers of discourse', see Elizabeth Jane Wall Hinds, 'Charles Brockden Brown and the frontiers of discourse', in David Mogen, Scott P. Sanders and Joanne B. Karpinski (eds), *Frontier Gothic: Terror and Wonder at the Frontier in American Literature* (Rutherford, NJ: Fairleigh Dickinson University Press, 1993), pp. 109–25.

25 Poe's 'The Man of the Crowd' was originally published in *Burton's Gentleman's Magazine* (December 1840), 267–70. My references to the story here and below will be to the online version available through the Edgar Allan Poe Society at *http://www.eapoe.org/works/tales/crowda1.htm*.

26 This potential unreliability of the narrator has been noted in critical readings of the tale, which emphasize not the narrator's failure to comprehend the man of the crowd but rather his own avoidance of introspection. The character that the narrator cannot or will not read, according to these interpretations, is in fact himself. See for example Dana Brand,

The Spectator and the City in Nineteenth-Century American Literature (Cambridge: Cambridge University Press, 1991); Jonathan Auerbach, *The Romance of Failure: First-Person Fictions of Poe, Hawthorne, and James* (New York and Oxford: Oxford University Press, 1989); Ray Mazurek, 'Art, ambiguity, and the artist in Poe's "The Man of the Crowd"', *Poe Studies*, 12/2 (1979), 25–8; and Patrick Quinn, *The French Face of Edgar Allan Poe* (Carbondale, IL: Southern Illinois University Press, 1957).

Bibliography

❧☙

I. Writings by Charles Brockden Brown

Alcuin: A Dialogue and *Memoirs of Stephen Calvert: Bicentennial Edition*, ed. Sydney J. Krause and S. W. Reid (Kent, OH: Kent State University Press, 1987 [1798]).

Wieland; or, The Transformation. An American Tale, with Related Texts, ed. Philip Barnard and Stephen Shapiro (Indianapolis: Hackett Publishing Company, 2009 [1798]).

Edgar Huntly; or, Memoirs of a Sleep-Walker, with Related Texts, ed. Philip Barnard and Stephen Shapiro (Indianapolis: Hackett Publishing Company, 2006 [1799]).

Ormond; or, The Secret Witness, with Related Texts, ed. Philip Barnard and Stephen Shapiro (Indianapolis: Hackett Publishing Company, 2009 [1799]).

Arthur Mervyn; or, Memoirs of the Year 1793, with Related Texts, ed. Philip Barnard and Stephen Shapiro (Indianapolis: Hackett Publishing Company, 2008 [Part I 1799, Part II 1800]).

Memoirs of Stephen Calvert: Bicentennial Edition, ed. Sydney J. Krause and S. W. Reid (Kent, OH: Kent State University Press, 1987 [1799–1800]).

Clara Howard in a Series of Letters: Bicentennial Edition, ed. Sydney J. Krause and S. W. Reid (Kent, OH: Kent State University Press, 1986 [1801]).

Jane Talbot; A Novel: Bicentennial Edition, ed. Sydney J. Krause and S. W. Reid (Kent, OH: Kent State University Press, 1986 [1801]).

Memoirs of Carwin the Biloquist, in *Wieland; or, The Transformation. An American Tale, with Related Texts: Bicentennial Edition*, ed. Sydney J.

Krause and S. W. Reid (Kent, OH: Kent State University Press, 1977 [1803–5]).

'Somnambulism. A fragment', in *Edgar Huntly; or, Memoirs of a Sleep-Walker, with Related Texts*, ed. Philip Barnard and Stephen Shapiro (Indianapolis: Hackett Publishing Company, 2006 [1805]), pp. 244–58.

II. Biographies of Brown

Barnard, Philip and Stephen Shapiro, 'Introduction', in Charles Brockden Brown, *Edgar Huntly; or, Memoirs of a Sleep-Walker, with Related Texts*, ed. Philip Barnad and Stephen Shapiro (Indianapolis: Hackett Publishing Company, 2006), ix–xlii. (See also Barnard and Shapiro's introductions to the Hackett editions of *Wieland, Ormond* and *Arthur Mervyn*.)

Chapman, Mary, 'Introduction', in Charles Brockden Brown, *Ormond; or, The Secret Witness*, ed. M. Chapman (Ontario: Broadview Press, 1999), pp. 9–31.

Clark, David Lee, *Charles Brockden Brown: Pioneer Voice of America* (Durham, NC: Duke University Press, 1952).

Kafer, Peter, *Charles Brockden Brown's Revolution and the Birth of the American Gothic* (Philadelphia: University of Philadelphia Press, 2004).

Warfel, Harry R., *Charles Brockden Brown: American Gothic Novelist* (Gainesville, FL: University of Florida Press, 1949).

III. Critical studies of Brown's writing

Achilles, Jochen, 'Composite (dis)order: cultural identity in *Wieland, Edgar Huntly*, and *Arthur Gordon Pym*', in Kevin L. Cope and Laura Morrow (eds), *Ideas, Aesthetics, and Inquiries in the Early Modern Era* (New York: AMS, 1997), pp. 251–70.

Anderson, Douglas, 'Edgar Huntly's dark inheritance', *Philological Quarterly*, 70/4 (1991), 453–73.

Arner, Robert D., 'Historical essay', in *Alcuin: A Dialogue* and *Memoirs of Stephen Calvert: Bicentennial Edition*, ed. Sydney J. Krause and S. W. Reid (Kent, OH: Kent State University Press, 1987), pp. 273–312.

Axelrod, Alan, *Charles Brockden Brown: An American Tale* (Austin: University of Texas Press, 1983).

Barnard, Philip, 'Culture and authority in Brown's historical sketches', in Philip Barnard, Mark L. Kamrath and Stephen Shapiro (eds), *Revising Charles Brockden Brown: Culture, Politics, and Sexuality in the Early*

Republic (Knoxville, TN: The University of Tennessee Press, 2004), pp. 310–31.

Barnes, Elizabeth, 'Loving with a vengeance: *Wieland*, familicide and the crisis of masculinity in the early Nation', in Milette Shamir and Jennifer Travis (eds), *Boys Don't Cry? Rethinking Narratives of Masculinity and Emotion in the US* (New York: Columbia University Press, 2002), pp. 44–63.

Bauer, Ralph, 'Between repression and transgression: Rousseau's *Confessions* and Charles Brockden Brown's *Wieland*', *American Transcendental Quarterly*, 10 (1996), 311–29.

Baym, Nina, 'A minority reading of *Wieland*', in Bernard Rosenthal (ed.), *Critical Essays on Charles Brockden Brown* (Boston: G. K. Hall, 1981), pp. 87–103.

Bell, Michael Davitt, '"The double-tongued deceiver": sincerity and duplicity in the novels of Charles Brockden Brown', *Early American Literature*, 9/2 (1974), 143–63.

—, *The Development of the American Romance: The Sacrifice of Relation* (Chicago: University of Chicago Press, 1980).

Bellis, Peter J., 'Narrative compulsion and control in Charles Brockden Brown's *Edgar Huntly*', *South Atlantic Review*, 52/1 (January 1987), 43–57.

Bennett, Charles E., 'Charles Brockden Brown: man of letters', in Bernard Rosenthal (ed.), *Critical Essays on Charles Brockden Brown* (Boston: G. K. Hall, 1981), pp. 212–23.

Bennett, Maurice, 'Charles Brockden Brown's ambivalence toward art and imagination', *Essays in Literature*, 10 (spring 1983), 55–69.

Bernard, Kenneth, '*Arthur Mervyn*: the ordeal of innocence', *Texas Studies in Language and Literature*, 6 (1965), 441–59.

Berthoff, Warner B., 'Adventures of the young man: an approach to Charles Brockden Brown', *American Quarterly*, 9 (1957), 421–34.

Berthold, Dennis, 'Charles Brockden Brown, *Edgar Huntly*, and the origins of the American picturesque', *The William and Mary Quarterly*, 41/1 (January 1984), 62–84.

—, 'Desacralizing the American Gothic: an iconographic approach to *Edgar Huntly*', *Studies in American Fiction*, 14/2 (1986), 127–38.

Bradshaw, Charles C., 'The New England Illuminati: conspiracy and causality in Charles Brockden Brown's *Wieland*', *The New England Quarterly*, 76/3 (September 2003), 356–77.

Brancaccio, Patrick, 'Studied ambiguity: *Arthur Mervyn* and the problem of the unreliable narrator', *American Literature*, 42 (1970), 18–27.

Bredahl, A. Carl Jr, 'Transformation in *Wieland*', *Early American Literature*, 12 (1977), 177–92.

—, 'The two portraits in *Wieland*', *Early American Literature*, 16 (1981), 54–9.

Brückner, Martin, 'Sense, census, and the "statistical view" in the *Literary Magazine* and *Jane Talbot*', in Philip Barnard, Mark L. Kamrath and Stephen Shapiro (eds), *Revising Charles Brockden Brown: Culture, Politics, and Sexuality in the Early Republic* (Knoxville, TN: The University of Tennessee Press, 2004), pp. 281–309.

Burgett, Bruce, 'Masochism and male sentimentalism: Charles Brockden Brown's *Clara Howard*', *The Arizona Quarterly*, 52/1 (1996), 1–25.

—, 'Between speculation and population: the problem of "sex" in Thomas Malthus's *Essay on the Principle of Population* and Charles Brockden Brown's *Alcuin*', in Philip Barnard, Mark L. Kamrath and Stephen Shapiro (eds), *Revising Charles Brockden Brown: Culture, Politics, and Sexuality in the Early Republic* (Knoxville, TN: The University of Tennessee Press, 2004), pp. 122–48.

Burnham, Michelle, 'Epistolarity, anticipation, and revolution in *Clara Howard*', in Philip Barnard, Mark L. Kamrath and Stephen Shapiro (eds), *Revising Charles Brockden Brown: Culture, Politics, and Sexuality in the Early Republic* (Knoxville, TN: The University of Tennessee Press, 2004), pp. 260–80.

Butler, David L., *Dissecting a Human Heart: A Study of Style in the Novels of Charles Brockden Brown* (Washington: University Press of America, 1978).

Butler, Michael D., 'Charles Brockden Brown's *Wieland*: method and meaning', *Studies in American Fiction*, 4 (1976), 127–42.

Cahill, Edward, 'An adventurous and lawless fancy: Charles Brockden Brown's aesthetic state', *Early American Literature*, 36/1 (2001), 31–70.

Carpenter, Charles A., 'Selective bibliography of writings about Charles Brockden Brown', in Bernard Rosenthal (ed.), *Critical Essays on Charles Brockden Brown* (Boston: G. K. Hall, 1981), pp. 224–39.

Cassuto, Leonard, '"[Un]Consciousness itself is the malady": *Edgar Huntly* and the discourse of the Other', *Modern Language Studies*, 23/4 (1993), 118–30.

Chase, Richard, *The American Novel and its Tradition* (Garden City, NY: Doubleday, 1957).

Christophersen, Bill, *The Apparition in the Glass: Charles Brockden Brown's American Gothic* (Athens, GA: The University of Georgia Press, 1993).

Clark, David Lee, 'Brockden Brown and the rights of women', *University of Texas Bulletin*, 22/12 (1922), 1–48.

Clark, Michael, 'Charles Brockden Brown's *Wieland* and Robert Proud's *History of Pennsylvania*', *Studies in the Novel*, 20 (1988), 239–48.

Cleman, John, 'Ambiguous evil: a study of villains and heroes in Charles Brockden Brown's major novels', *Early American Literature*, 10 (1975), 190–219.

Clemit, Pamela, *The Godwinian Novel: The Rational Fictions of Godwin, Brockden Brown, Mary Shelley* (Oxford: Clarendon Press, 1993).

Cody, Michael, *Charles Brockden Brown and the Literary Magazine: Cultural Journalism in the Early American Republic* (Jefferson, NC: McFarland, 2004).

Cohen, Daniel A., '*Arthur Mervyn* and his elders: the ambivalence of youth in the early Republic', *The William and Mary Quarterly*, 43 (1986), 362–80.

Comment, Kristin M., 'Charles Brockden Brown's *Ormond* and lesbian possibility in the early Republic', *Early American Literature*, 40/1 (2005), 57–78.

Cowie, Alexander, 'Historical essay', in *Wieland; or, The Transformation. An American Tale, with Related Texts: Bicentennial Edition* (Kent, OH: Kent State University Press, 1977), pp. 311–48.

Davidson, Cathy N., 'The matter and manner of Charles Brockden Brown's *Alcuin*', in Bernard Rosenthal (ed.), *Critical Essays on Charles Brockden Brown* (Boston: G. K. Hall, 1981), pp. 71–86.

—, *Revolution and the Word: The Rise of the Novel in America* (New York: Oxford University Press, 1986).

Dawes, James, 'Fictional feeling: philosophy, cognitive science, and the American Gothic', *American Literature*, 76/3 (September 2004), 437–66.

Decker, James M., 'Reassessing Charles Brockden Brown's *Clara Howard*', *Missouri Philological Association*, 19 (1994), 28–36.

Dill, Elizabeth, 'The Republican stepmother: revolution and sensibility in Charles Brockden Brown's *Wieland*', *The Eighteenth-Century Novel*, 2 (2002), 273–303.

Dillon, James, '"The highest province of benevolence": Charles Brockden Brown's fictional theory', *Studies in Eighteenth-Century Culture*, 27 (1998), 237–58.

Downes, Paul, 'Sleep-walking out of the Revolution: Brown's *Edgar Huntly*', *Eighteenth-Century Studies*, 29/4 (1996), 413–31.

—, 'Constitutional secrets: "Memoirs of Carwin" and the politics of concealment', *Criticism*, 39/1 (Winter 1997), 89–117.

Drexler, Michael J. and Ed White, 'Secret witness; or, the fantasy structure of Republicanism', *Early American Literature*, 44/2 (2009), 333–63.

Edwards, Justin D., 'Engendering a new Republic: Charles Brockden Brown's *Alcuin, Carwin* and the legal fictions of gender', *Nordic Journal of English Studies*, 2/2 (2002), 279–302.

Eiselein, Gregory, 'Humanitarianism and uncertainty in *Arthur Mervyn*', *Essays in Literature*, 22/2 (autumn 1995), 215–27.

Elliott, Emory, 'Narrative unity and moral resolution in *Arthur Mervyn*', in Bernard Rosenthal (ed.), *Critical Essays on Charles Brockden Brown* (Boston: G. K. Hall, 1981), pp. 142–63.

Ellis, Scott, 'Charles Brockden Brown's *Ormond*, property exchange, and the literary marketplace in the early American Republic', *Studies in the Novel*, 37 (2005), 1–19.

Emerson, Amanda, 'The early American novel: Charles Brockden Brown's fictitious historiography', *Novel: A Forum on Fiction*, 40/1–2 (2006), 125–50.

Ferguson, Robert A., 'Yellow fever and Charles Brockden Brown: the context of the emerging novelist', *Early American Literature*, 14 (1980), 293–305.

Fiedler, Leslie, *Love and Death in the American Novel* (New York: Anchor Books, 1992 [1960]).

Fleischmann, Fritz, *A Right View of the Subject: Feminism in the Works of Charles Brockden Brown and John Neal* (Erlangen: Verlag Palm & Enke, 1983).

Franklin, Wayne, 'Tragedy and comedy in Brown's *Wieland*', *Novel*, 8 (1975), 147–63.

Fussell, Edwin Sill, '*Wieland*: a literary and historical reading', *Early American Literature*, 18/2 (autumn 1983), 171–86.

Galluzzo, Anthony, 'Charles Brockden Brown's *Wieland* and the aesthetics of Terror: Revolution, reaction, and the radical Enlightenment in early American letters', *Eighteenth-Century Studies*, 42/2 (2009), 255–71.

Gardner, Jared, 'Alien nation: Edgar Huntly's savage awakening', *American Literature*, 66/3 (September 1994), 429–61.

Gilmore, Michael T., 'Calvinism and Gothicism: the example of Brown's *Wieland*', *Studies in the Novel*, 98 (1977), 107–18.

Goddu, Teresa A., 'Historicizing the American Gothic: Charles Brockden Brown's *Wieland*', in Diane Long Hoeveler and Tamar Heller (eds), *Approaches to Teaching Gothic Fiction: The British and American Traditions* (New York: Modern Language Association of America, 2003), pp. 184–9.

Goudie, Sean X., 'On the origin of American specie(s): the West Indies, classification, and the emergence of supremacist consciousness in *Arthur Mervyn*', in Philip Barnard, Mark L. Kamrath and Stephen Shapiro (eds), *Revising Charles Brockden Brown: Culture, Politics, and Sexuality in the Early Republic* (Knoxville, TN: The University of Tennessee Press, 2004), pp. 60–87.

Grabo, Norman S., 'Historical essay', in *Arthur Mervyn; or, Memoirs of the Year 1793, First and Second Parts: Bicentennial Edition* (Kent, OH: Kent State University Press, 1980), pp. 447–75.

—, *The Coincidental Art of Charles Brockden Brown* (Chapel Hill, NC: The University of North Carolina Press, 1981).

Hagenbüchle, Roland, 'American literature and the nineteenth-century crisis in epistemology: the example of Charles Brockden Brown', *Early American Literature*, 23/2 (1988), 121–51.

Hale, Dorothy, 'Profits of altruism: *Caleb Williams* and *Arthur Mervyn*', *Eighteenth-Century Studies*, 22 (1988), 47–69.

Hamelman, Steve, 'Rhapsodist in the wilderness: Brown's Romantic quest in *Edgar Huntly*', *Studies in American Fiction*, 21/2 (autumn 1993), 171–91.

—, 'Secret to the last: Charles Brockden Brown's *Ormond*', *Literature Interpretation and Theory*, 11/3 (2000), 305–26.

Harris, Jennifer, 'At one with the land: Charles Brockden Brown's *Wieland* and matters of national belonging', *Canadian Review of American Studies*, 33/3 (2003), 189–210.

Hedges, William, 'Benjamin Rush, Charles Brockden Brown, and the American plague year', *Early American Literature*, 7 (1973), 295–311.

—, 'Charles Brockden Brown and the culture of contradictions', *Early American Literature*, 9/2 (autumn 1974), 107–42.

Hesford, Walter, 'Do you know the author? The question of authorship in *Wieland*', *Early American Literature*, 17/3 (winter 1982–3), 239–48.

Hinds, Elizabeth Jane Wall, 'Charles Brockden Brown and the frontiers of discourse', in David Mogen, Scott P. Sanders and Joanne B. Karpinski (eds), *Frontier Gothic: Terror and Wonder at the Frontier in American Literature* (Rutherford, NJ: Fairleigh Dickinson University Press, 1993), pp. 109–25.

—, 'Charles Brockden Brown's revenge tragedy: *Edgar Huntly* and the uses of property', *Early American Literature*, 30/1 (1995), 51–70.

—, *Private Property: Charles Brockden Brown's Gendered Economics of Virtue* (Newark: University of Delaware Press, 1997).

—, 'Deb's dogs: animals, Indians, and postcolonial desire in Charles Brockden Brown's *Edgar Huntly*', *Early American Literature*, 39/2 (2004), 323–54.

Hobson, Robert W., 'Voices of Carwin and other mysteries in Charles Brockden Brown's *Wieland*', *Early American Literature*, 10 (1975), 307–9.

Hsu, Hsuan L., 'Democratic expansionism in *Memoirs of Carwin*', *Early American Literature*, 35 (2000), 137–56.

Hughes, Philip Russell, 'Archetypal patterns in *Edgar Huntly*', *Studies in the Novel*, 5 (1973), 176–90.

Hume, Robert D., 'Charles Brockden Brown and the uses of Gothicism: a reassessment', *ESQ*, 66 (1972), 10–18.

Hustis, Harriet, 'Deliberate unknowing and strategic retelling: the ravages of cultural desire in Charles Brockden Brown's *Edgar Huntly*', *Studies in American Fiction*, 31/1 (2003), 101–20.

Jehlen, Myra, 'The literature of colonization', in Sacvan Bercovitch (ed.), *The Cambridge History of American Literature, vol. I: 1590–1820* (Cambridge: Cambridge University Press, 1994), pp. 13–168.

Jordan, Cynthia S., 'On rereading *Wieland*: the folly of precipitate conclusions', *Early American Literature*, 16/2 (1981), 154–74.

Justus, James A., 'Arthur Mervyn, American', *American Literature*, 42 (1970), 304–24.

Kafer, Peter, 'Charles Brockden Brown and Revolutionary Philadelphia: an imagination in context', *The Pennsylvania Magazine of History and Biography*, 96/4 (October 1992), 467–98.

—, 'Charles Brockden Brown and the pleasures of "unsanctified imagination", 1787–93', *The William and Mary Quarterly*, 57/3 (July 2000), 543–68.

Kamrath, Mark L., 'Brown and the Enlightenment: a study of the influence of Voltaire's *Candide* in *Edgar Huntly*', *ATQ*, 5/1 (March 1991), 5–15.

—, 'Charles Brockden Brown and the "art of the historian": an essay concerning (post)modern historical understanding', *Journal of the Early Republic*, 21/2 (2001), 231–60.

—, 'American exceptionalism and radicalism in the "Annals of Europe and America"', in Philip Barnard, Mark L. Kamrath and Stephen Shapiro (eds), *Revising Charles Brockden Brown: Culture, Politics, and Sexuality in the Early Republic* (Knoxville, TN: The University of Tennessee Press, 2004), pp. 354–84.

—, *The Historicism of Charles Brockden Brown: Radical History and the Early Republic* (Kent, OH: Kent State University Press, 2010).

Kazanjian, David, 'Charles Brockden Brown's biloquial nation: national culture and white settler colonialism in *Memoirs of Carwin the Biloquist*', *American Literature*, 73/3 (September 2001), 459–96.

Kimball, Arthur G., 'Savages and savagism: Brockden Brown's dramatic irony', *Studies in Romanticism*, 6 (1967), 214–25.

—, *Rational Fictions: A Study of Charles Brockden Brown* (McMinnville, OR: Linfield Research Institute, 1968).

Kittel, Harald, 'Free indirect discourse and the experiencing self in eighteenth-century American autobiographical fiction: the narration of consciousness in Charles Brockden Brown's *Wieland'*, *New Comparison*, 9 (1990), 73–89.

Korobkin, Laura H., 'Murder by madman: criminal responsibility, law, and judgment in *Wieland'*, *American Literature*, 72/4 (December 2000), 721–50.

Krause, Sydney J., '*Ormond*: seduction in a new key', *American Literature*, 44/4 (January 1973), 570–84.

—, '*Ormond*: how rapidly and how well "composed, arranged, and delivered"', *Early American Literature*, 13 (1978–9), 238–49.

—, '*Clara Howard* and *Jane Talbot*: Godwin on trial', in Bernard Rosenthal (ed.), *Critical Essays on Charles Brockden Brown* (Boston: G. K. Hall, 1981), pp. 184–211.

—, 'Historical essay', in *Edgar Huntly; or, Memoirs of a Sleep-Walker: Bicentennial Edition*, ed. Sydney J. Krause and S. W. Reid (Kent, OH: Kent State University Press, 1984), pp. 295–400.

—, 'Penn's elm and *Edgar Huntly*: dark "instructions to the heart"', *American Literature*, 66/3 (September 1994), 463–84.

—, 'Brockden Brown's feminism in fact and fiction', in Klaus H. Schmidt and Fritz Fleischmann (eds), *Early America Re-Explored: New Readings in Colonial, Early National, and Antebellum Culture* (New York: Peter Lang, 2000), pp. 349–84.

Kreyling, Michael, 'Construing Brown's *Wieland*: ambiguity and Derridean "freeplay"', *Studies in the Novel*, 14 (1982), 43–54.

Larsson, David M., 'Arthur Mervyn, Edgar Huntly, and the critics', *Essays in Literature*, 15 (1988), 207–19.

Layson, Hana, 'Rape and revolution: feminism, antijacobinism, and the politics of injured innocence in Brockden Brown's *Ormond'*, *Early American Studies*, 2 (2004), 160–91.

Levine, Robert S., 'Villainy and the fear of conspiracy in Charles Brockden Brown's *Ormond'*, *Early American Literature*, 15 (1980), 124–40.

—, *Conspiracy and Romance: Studies in Brockden Brown, Cooper, Hawthorne, and Melville* (Cambridge: Cambridge University Press, 1989).

—, 'Race and nation in Brown's Louisiana Writings of 1803', in Philip Barnard, Mark L. Kamrath and Stephen Shapiro (eds), *Revising Charles Brockden Brown: Culture, Politics, and Sexuality in the Early Republic* (Knoxville, TN: The University of Tennessee Press, 2004), pp. 332–53.

Lewis, Paul, 'Charles Brockden Brown and the gendered canon of early American fiction', *Early American Literature*, 31/2 (1996), 167–88.

—, 'Attaining masculinity: Charles Brockden Brown and woman warriors of the 1790s', *Early American Literature*, 40/1 (2005), 37–55.

Lewis, R. W. B., *The American Adam: Innocence, Tragedy, and Tradition in the Nineteenth Century* (Chicago: University of Chicago Press, 1955).

Looby, Christopher, *Voicing America: Language, Literary Form, and the Origins of the United States* (Chicago: University of Chicago Press, 1996).

Luciano, Dana, "'Perverse nature'": *Edgar Huntly* and the novel's reproductive disorders', *American Literature*, 70/1 (March 1998), 1–27.

Luck, Chad, 'Re-walking the purchase: *Edgar Huntly*, David Hume, and the origins of ownership', *Early American Literature*, 44/2 (2009), 271–306.

Lueck, Beth L., 'Charles Brockden Brown's *Edgar Huntly*: the picturesque traveler as sleepwalker', *Studies in American Fiction*, 15/1 (1987), 25–42.

Lyttle, David, 'The case against Carwin', *Nineteenth-Century Fiction*, 26/3 (1971), 257–69.

Manly, William M., 'The importance of point of view in Brockden Brown's *Wieland*', *American Literature*, 35/3 (1963), 311–21.

McAlexander, Patricia Jewell, '*Arthur Mervyn* and the sentimental love tradition', *Studies in Literature*, 9 (1976), 31–42.

Morris, Mabel, 'Charles Brockden Brown and the American Indian', *American Literature*, 18/3 (1946), 244–7.

Murison, Justine S., 'The tyranny of sleep: somnambulism, moral citizenship, and Charles Brockden Brown's *Edgar Huntly*', *Early American Literature*, 44/2 (2009), 243–70.

Murley, Jane, 'Ordinary sinners and moral aliens: the murder narratives of Charles Brockden Brown and Edgar Allan Poe', in Margaret Sönser Breen (ed.), *Understanding Evil: An Interdisciplinary Approach* (New York: Rodopi, 2003), pp. 181–200.

Nelson, Carl W. Jr, 'A just reading of Charles Brockden Brown's *Ormond*', *Early American Literature*, 8 (1973), 163–78.

Newman, Robert D., 'Indians and Indian-hating in *Edgar Huntly* and *The Confidence Man*', *MELUS*, 15/3 (1988), 65–74.

Norwood, Lisa West, "'I may be a stranger to the grounds of your belief'": constructing sense of place in *Wieland*', *Early American Literature*, 38/1 (2003), 89–122.

Nye, Russel B., 'Historical essay', in *Ormond; or The Secret Witness: Bi-centennial Edition*, ed. Sydney J. Krause and S. W. Reid (Kent, OH: Kent State University Press, 1982), pp. 295–341.

O'Shaughnessy, Toni, "'An imperfect tale'": interpretive accountability in *Wieland*', *Studies in American Fiction*, 18/1 (1990), 41–54.

Ostrowski, Carl, "'Fated to perish by consumption'": the political economy of *Arthur Mervyn*', *Studies in American Fiction*, 32/1 (2004), 3–20.

Parker, Patricia L., *Charles Brockden Brown: A Reference Guide* (Boston: G. K. Hall, 1980)

Patrick, Marietta S., 'Charles Brockden Brown's *Ormond*: a psychological portrait of Constantia Dudley', *Journal of Evolutionary Psychology*, 5/1–2 (1984), 112–28.

—, 'Romantic iconography in *Wieland*', *South Atlantic Review*, 49/4 (1984), 65–74.

—, 'The doppelgänger motif in *Arthur Mervyn*', *Journal of Evolutionary Psychology*, 10 (1989), 360–71.

Person, Leland S., '"My good Mama": women in *Edgar Huntly* and *Arthur Mervyn*', *Studies in American Fiction*, 9 (April 1981), 33–46.

Prescott, Frederick C., '*Wieland* and *Frankenstein*', *American Literature*, 2 (1930), 172–3.

Rhombes, Nicholas Jr, '"All was lonely, darksome, and waste": *Wieland* and the construction of the new Republic', *Studies in American Fiction*, 22/1 (spring 1994), 37–47.

Ridgely, Joseph V., 'The empty world of *Wieland*', in Kenneth H. Baldwin and David K. Kirby (eds), *Individual and Community: Variations on a Theme in American Fiction* (Durham, NC: Duke University Press, 1975), pp. 3–16.

Ringe, Donald A., *Charles Brockden Brown* (Boston: Twayne Publishers, 1991 [1966]).

Roberts, Sian Silyn, 'Gothic Enlightenment: contagion and community in Charles Brockden Brown's *Arthur Mervyn*', *Early American Literature*, 44/2 (2009), 307–32.

Rodgers, Paul C. Jr, 'Brown's *Ormond*: the fruits of improvisation', *American Quarterly*, 26/1 (1974), 4–22.

Rosenthal, Bernard (ed.), *Critical Essays on Charles Brockden Brown* (Boston: G. K. Hall, 1981).

—, 'The Voices of *Wieland*', in Bernard Rosenthal (ed.), *Critical Essays on Charles Brockden Brown* (Boston: G. K. Hall, 1981), pp. 104–25.

Russo, James, 'The chameleon of convenient vice: a study of the narrative of *Arthur Mervyn*', *Studies in the Novel*, 11 (1979), 381–405.

—, 'The tangled web of deception and imposture in Charles Brockden Brown's *Ormond*', *Early American Literature*, 14 (1979), 205–27.

—, 'The chimeras of the brain: Clara's narrative in *Wieland*', *Early American Literature*, 16/1 (1981), 60–88.

Samuels, Shirley, 'Plague and politics in 1793: *Arthur Mervyn*', *Criticism*, 27/3 (1985), 225–46.

—, 'Infidelity and contagion: the rhetoric of revolution', *Early American Literature*, 22 (1987), 183–90.

—, '*Wieland*: alien and infidel', *Early American Literature*, 25/1 (1990), 46–66.

Scheiber, Andrew J., '"The arm lifted against me": love, terror, and the contruction of gender in *Wieland*', *Early American Literature*, 26/2 (1991), 173–94.

Scheick, William J., 'The problem of origination in Brown's *Ormond*', in Bernard Rosenthal (ed.), *Critical Essays on Charles Brockden Brown* (Boston: G. K. Hall, 1981), pp. 126–41.

Schulz, Dieter, '*Edgar Huntly* as quest romance', *American Literature*, 43/3 (1971), 323–35.

Seelye, John, 'Charles Brockden Brown and early American fiction', in Emory Elliott (ed.), *Columbia Literary History of the United States* (New York: Columbia University Press, 1988), pp. 168–86.

Seltzer, Mark, 'Saying makes it so: language and event in Brown's *Wieland*', *Early American Literature*, 8 (1978), 81–91.

Shapiro, Stephen, '"Man to man I needed not to dread his encounter": *Edgar Huntly*'s end of erotic pessimism', in Philip Barnard, Mark L. Kamrath and Stephen Shapiro (eds), *Revising Charles Brockden Brown: Culture, Politics, and Sexuality in the Early Republic* (Knoxville, TN: The University of Tennessee Press, 2004), pp. 216–51.

Shuffelton, Frank, 'Juries of the common reader: crime and judgment in the novels of Charles Brockden Brown', in Philip Barnard, Mark L. Kamrath and Stephen Shapiro (eds), *Revising Charles Brockden Brown: Culture, Politics, and Sexuality in the Early Republic* (Knoxville, TN: The University of Tennessee Press, 2004), pp. 88–114.

Sivils, M.W., 'Native American sovereignty and Old Deb in Charles Brockden Brown's *Edgar Huntly*', *American Transcendental Quarterly*, 14/4 (2001), 293–304.

Slotkin, Richard, *Regeneration Through Violence: The Mythology of the American Frontier, 1600–1860* (Middletown, CT: Wesleyan University Press, 1973).

Smith-Rosenberg, Carroll, 'Subject female: authorizing American identity', *American Literary History*, 5/3 (1993), 481–511.

Smyth, Heather, '"Imperfect disclosures": cross-dressing and containment in Charles Brockden Brown's *Ormond*', in Merril D. Smith (ed.), *Sex and Sexuality in Early America* (New York: New York University Press, 1998), pp. 240–61.

Soldati, Joseph A., 'The Americanization of Faust: a study of Charles Brockden Brown's *Wieland*', *ESQ*, 74 (1974), 1–14.

Spangler, George M., 'Charles Brockden Brown's *Arthur Mervyn*: a portrait of a young American artist', *American Literature*, 52 (1981), 578–92.

Stern, Julia, 'The state of "women" in *Ormond*; or, patricide in the new nation', in Philip Barnard, Mark L. Kamrath and Stephen Shapiro (eds),

Revising Charles Brockden Brown: Culture, Politics, and Sexuality in the Early Republic (Knoxville, TN: The University of Tennessee Press, 2004), pp. 182–215.

Strozier, Robert, '*Wieland* and other romances: horror in parentheses', *ESQ*, 50 (1968), 24–9.

Sullivan, Michael P., 'Reconciliation and subversion in *Edgar Huntly*', *American Transcendental Quarterly*, 2/1 (1988), 5–22.

Temple, Gale, 'Carwin the onanist?', *Arizona Quarterly: A Journal of American Literature, Culture, and Theory*, 65/1 (2009), 1–32.

Teute, Fredrika J., '"A Republic of intellect": conversation and criticism among the sexes in 1790s New York', in Philip Barnard, Mark L. Kamrath and Stephen Shapiro (eds), *Revising Charles Brockden Brown: Culture, Politics, and Sexuality in the Early Republic* (Knoxville, TN: The University of Tennessee Press, 2004), pp. 149–81.

Toles, George, 'Charting the hidden landscape: *Edgar Huntly*', *Early American Literature*, 16/2 (autumn 1981), 133–53.

Tompkins, Jane, *Sensational Designs: The Cultural Work of American Fiction 1790–1860* (Oxford: Oxford University Press, 1985).

Traister, Bryce, 'Libertinism and authorship in America's early Republic', *American Literature*, 72/1 (March 2000), 1–30.

Van der Beets, Richard and Paul Witherington, 'My kinsman, Brockden Brown: Robin Molineux and Arthur Mervyn', *American Transcendental Quarterly*, 1 (1969), 13–15.

Verhoeven, W. M., 'Displacing the discontinuous; or, the labyrinths of reason: fictional design and eighteenth-century thought in Charles Brockden Brown's *Ormond*', in W. M. Verhoeven (ed.), *Rewriting the Dream: Reflections on the Changing American Literary Canon* (Amsterdam: Rodopi, 1992), pp. 202–29.

—, '"This blissful period of intellectual liberty": transatlantic radicalism and enlightened conservatism in Brown's early writings', in Philip Barnard, Mark L. Kamrath and Stephen Shapiro (eds), *Revising Charles Brockden Brown: Culture, Politics, and Sexuality in the Early Republic* (Knoxville, TN: The University of Tennessee Press, 2004), pp. 7–40.

Vickers, Anita, 'Patriarchal and political authority in *Wieland*', *AUMLA: Journal of the Australasian Universities Modern Language Association*, 90 (1998), 1–19.

—, '"Pray Madam, are you a Federalist?" Women's rights and the Republican utopia in *Alcuin*', *American Studies*, 39/3 (1998), 89–104.

Voloshin, Beverly R., '*Wieland*: "accounting for appearances"', *The New England Quarterly*, 59/3 (1986), 341–57.

—, '*Edgar Huntly* and the coherence of the self', *Early American Literature*, 23/3 (1988), 262–80.

Wallach, Rick, 'The manner in which appearances are solved: narrative semiotics in *Wieland, or the Transformation*', *South Atlantic Review*, 64 (1999), 1–15.

Warfel, Harry R., *Charles Brockden Brown: American Gothic Novelist* (New York: Octagon Books, 1974 [1949]).

Waterman, Bryan, '*Arthur Mervyn*'s medical repository and the early Republic's knowledge industries', *American Literary History*, 15 (2003), 213–47.

Watts, Steven, *The Romance of Real Life: Charles Brockden Brown and the Origins of American Culture* (Baltimore: The Johns Hopkins University Press, 1994).

Weldon, Roberta F., 'Charles Brockden Brown's *Wieland*: a family tragedy', *Studies in American Fiction*, 12/1 (1984), 1–11.

White, Ed, 'Carwin the peasant rebel', in Philip Barnard, Mark L. Kamrath and Stephen Shapiro (eds), *Revising Charles Brockden Brown: Culture, Politics, and Sexuality in the Early Republic* (Knoxville, TN: The University of Tennessee Press, 2004), pp. 41–59.

Wiley, Lulu Rumsey, *The Sources and Influence of the Novels of Charles Brockden Brown* (New York: Vantage Press, 1950).

Williams, Daniel E., 'Writing under the influence: an examination of *Wieland*'s "well authenticated facts" and the depiction of murderous fathers in post-Revolutionary print culture', *Eighteenth-Century Fiction*, 15/3–4 (April–July 2003), 643–68.

Witherington, Paul, 'Benevolence and the "utmost stretch": Charles Brockden Brown's narrative dilemma', *Criticism*, 14 (1972), 175–91.

—, 'Brockden Brown's other novels: *Clara Howard* and *Jane Talbot*', *Nineteenth-Century Fiction*, 29 (1974), 257–72.

—, 'Charles Brockden Brown's *Ormond*: the American artist and his masquerades', *Studies in American Fiction*, 4 (1976), 111–19.

—, '"Not my tongue only": form and language in Brown's *Edgar Huntly*', in Bernard Rosenthal (ed.), *Critical Essays on Charles Brockden Brown* (Boston: G. K. Hall, 1981), pp. 164–83.

Wolfe, Eric A., 'Ventriloquizing nation: voice, identity, and radical democracy in Charles Brockden Brown's *Wieland*', *American Literature*, 78/3 (September 2006), 431–57.

Ziff, Larzer, 'A reading of *Wieland*', *PMLA*, 77/1 (1962), 51–7.

IV. Other works cited

Auerbach, Jonathan, *The Romance of Failure: First-Person Fictions of Poe, Hawthorne, and James* (New York and Oxford: Oxford University Press, 1989).

Becker, Susanne, *Gothic Forms of Feminine Fiction* (Manchester: Manchester University Press, 1999).

Bloom, Clive (ed.), *Gothic Horror: A Guide for Students and Readers*, second edn (New York: Palgrave Macmillan, 2007).

Bradford, William, *Of Plymouth Plantation 1620–1647*, ed. Samuel Eliot Morison (New York: Alfred A. Knopf, 1953).

Brand, Dana, *The Spectator and the City in Nineteenth-Century American Literature* (Cambridge: Cambridge University Press, 1991).

Burrows, Edwin G. and Mike Wallace, *Gotham: A History of New York to 1898* (New York: Oxford University Press, 1998).

Carter, Boyd, 'Poe's debt to Charles Brockden Brown', *Prairie Schooner*, 27 (1953), 190–6.

Clark, David Lee, 'The sources of Poe's "The Pit and the Pendulum"', *Modern Language Notes*, 44/6 (June 1929), 349–56.

Crèvecoeur, J. Hector St John de, *Letters from an American Farmer* (New York: Fox, Duffield and Company, 1904 [1792]).

DeLamotte, Eugenia C., *Perils of the Night: A Feminist Study of Nineteenth-Century Gothic* (New York: Oxford University Press, 1990).

Doody, Margaret Anne, 'Deserts, ruins, and troubled waters: female dreams in fiction and the development of the Gothic novel', *Genre*, 10 (winter 1977), 529–72.

Dunn, John, *Locke: A Very Short Introduction* (Oxford: Oxford University Press, 1984).

Ehrlich, Heyward, 'The "Mysteries" of Philadelphia: Lippard's *Quaker City* and "Urban" Gothic', *ESQ*, 18/1 (1972), 50–65.

Ellis, Kate Ferguson, *The Contested Castle: Gothic Novels and the Subversion of Domestic Ideology* (Urbana: University of Illinois Press, 1989).

Fisher, Benjamin F., 'Poe and the Gothic tradition', in Kevin J. Hayes (ed.), *The Cambridge Companion to Edgar Allan Poe* (Cambridge: Cambridge University Press, 2002), pp. 72–91.

Fitzgerald, Neil, 'Philadelphia Gothic: Charles Brockden Brown'. Online, accessed 5 July 2010, *http://www.librarycompany.org/gothic/brown.htm*.

Gilbert, Sandra M. and Susan Gubar, *The Madwoman in the Attic: The Woman Writer and the Nineteenth-Century Literary Imagination* (New Haven, CT: Yale University Press, 1979).

Halttunen, Karen, *Confidence Men and Painted Women: A Study of Middle-Class Culture in America, 1830–1870* (New Haven, CT: Yale University Press, 1982).

Harris, Susan K., *Nineteenth-Century American Women's Novels: Interpretive Strategies* (Cambridge: Cambridge University Press, 1990).

Hawthorne, Nathaniel, 'The Hall of Fantasy', in *Mosses from an Old Manse* [1846]. Online, accessed 5 July 2010, *http://www.ibiblio.org/eldritch/nh/hall.html*.

Heller, Tamar, *Dead Secrets: Wilkie Collins and the Female Gothic* (New Haven, CT: Yale University Press, 1992).

Hirsch, David H., 'Another source for "The Pit and the Pendulum"', *Mississippi Quarterly*, 23/1 (winter 1969–70), 35–43.

Hoeveler, Diane Long, *Gothic Feminism: The Professionalization of Gender from Charlotte Smith to the Brontës* (University Park, PA: Pennsylvania State University Press, 1998).

Irving, Washington, 'The Legend of Sleepy Hollow', in *The Sketch-Book of Geoffrey Crayon, Gent* (New York: G. P. Putnam's Sons, 1880 [1820]), pp. 382–419.

Kahane, Claire, 'The Gothic mirror', in Shirley Nelson Garner, Claire Kahane and Madelon Sprengnether (eds), *The (M)other Tongue: Essays in Feminist Psychoanalytic Interpretation* (Ithaca, NY: Cornell University Press, 1985), pp. 334–51.

Kerber, Linda K., *Federalists in Dissent: Imagery and Ideology in Jeffersonian America* (Ithaca, NY: Cornell University Press, 1970).

Kilgour, Maggie, *The Rise of the Gothic Novel* (London: Routledge, 1982).

Leeuwen, Frederike van, 'Female Gothic: the discourse of the Other', *Revista Canaria de Estudios Ingleses*, 14 (1982), 33–44.

Mather, Cotton, *The Wonders of the Invisible World*, reprinted in Paul Lauter *et al.* (eds), *The Heath Anthology of American Literature*, third edn, vol. 1 (New York: Houghton Mifflin, 1998), pp. 421–5.

Mazurek, Ray, 'Art, ambiguity, and the artist in Poe's "The Man of the Crowd"', *Poe Studies*, 12/2 (1979), 25–8.

Melville, Herman, 'The Paradise of the Bachelors and the Tartarus of the Maids', *Harpers New Monthly Magazine*, 10 (April 1855), 670–8. Online, *http://etext.virginia.edu/toc/modeng/public/MelPara.html*.

Mighall, Robert, *A Geography of Victorian Gothic Fiction: Mapping History's Nightmares* (Oxford: Oxford University Press, 1999).

—, 'Gothic cities', in Catherine Spooner and Emma McEvoy (eds), *The Routledge Companion to the Gothic* (New York: Routledge, 2007), pp. 54–72.

Milbank, Alison, 'Female Gothic', in Marie Mulvey-Roberts (ed.), *The Handbook of the Gothic*, second edn (New York: New York University Press, 2009), pp. 120–4.

Miller, Richard G., 'The Federal city, 1783–1800', in Russell F. Weigley (ed.), *Philadelphia: A 300-Year History* (New York: W. W. Norton & Company, 1982), pp. 155–208.

Modleski, Tania, *Loving with a Vengeance: Mass-Produced Fantasies for Women* (Hamden, CT: Archon Books, 1982).

Moers, Ellen, *Literary Women* (Garden City, NY: Anchor Books, 1976).

Mogen, David, Scott P. Sanders and Joanne B. Karpinski, 'Introduction', in D. Mogen, S. Sanders and J. Karpinski (eds), *Frontier Gothic: Terror and Wonder at the Frontier in American Literature* (Rutherford, NJ: Fairleigh Dickinson University Press, 1993), pp. 1–27.

Mulvey-Roberts, Marie (ed.), *The Handbook of the Gothic*, second edn (New York: New York University Press, 2009).

Nash, Gary B., *First City: Philadelphia and the Forging of Historical Memory* (Philadelphia: University of Pennsylvania Press, 2002).

Poe, Edgar Allan, 'William Wilson. A Tale', *Burton's Gentleman's Magazine* (October 1839), 205–12. Online, accessed 4 July 2010, *http://www. eapoe.org/works/tales/wilwilb.htm*.

—, 'The Man of the Crowd', *Burton's Gentleman's Magazine* (December 1840), 267–70. Online, accessed 5 July 2010, *http://www.eapoe.org/ works/tales/crowda1.htm*.

Pritchard, Allan, 'The Urban Gothic of *Bleak House*', *Nineteenth-Century Literature*, 45/4 (1991), 432–52.

Quinn, Patrick, *The French Face of Edgar Allan Poe* (Carbondale, IL: Southern Illinois University Press, 1957).

Radway, Janice, 'The utopian impulse in popular literature: Gothic romances and "feminist" protest', *American Quarterly*, 33/2 (summer 1981), 140–62.

Restuccia, Frances L., 'Female Gothic writing: "under cover to Alice"', *Genre*, 28 (autumn 1986), 346–66.

Rowlandson, Mary, *A Narrative of the Captivity and Restoration of Mrs Mary Rowlandson*, in Paul Lauter *et al.* (eds), *The Heath Anthology of American Literature*, third edn, vol. 1 (New York: Houghton Mifflin, 1998), pp. 343–65.

Showalter, Elaine, *A Literature of their Own: British Women Novelists from Brontë to Lessing* (Princeton, NJ: Princeton University Press, 1977).

—, *Sister's Choice: Tradition and Change in American Women's Writing* (Oxford: Clarendon Press, 1991).

Spencer, Kathleen, 'Victorian Urban Gothic: the first modern fantastic literature', in Eric S. Rabkin (ed.), *Intersections: Fantasy and Science Fiction* (Carbondale, IL: Southern Illinois University Press, 1987), pp. 87–96.

——, 'Purity and danger: *Dracula*, the Urban Gothic, and the late Victorian degeneracy crisis', *ELH*, 59 (1992), 197–225.

Todorov, Tzvetan, *The Fantastic: A Structural Approach to a Literary Genre*, trans. Richard Howard (Ithaca, NY: Cornell University Press, 1973).

Warner, Sam Bass Jr, *The Private City: Philadelphia in Three Periods of its Growth*, second edn (Philadelphia: University of Pennsylvania Press, 1968).

Weigley, Russell F. (ed.), *Philadelphia: A 300-Year History* (New York: W. W. Norton & Company, 1982).

Weinstock, Jeffrey Andrew, 'Lostness (Blair Witch)', in Sarah L. Higley and Jeffrey Andrew Weinstock (eds), *Nothing That Is: Millennial Cinema and the* Blair Witch *Controversies* (Detroit: Wayne State University Press, 2004), pp. 229–44.

Williams, Anne, *Art of Darkness: A Poetics of Gothic* (Chicago: University of Chicago Press, 1995).

Index

༉༙

Index

Index

Volney, Comte de 11
Voloshin, Beverly R. 97–8
Voltaire 20

Wallace, Mike 124–5
Walpole, Horace 98, 137
Warfel, H. R. 2, 20, 62
Washington, George 15, 67,
    162n75
Weigley, Russell F. 168n17
Weinstock, Jeffrey Andrew 167n70
West Indies 13, 14, 17
Whig Party 18
Whiskey Rebellion 16, 17, 18, 67,
    162n75
Whitman, Walt 151
Whittier, John Greenleaf 4, 149
Wilcocks, Alexander 8, 9, 160n52

Wilder, Billy 54
Wiley, Lulu Ramsey 19
Williams, Anne 121–2, 174n18
Williams, Helen Maria 13
Winthrop, John 31
Witherington, Paul 97, 160n49
Wollstonecraft, Mary 10, 13–15,
    24, 93, 124–5, 126, 127, 131,
    133–4, 140, 161n68, 161n70
Women's Rights *see* Feminism

X-Files, The (TV programme)
    91–2, 98
XYZ Affair 15–16, 17

Yellow Fever 9, 10, 12, 18–19, 23,
    60–5, 68, 70–2, 74–7, 79–80,
    82–3, 87–9, 96, 153, 154